I'm a Fan:

How I married U2 into my life
without going to the altar

A memoir by Eric Shivvers

I'm a Fan:
How I married U2 into my life without going to the altar.

Cover photo: Joseph Cable
Author photo: Amy Shivvers
Book design: 822design.com

Shivvers, Eric.

I'm a fan : how I married U2 into my life without going to the
altar : a memoir / by Eric Shivvers. -- 1st ed.

p. ; cm.

ISBN-13: 978-1-4565-3315-1
ISBN-10: 1-456-53315-0

1. Shivvers, Eric. 2. Rock music fans--United States--Biogra-
phy. 3. U2 (Musical group)--Influence. 4. Rock music--Social
aspects. I. Title.

ML429 .S55 2011
782.42166/092
2011900731

Me, mom and Johnny Cash

I dedicate this book to my mom,
Shari Benstock.

To my parents, Dad, Linda, Mom, Berni and Tom,
thanks for giving me direction in life.

To my life companion Amy, I thank you for
your love, patience and sending me to the
Iowa Summer Writing Festival to hone my craft.

Chapters

1: a lost boy

I don't have an exact date or time when I caught the music bug, especially when it comes to the Irish quartet, U2. Nor can I tell you my favorite song or album, U2 or otherwise; it changes daily depending on my mood. I can, however, point to my stepfather, Stefano, as the person who had the greatest impact on me when it comes to my passion for the band hailing from the Northside of Dublin. The irony lies in his scholarly work. He was one of the foremost leading scholars on James Joyce, the Irish novelist. With that in mind, you'd think his academic forte would be the gateway to this Irish rock band. Certainly, that is not the case here. It was the travel benefits of Stefano's academic career, not his specialty in Irish studies, which was my linchpin connection to U2.

We traveled to Europe on several trips, including two sabbatical years, where I witnessed events that also made an impact on the four young lads who founded U2: Paul Hewson, David Evans, Larry Mullen, Jr., and Adam Clayton. Others along the way have spurred my interest in music in general, like my mother's musical gifts or my father's passion for 50s rock 'n' roll. Of course, this is all hindsight now, but the journey I'm about to take you on wouldn't have been possible if my stepfather hadn't entered the picture.

I was six years old on the fateful day when Mom married Stefano, fourteen years her senior, in Kent, Ohio. Mom had been divorced from Dad for three years and yearned to get on with her academic life. My father, a very loving man, who's influential in his own right in my life when it comes to music, had no ambition to travel to Europe, let alone partake in Mom's academic desires. Although ultimately the divorce would lead to adding Stefano to my family, it also took Dad away from me. I loved being a kid in the back yard in Iowa with Dad, playing with my Tonka trucks or building model airplanes in the basement. Stefano had no interest in such activities. He was a true academic who lived his life in the confines of the university and who then escaped to Europe during the summers. When he married my mom, who had scholarly aspirations of her own, my whole life changed. Stefano had two older girls from a previous marriage, but he saw me as moldable clay. He could make a young academic out of me by introducing me to his passions of travel and by feeding an adventurous appetite, something he couldn't do with his girls. Mom was already onboard with all of the new changes; I was the one dragging my feet. Having Mom marry someone who took over Dad's shoes was hard to comprehend, especially on the day of their wedding when all I really wanted to do was run a lemonade stand.

It was the first weekend of May, 1974. Spring had finally arrived. The weather was perfect for opening my first lemonade stand with my next-door friends Greg and Katy Wolzniak. Under a cloudless sky, Mrs. Wolzniak brought out their card table from the garage, while Katy and I got the Dixie cups from the kitchen. Greg, who was older and finishing second grade, put himself in charge of making the lemonade. We set up shop along the sidewalk. Katy made a handmade sign, which Mrs. Wolzniak taped to the table. It dangled from the edge and fluttered with the passing breeze.

The street we lived on was fairly busy with traffic, but no one who was driving by was going to stop just to buy a glass of lemonade. However, having the A&P down the street was a benefit. We talked to prospective sales walking to the grocery store with the hope they would return to buy some of our delicious, citrus drink. After setting up and making only our first sale, mom's brown Buick Electra rolled up next to us from the back alley, which ran between our house and Greg and Katy's. The electric window on the driver's side retracted into the door, shuddering and squeaking.

"Eric!" mom shouted from behind the steering wheel. "Get in the car. We're going to be late."

"Why, Mom?"

"You know it's my wedding day. We're going to the Lombardi's house where the rabbi is waiting to begin the service."

"Mom! I can't go. I'm running the lemonade stand with Greg and Katy," I said, as I pointed blindly behind me. "We just got started."

"Eric, I'm sorry, but you've got to give it up. I don't want to leave you behind."

"But Mooooooooooooom."

My future stepfather, Stefano, leaned forward from his seat on the passenger side. He glanced at me from behind mom.

"Aheemm," he noised, clearing his throat. "Eric, get in the car now!"

"Yeah, the lemonade stand will be here when we get back,"

mom barked, looking through her oversized brown-tinted sunglasses, with her hair just a shade of blonde away from looking like Mia Farrow.

I quickly said good-bye to my lemonade-stand gang. By now, they were knee-deep in customers and probably wouldn't notice my absence. I ran around to the rear of the car, careful not to trip on any of the ill-shaped rocks in the alley. The open passenger door greeted me as my soon-to-be-stepfather leaned forward in his seat, allowing me to climb into the back. For a six-year-old boy, mom's car seemed like a small shipping vessel. The back seat was huge, with room for me to roam from side to side depending upon which view I wanted from the rear windows.

As I plopped myself down on the seat, mom hit the gas. I turned around in the back seat and stared out the rear window. The lemonade stand was fading from sight. We were on our way to the Lombardi's for the backyard wedding. Along the way, we had to make one quick stop to pick up Stefano's two daughters, Jolene and Roberta, who lived across town with their mother. Jolene was closer in age to me as she was in second grade and I was just finishing kindergarten. Roberta, on the other hand, was much older. She was in junior high. For the most part, they seemed to get along with each other and, unlike my parents, Stefano and his ex-wife Genevieve had a civil relationship, even living in the same town. Jolene and Roberta's only contact with me would be on weekend visits to our house. Life was going to be complicated enough with a new father in my life, let alone with two new siblings, but we made it work.

I only vaguely remember mom and dad as a married couple. Memories of their union stay alive in discolored Polaroids housed in musty, burlap-covered photo albums that are now scattered throughout both sides of the family. Most of the images captured relatives with my parents, as they huddled together around a dining room table covered with dishes from that day's feast. I was never sure what purpose the dirty table played in the images, but it was always the central subject. At the last moment, someone must have thought it would be great to get a picture while everyone was in the same room. I'm not sure about my theory, but the images provide me a time capsule whenever I need to see my parents together during happier times.

Photography was a hobby for dad. He'd find a moment of my life to capture in pictures and the Polaroid camera would appear from out of nowhere. Most of the early shots caught me fascinated with new things, like playing with my grandfather's pipe or sitting with my Uncle Dan while he tape-recorded my voice. The images captivate me to this day, but I don't remember being an active participant. I do, however, recall a year or two after the divorce when dad would pose me next to his new Ford Thunderbird. While behind the camera, dad would squint one-eyed through the viewfinder with one finger on the shutter button while his other hand gently moved the bellows back and forth to get me in focus.

"Hold it," he'd say out of the side of his mouth while framing the picture just how he wanted.

Pop! The flash above the camera burst a shot of light toward me. Out of the back of the camera appeared a plastic tab, which dad tugged on as the camera made a grinding noise, revealing a piece of rectangular paper. He'd look at his watch and then vigorously waved the paper in the air. After he pulled the paper negative from the print, voila! I was bewildered, as if I was attending some kind of magic show. The image came to life. There I was, caught forever on a Polaroid print and frozen in time.

Dad's other interest was recording my first words on his reel-to-reel tape deck. In the deep reaches of his stereo cabinet are the tapes of my first spoken words. Every now and then, dad still extracts a few when I visit. He places them with loving care onto the spindles and hits the play button. Out of the speakers rolls an interview shortly after I began to talk.

"Eric, how old are you?" dad asked.

A thumping comes through the microphone. Laughter arrives out of the left speaker followed by more thumping.

"Speak into the microphone," dad prompts to my interest in the metallic object and not the question. There would be another pause.

"Two!" I shout with glee.

"Right on! Lookey, Eric, who's that over there?"

Obviously, the pause after the question speaks volumes about my attention span. Laughter, again, breaks out in the background.

"No, who's that over there?" he repeats the question.

"Mommy!" I say with determination.

"That's right, Eric," mom says with a chuckle.

These recordings go on for hours. I guess I was the opening act for any evening's festivities. Other voices and laughter sporadically come in and out of the speakers. I wasn't just doing my one act show for my parents, but for their friends as well. These were happy times. They just didn't last very long.

Once the divorce decree's ink dried at the Des Moines courthouse, mom pulled up to what would now be dad's house and loaded her life, with the help of her graduate student friends, into the back of her rented van. For whatever reason, after only a few years of marriage, she was desperate to move on with her life, chasing academia. We moved into a tiny, cramped two-bedroom apartment on the other side of town, away from dad. The place had just enough room for mom and me. Left behind were reminders of happier times, my fire trucks and bulldozers that dad and I had played with, in the backyard, the previous summer. Mom could only think about herself and her need to separate from the past. Once the move was completed, pain began to overtake me. I cried a lot and dragged my feet in resistance to this new life.

"Mom, I want dad back!" I'd complain over my cereal.

"You can go visit him next week. That's the plan," she said over her shoulder, as she plopped bread into the toaster. She was protecting me from the jargon and rules of the divorce decree.

"Mooooom, I want to be with dad right now!" I'd uncontrollably stammer.

She turned and looked at me. She knew I was too young to comprehend the intricacies of a divorce, but she tried.

"Eric, I'm no longer married to your father," she tried to explain through her own pain. "You're with me now. I have custody of you. Your father has you on the weekends."

"Mom, get dad on the phone now. I wanna to talk to him."

"Eric, Pickle, it's not that easy," she said, as she tightened the belt on her robe "You've to go get ready for preschool. We need to be at Margaret's in an hour. I'll pick you up at four this afternoon." She turned to the toaster, coffee cup in hand.

"Mom, it's not fair." I began to cry in earnest.

Mom put her coffee cup onto the counter, coming over to comfort me. She could not hide the grief of her decision. She too was crying, worried if she'd done the right thing.

I thought I could find some magic glue to bring my parents back together, but never did. My hurt wouldn't cease. I would see dad every weekend, but the pain just wouldn't go away. Nights were the hardest. Each evening, a sliver of light from the living room would enter my bedroom while mom played her Martin guitar. The light, combined with the sound of the guitar, was my safety blanket as I lay under a poster of Johnny Cash. Mom pulled tunes from Simon and Garfunkel, Joan Baez, and Bob Dylan. *Bridge Over Troubled Water* was heavy in the rotation. Her harmonic voice made the suffering a little easier. There would be evenings when she would let me stay up for one song. Actually, I had a request list of one: Don McLean's *American Pie*. Why was I attracted to the song? I don't know. Maybe it was the lyric, almost nursery rhyme-like in it's storytelling. More likely, mom made it that way by how she sung it. Unbeknownst to me, the song began with the death of one of dad's musical heroes, Buddy Holly. It was a song of loss and I was attracted to it. As mom strummed the tune, the Martin seemed to play by itself as her long fingers, moving with ease on its neck, formed the song's chords. Her voice was mesmerizing. She was always on key and in perfect pitch, something drilled into her from her own mother's insistence. My grandmother had been the church choir director. It would be an insult, even at mom's age of twenty-six, not to hit the notes perfectly. More amazing was her ability to play the song as if it was her own. For all I knew, Don McLean was playing her song.

It would only be another year before mom and I were once again on the move. Our vagabond lifestyle would lead us to Kent, Ohio, where she would pursue her doctorate and unearth the next love of her life, Stefano. As she worked toward her advanced degree, I honestly didn't know what dad was doing. Mom tried hard to sever her relationship with dad. In doing so, I became lost in what my role was in the bigger picture. Iowa and dad seemed a million miles away from me. The physical and emotional distance from my father only deepened my sorrow. I felt as though I was in a tunnel with a light at both ends. As I would go one direction, the light would become brighter. I would then turn around only to see the light behind me fading away. I knew I was loved, but lost in the shuffle of two people trying to put their own lives back together.

I saw dad on very rare occasions when I lived in Kent, Ohio. I remember taking a trip with him to Rhode Island to see my aunt, uncle and cousins. It was one of the few times I was allowed to see my father. He met me at the tiny Kent airport and we hopped the last leg of the trip together. As I sat in the window seat next to him, tears rolled down his face while he caressed my head, so happy to be with me. Flying was new to me. I stared out the window at the sky and asked if we jumped out of the plane, could we hang out on a cloud. Dad told me we would fall through to the ground. Tears were still streaming down his face. To me, tears were a sign of pain, not joy. Dad had me for four days. Mom was not making our relationship easy. Her separation agreement only allowed dad and me small windows of time together. We made that plane ride our time and escape from the hurt we were both feeling. I knew he was crushed. As I write this, I cannot imagine what it would be like to have your family taken from you. Somehow, dad forged on. He probably dug himself deeper into his career of architecture or one of his many hobbies such as woodworking. But, whatever he immersed himself in, it wasn't enough to flee from the pain of losing his son.

As the marriage ceremony and the festivities came to a close that May afternoon in the Lombardi's back yard, it was clear to me, even then, that my life was in flux yet again. After dropping my newly anointed stepsisters off at their mother's house, our car pulled into alley where my day's journey began. Dusk was encroaching and the lemonade stand was long gone. Whether I wanted to think about it or not, I was forced to open a new chapter in my life. Mom was now remarried. She, once again, chose to wed someone older by at least a decade. I'm not sure if this is more telling of mom's need for a father figure or her search for stability. Stefano's career as a professor was saner than dad's career as an architect. Architecture induced long hours and demands outside of the marriage. As an architect, dad often faced unrealistic deadlines, which meant he would stay up at all hours of the night playing some Johann Sebastian Bach symphony while executing drawings for the following day's client meetings. The career added to his creative mania, the up and down mood swings depending on how work was going. Mom couldn't handle the anxious behavior. It would only induce her anxieties. She deeply desired to pursue her education beyond her master's degree but more importantly, she needed emotional stability. In time, she'd profit from Stefano's academic status, creating a career of her own as an Edith Wharton scholar. Moreover, she benefited from his even-keeled persona. For me, however, I was on shaky ground, learning what it was like to have another father and to be his third child. I was attached to mom's hip and obviously her little boy. It wasn't easy. I still wanted dad back. I walked on emotional eggshells because the pain inside hurt so much. I was a very expressive young boy who came from emotional parents. I would sometimes cry at the drop of a hat. My stepfather was the opposite. He was not an openly demonstrative man.

Within days after the wedding, the three of us were in Europe for the summer. Jolene and Roberta didn't join us because they had already been abroad. It was now time for Stefano to step in as a second father and give me my first taste of international travel. We were not hotel rats. Instead, we visited Stefano's friends and colleagues, who would take us in for days at a time. Some, not all, had previously met my mother but she, and I, charmed them all. For me, it was a whole new experience. I became an explorer. I was off to new lands where no one except mom and Stefano spoke English. With the kids I befriended, spoken words were not needed. When it came to communication, hand signals and unified gestures, whether for hunger or for wanting to go outside to play, were the name of the game. Without realizing it, I was starting to break my own boundaries and fears. Cannes, in the South of France, and stonewalled villages isolated by water, like those along the Adriatic coast near the former Yugoslavia, were the highlights of the three-month "family" honeymoon. Picturesque villages like these offered me opportunities to start leaving my mother's side and explore on my own.

Klaus, Stefano's good friend in Switzerland, often traveled with us and, like dad, always carried a camera. But, Klaus was subtle with his single-lens reflex. He often captured me at the right moment, as I was investigating my new world. Stefano knew I was at the right age to soak in all of the culture. He was a first-generation American. His parents emigrated from Poland a few years after World War I and he was born in Brooklyn shortly thereafter. He longed for culture and found it traveling across Europe. He may not have spoken his love for me, but I realize now that travel is how he professed it, by giving me the opportunities to voyage at a young age, offering Paris, Zurich, Bologna, and the like, which became familiar territory for me.

In the coming fall, after our return from Europe, we began anew in Champaign, Illinois, where Stefano had been hired as the chair of the Modern Languages Department the previous spring. Sadly, mom, with a freshly minted doctorate in hand, had to accept an administrative position at the same university. She was deeply frustrated being a secretary in the Political Science Department, but she didn't let her push for a professorship stop her from being a good mother. She always walked me halfway to school in the morning, where I would meet up with other kids in my school. When I arrived home in the afternoon to our stately Victorian mansion, she wouldn't be that long behind. Her boss, Phillip Cullinan, lived only a half a block away with four boys – Michael, Dylan, Alan, and Paul. I was Michael's age, and two years younger than Dylan. The other two boys were quite older.

Michael, Dylan, and I became instant friends, riding our bikes through the neighborhood or playing army on the Cullinan's sprawling lawn. They helped with the pain of missing dad, but beginning first grade was still difficult.

I was again a new student in a new school. I had separation anxiety as I entered Mrs. Blum's classroom at South Side Elementary School. I bawled when mom dropped me off for kindergarten in Kent, Ohio, but this year, I tried to hold back the tears. I didn't succeed. They rolled down my face as class began. The emotions were a reaction to the separation. Once again, I had to forge onward. Luckily, a few of my fellow classmates were even more emotional than me. I could empathize with them; the comfort of familiar surroundings being taken away as you're thrust into a room with nineteen five-year-old strangers. The separation is not finite like divorce, but acts upon the same emotions. When the school bell rings, you head back home, unlike when the judge's gavel falls deciding your fate in the court of law. Mom leaving dad resulted in my separation anxieties as a young child, which made first days of school, or first anythings for that matter, harder on me. Knowing dad was now only a state away, instead of three states, made the first day of first grade more bearable.

Mom started to ease the restrictions on dad. First, dad and I were allowed to have once-a-week phone calls, which eventually lead to a once-a-month visit, thanks to mom and dad working out an agreement through the courts. On one of his first visits, he brought me my very own stereo console, giving me a gift that grew my love of music, though I didn't know it at the time. There was a turntable, an 8-track tape player, and an AM/FM radio, all built into one unit. Added to the stereo gift was a pair of oversized KOSS headphones, which I could plug into the headphone jack and blare my records or dad's favorite 50s tunes without disturbing mom or Stefano. I had a bevy of my own records, including The Beach Boys, Elvis, and The Osmond Brothers, along with albums of Canned Heat and The Who that I had inherited from Stefano. It wasn't the greatest collection of albums...yet...but it was a start. As the tunes blared into my audio cortex via the squiggly headphone cord, music would soon free me of the pain of my parents' divorce and the confusion of working out a relationship with a stepfather. Music was becoming my outlet, my escape. It taught me how to be alone without being lonely.

2: behind the face paint

I stared into the television set, centered under the north window, in our guest bedroom aptly named the "TV room." Crossed legged, I sat on the double bed my parents would lounge on late at night watching *Kojak* or *Columbo*. It was early Saturday morning and the local ABC affiliate awakened the airwaves with the national anthem, which greeted the first rays of daylight glistening the room. Between my legs, sat a cereal bowl, which my spoon would visit every so often as I readied myself for cartoon entertainment beginning with *Looney Tunes* followed by *Hong Kong Phooey*, *Scooby-Doo!* and eventually *Super Friends*. Like me, every other kid in America was up at the crack of dawn as not to miss a minute of cartoon heaven as there was no Cartoon Network back in 1974. If we missed our Saturday morning cartoons, we would have to wait a week to catch up with our television pals. Some mornings, I would giggle at Bugs Bunny. The lighthearted competition Bugs had with his fellow cohorts, such as Daffy or Marvin the Martian, had a sophomoric, comedic slant. On another level, the cartoon carried a very adult like narrative wrapped around great symphonies or operas like *The Barber of Seville*, which my father would play for me, upon request, on his reel-to-reel player whenever I would visit him.

On this particular Saturday morning, the door opened softly. Mom peaked into the room.

"Eric," she said in a loud whisper with her singsong vocals.

"Yes, Mom," I replied with a quick glance. Her hair was disheveled, but she still looked like a beauty queen while wearing a maroon-colored, terry cloth robe.

"Can you turn down the volume?"

"Mom, it's as low as it can go."

"Turn it down just a little bit. Stefano's still sleeping. I don't want you to wake him up," she said with a sterner whisper.

I removed the cereal bowl from between my legs and crawled off the bed. I scooted across the floor to turn the volume knob ever so slightly to appease my mother.

"Is that better, Mom?" I asked while in a deep trance, staring into the television.

"Yes, thank you. I'm going to close the door tightly. Remember, you've got to rake and bag the leaves in the front yard today."

I turned and looked back at the door. "Yes, Mom," I said with a grin.

I resumed my cross-legged position on the bed and stared back into the abyss of the glowing box as the door shut tightly behind mom. When I heard the latch catch, I knew it was safe to crawl back to the television and turn up the volume. I was a good kid aware of the wrath I'd create by stepping out of line with my stepfather. I was now protected from my parents with my cartoon friends. The knowledge of raking leaves sat in the back of my mind, but was not imperative. I would eventually get out and execute the chore, but for now, I was caught up in a world of imagination, which would help fuel my creativity with my friends on the playground in the coming week.

Our house on University Avenue was like every other residence on the block. It was no bigger, or smaller, than any of the other dwellings on our street. However, the slight difference was we were one of the only houses which had a converted attic made into tiny apartments rented primarily by graduate students. The rest of the house was spacious and had a lot of charm. Mom chose my room before they even closed on the purchase of the property. I was granted the solarium on the second floor, which sat at the end of a long, narrow hallway at the back of the house. Two of the four walls in the room were windows running from my waist to the ceiling and flanked by fire engine red drapes. Underneath the longest wall, housing the five windows, sat a desk from a build-it-yourself furniture store, which mom painted a sky blue. Across the floor, lay a black carpet remnant unable to cover the entire wooden floor. The wall, running parallel to the longest wall of windows, was painted a nondescript white and abutted the narrowest wall in the room covered by stereoscopic checkered wallpaper, which seemed to move whenever you walked across the room. A small closet tucked itself away in the corner and it too had windows facing out to the back yard. It was my first true bedroom where I could hang out on my bean bag chair and escape into the world of my *National Geographic* magazines, which came monthly thanks to my grandparents.

I felt secure within my four walls. It was my space where I could let my tears flow without being punished for them. Meanwhile, dad was a state away from me and, as stated previously, mom granted him once a month visitation. He would come pick me up early on a Saturday morning; first we would go out for breakfast and then to the mall. If I had a Gray-Y basketball game at the YMCA, we would do that first. Dad allowed me to do everything that I normally didn't do at home with mom: eat tons of candy, stay up late watching television and drink a couple sodas along the way. I was with dad. The three weekends in-between dad's trips to Champaign were the longest. I submerged myself into small escapes. Dad bought me a bike and shipped it through Sears to our house. I traversed our neighborhood with Michael and Dylan, Phillip Cullinan's kids up the street, and other classmates whom I walked back and forth to school with each day. My bike allowed me to be an explorer. My two-wheel freedom was allowing me to build an independent, geographic landscape around my house.

While I built a stable of friends from school, my parents integrated me with their academic peer's kids, either on the University of Illinois campus or at other institutions in the Midwest. One such academic child, Blake, was a son of an English professor at the University of Wisconsin and a grade older than I. When I visited Blake, in the spring of second grade at his home in Madison, my musical world took off. Blake and I shared interests in building model airplanes and watching cartoons, along with having vivid backyard imaginations. Ian, Blake's older brother, steeped himself into music. He was only seen in the Fisk's house on occasion, but his musical influence, on Blake, was enormous. Ian listened to David Bowie, KISS, Alice Cooper and many more avant-garde artists of the mid-seventies. The effect this had on Blake was paramount. Blake sang and created band noises, mostly imitating the guitars and drums, as we were building with his Legos.

"Na-na-na-naaaaaaa. Dsht. Dsht. Dsht," Blake sang. Humming along as his Lego project became bigger and bigger.

"Blake, what are you singing?" I asked.

"KISS!" He fired back without looking up from the gigantic, rocket-propelled house he was building while resuming the drumbeat bouncing around inside his head.

"I think I know who you're talking about. Who are they again?" I inquired with curiosity. I felt safe asking someone whose barriers were easy to overcome.

"Ahhh man, they're so cool. They're a rock band with four dudes dressed up as different characters," he replied. "My brother Ian listens to them all the time."

"Got any of their records?"

"Nope, but Ian does. Wanna listen to 'em?" Blake asked, while making more ambient band noises with his mouth.

"Sure!"

"Great! Let me go into his room and get one," Blake responded to my enthusiasm.

Blake got up from the card table where we were working at and headed to his brother's bedroom. Delores, Blake's mom, caught him crossing the living room upon entering Ian's abode. I could hear his mother questioning him. She was concerned Blake would disrupt Ian's space. Blake was everything his parents wanted. In Ian's eyes, Blake could do no wrong. The Fisk boys got along most of the time, but Ian had a short fuse to his powder keg emotional outbursts. He could set off into a rage at the slightest of things. Delores, on this day, was making sure this wouldn't happen while we were visiting. I heard snippets of the conversation.

"Mom, I'll put it right back where I found it," Blake pleaded.

"Well, I'm not sure what to say. Ian's very possessive about his stuff. You know that. I'll let you do it this time, but you've got to ask Ian if he minds you borrowing his things whenever he's not around," she retorted.

Around? Ian? He was never around when we visited. In fact, on the trips back from Madison, where the Fisk's lived, our car was infused with stories about Blake's older brother and the unrest he caused in the Fisk's home. Anyway, Blake went in and found the album of the hour, *Destroyer*, which KISS had just released a few months prior. It was the lifeblood of Blake.

"You've never heard of KISS before?" Blake asked me again as we ventured into his room for a listen while leaving our Lego creations behind.

"No. I've seen them on covers of magazines. One of my classmates brought them in for show and tell once," I replied.

"Brought in the band? How'd they do that?"

"No, not the band, dufus. He brought in an album," I said, as Blake pulled the record out of the sleeve, which was adorned with an oversized, KISS Army logo. He put the disc on the record player. I simultaneously grabbed the album cover from him as he dropped the needle on his turntable. The crunching of the vinyl grooves could be heard through the speakers. What audio followed seemed like a radio report with some clinking of glasses in the background. What I was really listening to was the opening track, *Detroit Rock City*.

All of a sudden, a car crash exploded from the speakers followed by a pulsating bass line. It lasted for a few seconds before a guitar, with a repeating riff, and the drums took over the tune. Over the racket, a soprano scream arrived out of the speakers, leading us into the verse. I looked at the album cover, adorned with a photographic illustration of the band, wearing their stage costumes while floating above chard-concrete debris. I then looked at Blake.

"Which one of these guys is singing?" I asked.

"The one on the left, Paul Stanley," Blake replied as the needle of the phonograph moved deeper into the song.

"Hmmm. Seems to be the most boring of all of the dudes in the picture. Who's the guy in the space boots?" I queried.

"Him?" Blake said, pointing to the guy showing four fingers on one hand while pointing to us with the other. "That's Ace Frehley, Space Ace, he's the guitar player. He's got a solo coming up."

We intently listened to the track. As the band moved through the second chorus, they greeted me with Da-da-dadaaaaaa-na-na-nana-naaaah. Unbeknownst to me, I was listening to something unfamiliar in my musical experience, the guitar solo. I was like an archaeologist unearthing a new reverberation and adding it to my aural dictionary. All the while, Blake was turning into my big brother. He was introducing me to KISS, who would stay with me during my elementary school years as my band of choice. I would lose grip of dad's influence of Elvis, Buddy Holly, Jerry Lee Lewis and others while trading in my greaser look, consisting of a leather jacket and white T-shirt, for anything resembling the dudes in KISS.

Every Halloween, from second grade to fifth, I chose to dress up as a specific KISS band member. I couldn't get up the nerve to ask my parents to buy me the official KISS face paint. So, I created my own by digging through my parent's bathroom cabinet collecting items, which I thought would work. I unearthed a white, paste-like substance, which I would use as a substitute for the base color that makes up sixty percent of the KISS look, and snagged mom's extra tube of mascara, to finish out my make-up needs. I took my costume, along with the items from my parent's bathroom, to school with me the following day. As I began to dress up in costume for our afternoon Halloween party, two doors away from our classroom, I adhered the white, paste-like substance to my face. Unbeknownst to me, the white substance I used as a base was really mentholated foot cream. My cheeks and forehead began to burn. I tried to wash it off with soap and water, but it didn't help as the scrubbing of my face only acerbated the situation. The pains I went through to be like my altar ego, Peter Criss.

I turned to Blake and began to inquire about the others in the band.

"Blake, they're great. Who's the dude wearing the dragon boots?" I asked.

Blake grabbed the album cover from my hand.

"Ahhhh, that's Gene Simmons. He's the bass player. He's kind of a devil-like character. My brother Ian told me he breathes fire and spits blood in concert."

"No way. That's so cool," I said, as I reviewed the band members more closely. "Who's this guy?" I asked, pointing to the dude, looking like he was driving a motorcycle.

"He's the drummer," Blake said, pointing to Peter Criss with cat-like make-up on.

"Peter sings the song *Beth* on the second side of the album."

Thanks to Blake, I was becoming a full-fledged fan of KISS and was dead set on buying the album, *Destroyer.* Since I didn't have enough pocket money, I had to wait for dad to come visit. I knew if I begged the right way, he would buy the album for me. Dad heard the band once and has hated them ever since, but he never refuted a future KISS acquisition. He could tell that I would play them incessantly and it was cash well spent. When I arrived home from one of dad's monthly visits with my newly acquired KISS record, I bypassed mom and Stefano with a quick "hello" as my record player was calling my name. I took the album straight to my room and put it on my turntable. I plugged in my headphones and turned up the volume as high as I could stand it.

KISS was an escape. I would listen to them all the time like when I sorted my baseball card collection or built model airplanes. I'm sure I looked kooky wearing my oversized KOSS headphones while drawing in my sketchbook or staring out the window into the back alley, running behind our house. I was a scrawny kid with oversized ear goggles, which roared with either Gene Simmons' bass or Paul Stanley singing his heart out. I was now closer to the emotion and the lyrics without interruption. Without a doubt, I thought KISS was the best band in the world. Better yet, I thought Peter Criss couldn't be beaten behind the drum kit. It would take a while for me to find out that there were a bevy of other drummers in the music world, but since I was an only child, and had no older siblings to influence me or introduce me to The Beatles or Led Zeppelin, KISS was it for me.

Overtime, I found out why KISS appealed to my fellow classmates. It was the fantasy they created by their stage personas. Everyone had a favorite band member. There was the Gene fan club or the Paul fan club. We would bring our KISS records to school and huddle around the phonograph in the back corner of the library during our lunch hour, sharing headphones just for a listen. Sometimes, our group would grow to six or seven and we would use the headphones as small speakers while ever so slowly increasing the volume of the player to hear the tunes, causing the librarian to raise an eyebrow towards us. A loud shush would come from her every now and then to remind us that we were still in the library and not to disturb others. It was obvious to everyone that the rock band, KISS, was creating a small gang of rocker wannabes. If the carting of KISS records wasn't enough evidence, then the addition of Gene, Peter, Paul and Ace into our cartoons we drew at lunch, which already included the likes of Batman or Superman, was even more validation that the band made inroads into South Side Elementary School. As soon as I had enough money, I would find my pal Jeremy, who not only shared my love for KISS, but also collecting baseball and football cards, and pleaded with his mom to take us to the record store. She would easily give into our KISS hysteria.

Gene, Peter, Paul and Ace could only take me away from the pain so far. I still longed for my father. He would call on the Sunday nights between his monthly visits. It was dad and Eric time on the phone. Dad was like clockwork. I knew when the phone rang at seven o'clock on any given Sunday night, it was him. I would usually run upstairs to my parent's room to catch the phone call. Their bedroom was a space where I had the most privacy while mom and Stefano finished dinner downstairs.

Dad and I talked about everything. I would ask about Grandma Irene and Grandpa Carl, his parents. He would fill me in on their lives as well as his. We had our own dialect too. He had me say phrases that he created while I visited him on vacation.

"Eric, what's the word?" he asked, over the phone.

"Thunderbird!" I would shout in response.

The silly call-and-response style was a way for dad to reconnect with me. Every now and then, he requested to speak with mom. Those were the toughest calls to listen in on. They weren't casual conversations about PTA, but discussions about child support payments or when I could visit him for Christmas. My father was allowed to have me visit Des Moines for the holidays, but my mom added on extra rules outside the divorce decree to make it difficult on him. She'd ask for a cashier's check of two thousand dollars in order for my safe return. She knew dad didn't have the money and he would have to take out a loan to cover it. Also, she would dictate the days in which I could visit him, making the purchase of airplane tickets more expensive. Mom knew what she was doing, playing me against my father while my stepfather was pulling the strings. The times were emotionally hard on me. I had to make them work. I had nowhere to turn to except my favorite escape, music, which now had an identity to fall behind, KISS.

3: god saves

I propped my foot up on the luggage carousel as mom, Stefano and myself waited patiently for our bags to be unloaded from our New York flight. We had just landed at Heathrow for a yearlong sabbatical leave, a benefit of Stefano's professorship. The year abroad would encompass my fourth grade year back home, at Southside Elementary School, and would not penalize my entering fifth grade upon my return home. However, this sabbatical would be the first of two years living abroad as a child and probably the easiest since there was no real language barrier other than having to learn how to spell color as 'colour' or airplane as 'aeroplane.' The only difficulty I would eventually have would be the integration into a new school, but that wouldn't be for a few weeks as today, I was assigned the duty to keep an eye out for our baggage.

We had twelve pieces filled to the gills for the year's absence from America and there was no vanity in our travel collection, just a lot of weight. Unloading the utilitarian objects from the unforgiving carousel was another issue. While some of the luggage weighed less than I, heaving the heavier ones off the stainless steel monster proved to be more difficult and strenuous. I wanted to turn in my slave labor card and hire an airport porter. My stepfather would not hear of it. In fact, Stefano brushed one porter aside when the man saw me struggling with our hanging bag, which was made of vinyl and about to split at the seams. Stefano thought children should bear some of the load of travel. Since I had no other siblings, and my stepsisters were not joining us, I was it and the complaint department was closed. I couldn't grumble because I was about to live in Europe, an opportunity other classmates at South Side Elementary School in Champaign didn't have.

While on jet lag, the mechanical ogre moving our luggage didn't want to stop. I resisted its temptation to put me to sleep. I kept an eye out for my duffel, filled with my art supplies, magazines and card games. The motor running the stainless steel beast would suddenly stop and start without notice. A conveyer belt, from below baggage claim, belched out our bags, one of which was mine. I prepped myself for its arrival, as I would need to muscle all my strength to pull it towards me upon approach. The carousel tested my preparedness. My luggage came closer. I saw its handles and grabbed one. The bag was lifeless as I pulled and tugged it over the lip of the monster. It then fell onto the floor in front of me. My job was done. All twelve pieces of baggage lay at our feet. I looked at the odd pile and began to help Stefano heave them onto a handcart we secured a few minutes before our arrival into baggage claim. Whatever bag didn't make the cart, I was held responsible for carrying. I chose my own duffel, which survived the eight-hour flight, but the shoulder strap broke in transit. Like a dog, I dragged it behind me on the way to the taxi stand where we would soon stand in a British queue to get a ride into the city.

Stefano, mom and I were embarking upon our third trip together to the United Kingdom in as many years. The previous two were over the Christmas holidays, getting myself acquainted with the country. This time, however, our sabbatical in Reading, just outside London, would last exactly twelve months, from August, 1977 to August, 1978. Although exciting, the new experience would take away my weekly phone calls from dad. I was now down to postal communication with him. His voice would remain silent until the following summer when I got back to the states. A fleeting thought of sorrow crept into my soul as we poured our luggage into the back of the taxi and headed into London to bunk in with our friends, the Stocktons, for a week's stay before moving onto our final destination, Reading.

We knew the Stocktons from back home. Every year, over Thanksgiving weekend, we would drive from Champaign to their house in Tulsa, Oklahoma to celebrate the holiday. Avery Stockton, an academic pal of Stefano, was a Joycean as well and decided to extend his summer vacation in London with his family. His wife, Corkie, flew over with their four children six weeks prior to our arrival and hunkered themselves down in a three-story house in Greenwich. The home was modestly decorated on the first and second floors, but as one ventured to the third floor, you could tell an artist lived in the residence. Half-painted canvases rested on easels throughout the loft-like workspace while stalls filled with nearly completed work flanked each side of the vast space. Tabletops of various heights were littered with jars holding paintbrushes of all sizes and shapes. Painter's palettes were scattered about the room covered with plops of oil paint, waiting to be brought back to life. Mom mentioned in passing whom the owner of the house was, but I really didn't care. It was a cool place to go explore, especially the studio.

Kip, Avery and Corkie's youngest child with fire-red hair and freckles, was about my age. We had a fondness for music, which immediately connected us at the hip. Kip and I were eight weeks apart in age and, like Blake back in Madison, he possessed an enticing mischievous side as well. We would find ways to get into trouble and devised a system of lies to get out of whatever we had done. Sometimes, we escaped unharmed and sometimes not. The penalties were not that harsh. It was the fury in which they were delivered to us that scared the crap out of us, which is why we continuously did it.

Kip integrated himself, along with his siblings, into the Greenwich scene with ease. He got a leg up on the Teddy Boy/Punk boom taking over the London streets. Punks and Teds, street slang names, were the two categories London teens applied themselves to depending on their musical interest and fashion. In fact, when I arrived on the Stocktons' doorstep in Greenwich, Kip gave me the once over. When he saw my shoes, he started in on me with his phony London accent.

"Yo're a Teddy Boy, Eric!" Kip said, as he stood three steps above me on the porch while casting his body over me like a gargoyle and pointing at my shoes.

"What do you mean, Stockton?" I queried Kip.

"Yore shoes look like those worn by Teddies," Kip said with a shitty, childhood smirk.

"Teddies? Who are they, Kip?"

"Ah, Teddy Boys are the opposite of Punkers. They're into 50s music," he replied still holding onto his fake accent.

"Corkie, so good to see you," mom said over me as she greeted Kip's mother, standing behind her son.

"Well, I like Punkers, Kip! Not Teddy Boys," I said in disgust.

"Shari, you look ravishing. Stefano, great to see you as well," Corkie said, greeting my parents while she leaned over her son to peck my stepfather on the cheek.

"The Punkers'll beat you up. They hate Teds!" Kip exclaimed. "Looks like the boys are going to be just fine. Come on in. We'll put you up on the second floor. Avery is in the back library, awaiting your arrival," Corkie said, as she turned to the front door and led us into the grand entrance. I looked at mom for validation to follow Kip into the deep reaches of the house. I was now released from the parental leash and allowed to wander with my red-haired friend.

Since I was younger than Kip, I was his whipping post. I'm sure his welcome was how he took out the frustration of being the youngest of his three Catholic siblings. We made-up moments later and over the coming days, wandered London together with our parents. Mom and Stefano kept it interesting for us kids by making sure a museum or two were on the daily trek into the city. It was during these excursions when we often ventured into London's West End, the home of London's punk movement, a youth-based reaction towards the celebrity of the monarchy and class status.

Kip and I would gawk at the misfits hanging out on street corners with their multi-colored Mohawks sprouting above their black leather jackets inscribed with scrawl and defamed Union Jacks. Most punkers wore a standard dress code, consisting of a leather jacket, a ripped T-shirt and a pair of tartan pants. The tartan-patterned fabric, a representation of aristocracy, was integrated into the punk look and denigrated often by ripping it and then safety pinning it back together. It was their way of displaying dissatisfaction with the ruling class. Punker's also had another self-identifier, safety pins, which they either pierced through their ears or their nose. Both genders wore boots and leather jackets. From a distance, these kids seemed approachable, but one got a sense that there was a vicious underbelly to them.

Kip and I didn't care. Maybe our adolescence was the saving grace as we stared at the punkers in awe. I'm sure a pair of nine-year-olds posed no threat to them. They probably liked the attention since they weren't getting it from home. Kip and I found it sport in spotting these tribes of misfits on the streets and pointing them out to our parents. Punkers were the outsiders we wanted to be. I'm sure our parents would have freaked out if we bleached our hair, died it some unnatural color and came home with a safety pin through our nose. I can almost guarantee Kip would have egged me on to do it and would have walked away while I got into trouble. He was an instigator. I had to be careful. His Catholic schoolboy charm was intoxicating.

Seven days after our arrival in London, Stefano, mom and I left the confines of the Stockton's abode and embarked on our journey to Reading where we were welcomed into our sabbatical home with the announcement of the death of Elvis Presley. British television brought the passing of The King into our little bungalow house on Ridgeway Road. We watched it all unfold as hordes of people descended on Graceland, like flies to a dying carcass, to mourn his death. An era had ended. Elvis was the face of the youth movement of the 50s and fans fawned over him like he was the second coming of Christ. Everywhere Elvis went throughout his life; he was haggled. In the end, he wasn't the sex symbol he once was, but he was still Elvis, adorned in Rhinestones and adored by his fans. My father admired Elvis, but he wasn't fanatical. Whenever I brought up KISS, or any other band dad didn't like, he reminded me how nothing could compare to his era of music, including Elvis.

"That's real music. That's rock 'n' roll. What you have today is just crap. I grew up with Elvis, Carl Perkins, Buddy Holly and Little Richard. You've got nothing that even compares to them in today's music," dad would say.

I tended not to agree. I thought I knew better. But now, as I look in the rearview mirror of life, my father was right. Instead of giving me his coveted Elvis 45 rpm records when I was eight, he bought me *Elvis Pure Gold* instead. Elvis Aaron Presley graced the record jacket dressed in a Rhinestone outfit from Vegas. It wasn't the Elvis I admired. The fat, bloated man captured on the cover was past his prime. In first grade, and before my peers filled my head with KISS, I was so caught up in the Elvis craze that I begged my dad to buy me a leather jacket. He did. Once the jacket was in hand, I would succumb to slicking back my hair, put on a white T-shirt and became a greaser. I was a cross between television's The Fonz and Elvis, but even cooler.

Ironically, Elvis' death took a minute, or two, out of the Queen of England's Silver Jubilee celebration during the month of September when we arrived. The commemoration was an escape for Britons from the social turmoil and unrest existing under the rule of Prime Minister Leonard Callaghan's Labor Party. His political machine was ruining the country as the Silver Jubilee tried to do the opposite, help unite the spirit of the United Kingdom. Punk, on the other hand, was anti-everything: monarchical, government or anything pertaining to an establishment. The conflict among the classes, plus the celebration of a monarch, was the perfect seed for this rebellion. In fact, the Sex Pistols, one of punk's notorious bands and poster children for the genre, pulled a publicity stunt performing their anti-monarchy anthem *God Save The Queen*, at high volume, as the band floated down the River Thames on a barge. It was a brilliant marketing idea for punk. Malcolm McLaren, who managed the Sex Pistols, pushed punk fashion from his boutique, SEX in London's Chelsea neighborhood, to music, using the Pistols as his foray into the genre.

None of what I had witnessed in London's punk movement existed at Ridgeway Primary School in Reading where I went to school. When I stepped onto the playground on my first day of school, I stood out. I was an American and the kids glommed onto me. As I wandered the playground, being introduced by the headmaster, I would be interrupted by a passing question wanting to know whether I knew *Starsky & Hutch* personally or if *Kojak* really ran New York City. I was hounded on all sides. I was taken aback by how much they knew about my country and how little I knew about their society other than what I had seen in London. The only preparation I had for my year abroad in the United Kingdom was found in the musty pages of mom's hand-me-down encyclopedias. Each night, months before we left for the United Kingdom, I had to read a new entry. One night was about the history of the Norman Conquest while another was spent researching Sir Walter Raleigh or Lord Nelson. None of which would come into my lunchtime conversations with my working class counterparts nor on the football pitch after school. What these kids really wanted to know was if we had a red sports car, like the one in *Starsky & Hutch*, parked in our driveway back home.

Overtime, the American inquisition would cease. I would be granted entry into my fellow schoolmate's lives. Living near a working class neighborhood was new for me. Actually, it lived behind our bungalow and only visible from the farthest reaches of our back yard behind the pear trees and gooseberry bushes. All of their houses were made of cinder block and linked together. The only differentiation, from one property to the other, was the color of the door. Spencer, a classmate of mine, and his parents lived in the midst of these concrete row houses. His older brother Sam, who went to the Upper School, was deeply rooted into the punk movement, but didn't wear the uniform in any means. He definitely knew of The Stranglers, The Clash and the Sex Pistols. From an outside observation, I would say Spencer was the darling of the two kids, but had a rough mentality, part of which was being in the working class. He would often be in the living room showing his mom new Teddy Boy dance moves that he picked up from his cousins, whom he visited often, much to the chagrin of his older brother. While keeping the left leg stiff and sort of po-going on it forward and backward, he took his right foot and did a heel-toe combination that crossed the left foot on alternate beats. I'm not sure if this was a partnered dance or something you would do solo, but it caught on quick. I brought it home to show my parents. As usual, they glazed over it and moved onto whatever academic project was in the mix. Whenever I was in our back yard playing, I would take Spencer's dance moves and create my own version. I didn't need the music. I had a set rhythm and added more moves to the steps that I had already seen. Since I was in my own space, both in my head and in private, I felt safe.

My year in Reading was coming to an end. After living in the United Kingdom for twelve months, I was now a europhile. Upon my reentry into South Side Elementary School, I was greeted by my friends and again, bullied by my enemies. It was as if my being gone for a year didn't happen. The KISS phenomenon, which I was deeply rooted into before I left for Reading, was now starting to diminish with my classmates. The relationship I had with Gene, Peter, Paul and Ace would come to a complete halt as I started middle school the following year. It would be during those middle school years when I would witness my mother crying over the death of John Lennon, her musical hero. She had as much of a connection to him as my father did to Elvis. My musical horizon was changing as well. I moved from KISS to AC/DC in about a year and never looked back. Although I had seen punk first hand, the interest in the genre didn't follow me back to the states. The style was such a juxtaposition to mainstream American music, which was becoming enraptured with disco.

I wasn't the only one taking notice of the change in music during the late seventies. So were a group of kids, from North Dublin, brought together by a youthful Larry Mullen, Jr., when

Larry posted a note on Mount Temple Comprehensive School's notice board. He requested fellow classmates interested in music, and wanting to start a band, to come over to his house. Paul Hewson and David Evans showed up in the Mullen's kitchen for auditions. Adam Clayton came along later, wearing an afghan coat, funky glasses and sporting a bass guitar, which garnered his entry into the band immediately. All four future members of U2 were inspired by music, as the punk movement was the glue of the time. Paul and David felt akin to The Ramones, Television, Patty Smith and a handful of others housed in New York's CBGBs. These bands, along with The Clash and a few others, laid the groundwork for what the four Dublin lads wanted to create, a rock band. Harnessed with the inability to play their instruments, except for Larry, they soaked it all in and created their own sound.

Within a few short weeks, of the initial meeting in Larry's parent's kitchen, the band configuration was set. Larry, involved in his youth in the Artane Boys Band, a Dublin marching band, was on the drums. Afro wearing Adam played the bass. David, now nicknamed The Edge, played the Gibson Flying V guitar. Paul, nicknamed Bono Vox, became the front man. They regurgitated punk to the world in a rock band initially named Feedback, then The Hype and finally, as U2.

4: a witness to solidarity

We landed at Amsterdam's Schiphol Airport, in September, 1981, for another yearlong sabbatical adventure, on the Côte d'Azur, in the South of France. Stefano's love affair with France was the driving force for this nine-month escapade away from America. My parent's desire was to live half of the year in the United States and the other half in Paris. On paper, it was a great idea. However, it was almost impossible to achieve. Instead, they settled for a year abroad in France, which was the closest way to achieve their dream. Within a few weeks of our arrival in the Netherlands, we would take up residency at the Camargo Foundation housed in Cassis, a small fishing village located on the Mediterranean Sea about 20 kilometers east of Marseilles. In the meantime, we traveled slowly to Cassis, picking up mom's new Audi and meeting up with some old friends along the way.

Two years prior to our French expedition, mom and Stefano enrolled me into advanced French classes, at a local high school in Champaign, while being visited weekly by a private tutor at home. The culmination of these studies would plant me into a French speaking school, forcing me, a thirteen-year-old, to converse with classmates in French and help me survive an education in a foreign tongue.

Within days of our arrival, on the southern coast of France, my parents made an appointment with the principal of the C.E.S. de Cassis, my future school. Mom and Stefano towed me along for the introduction where the conversation was completely versed in French. I was lost, but my parents referred to me as their jeune fil or young boy. Seated between my parents, I smiled on cue and never let on to how much trouble I could get into. Saintly is what my parents wanted me to be while anxiety ran through me. I now realized speaking French meant survival. There was no opportunity to turnaround and go back to the States. I was here to stay and the function of enduring the new challenges ahead of me was part of my education.

I knew what to expect on the first day of school in a foreign country. I had been thrust into this situation before, knowing no one on the playground and having to make friends. Now, I had to do it speaking French. Luckily, the kids I met on the playground were no different from those I had met in Reading, four years prior, except for their deep fascination with Marilyn Monroe, James Dean and the Marlboro Man, an America unfamiliar to me. I, on the other hand, became interested in French soccer, which helped me grow a close-knit group of friends. They were a cool gang of kids to hang out with, but I yearned to speak English. I found relief when I met François, a playground advisor, who within weeks of my arrival, revealed to me that he spoke pretty fluent English. We became instant friends. François was studying English at a collegiate level and leaned on me to advance his intonation for his oral exams. On occasion, he would give me a handful of paragraphs to record on cassette tape. I would take them home and read them into our cassette recorder. In return for the recorded cassette, he bought me an AC/DC T-shirt. François was my saving grace to the year abroad. Whenever I felt like speaking my native tongue, slang included, he was there for me by providing an escape from the burden of conjugating verbs in my head as I carried on with my classmates.

After the first trimester, the Christmas holidays arrived and it was time to vacate our little French fishing village nestled along the Mediterranean coast. We headed north to England where my parents would leave me, with their friends in London, as they flew to New York in order to make their annual trek to the Modern Language Association Convention, a collection of like-minded intellectuals, giving papers in their areas of expertise. Our first stop on the journey had to be Paris. After five hours of driving from Cassis, we checked into our quaint, Left Bank hotel and equipped ourselves for an afternoon jaunt across the city under a cold, grey sky. We sauntered through some of Stefano's beloved areas of the Rive Gauche, taking in as much as we could in one afternoon, following the winding streets leading from one arrondissement to another. Paris, no matter what the weather, was always beautiful, especially in the parks. This day was no different as we ventured to L'Esplanade des Invalides, an amalgamation of buildings, surrounding a park, paying homage to the military history of France, including Napoleon Bonaparte's burial site.

Upon our entering the park, we noticed a group beginning to gather on a side street to our right. Protestors, maybe forty in size, were carrying banners covered in red scrawl while others were hoisting red and white flags. The crowd grew and began shouting. One moment, their voices were loud then silent. During the lull, an unseen protestor led a chant with a bullhorn. The group responded. The crowd was now entrenched in a call-

and-response style protest. Even if we wanted to get closer, the narrowness of the street, filled with onlookers, hampered our ability to go forth into the crowd. So, we stood afar and observed. The scene was reminiscent of those I had seen at soccer matches, which I watched on television, where passionate fans would sway back and forth in the stands at their home pitch, provoking the competition. Stefano, a person who was interested in any uprising, paused for a moment. He became engrossed in the commotion while mom, dressed in my grandmother's full-length mink coat to keep out the Paris chill, stood by his side.

"Stefano, what's this protest about?" mom inquired, clutching the collar of her coat as not to allow the chill of the winter air to grace her neck.

"I'm not sure ma cheri. I can't make anything out while their backs are to us. I think they're shouting in Polish because I see familiar red and white flags in the distance and we are near where all of the consulates of foreign countries have offices," he replied.

"Only in Paris would you see this," she muttered with a sigh.

I was glued, waiting for the crowd to turn ugly. The chill in the air became extinct.

"Mom, it's a protest!" I shouted under my breath as I kept an eye on the energy, emanating from the crowd.

"Shari, love, I'm curious to find out what this is all about, but I'd think we'd better stay here and not venture any closer," Stefano said. He too was absorbed.

Mom looked regal in her mink coat. She lost interest in the now-growing mob half a block away and turned to her left with disinterest while still clutching my stepfather's arm. She began to take notice of other Parisians in the park huddled on benches, talking in groups and going about their daily lives feeding the pigeons. What was happening on that tiny side street of Rue de

Talleyrand was nothing new to the locals. These sorts of disturbances were commonplace and became part of the city's daily chatter. Mom returned her attention to us.

"Really, you two are so enraptured. It's like you're watching a car crash in slow motion. You can't get enough. I'm getting cold. My feet are freezing and I need to keep moving," she said, tugging on Stefano's arm while hopping slightly to stay warm.

"Come on Gonfalon. Your mother's lost interest," Stefano said, as he put his hand, shrouded in a leather glove, on my shoulder and gently nudged me. I was still staring at the horde, unwilling to move.

Slowly, I turned away from the visual disturbance while the nickname Gonfalon rattled around inside my brain. Only a son of an academic would get such a moniker. It was a cool name, but I had no idea where it came from. Maybe, Stefano called me such because Gonfalon was unique. The thought was fleeting as I reran the images of the protestors through my head. I could hear cars passing by and Parisians talking on the streets, but it was all background noise. Something inside was telling me to remember what I just witnessed as I held back a few paces from my parents while we trooped south to Rue de Grenellea and hung a left on a small side street, Rue de Saint-Simon. We eventually found ourselves on Boulevard Saint-Germain and headed back into the heart of the Left Bank of Paris, an area known as a haven for scholars, prophets and artists. Eventually, we made our way to Café de Flore, which was seated at the corner of Boulevard Saint-Germain and Rue St. Benoit.

We planted ourselves just outside the front door, facing Rue St. Benoit, which was now enclosed for winter. Mom seated herself first followed by Stefano. She rolled her mink coat over the back of her chair. As usual, I flanked Stefano facing my mother and looked into the café. We were being Parisians, for one night, having a pre-dinner drink before moseying to my favorite Parisian restaurant, Le Petit Zinc, just around the corner. No matter where we traveled, my parents always integrated themselves into the country they were visiting. They strived not to be noticed as Americans. Even Stefano smoked the local cigarettes, Gauloises. On this night, like any other, he extracted a crisp, blue Gauloises box out of his blazer. He rapped it against the table then proceeded to pick up the matches off the table next to us. He leaned over and lit mom's cigarette, Merit's of course. He then lit his own. A huge plume of smoke came out of his mouth as he forced it upward into the air. As the cloud of smoke hovered over us, and then slowly wafted down, my parents began to entangle themselves into a conversation regarding their upcoming trip to New York while I was to be left behind with friends in London. I paid little attention to their conversation as I began to drift to the outside world in my own silence. It was commonplace for me to do this while my parent's held court in conversation.

On this night, I turned around in my chair and faced the street. Lost in thought while Parisians walked by, I reflected on life and how, to this date, it had been so jumbled. I hadn't lived in one house for more than five years. Compared to my friends, living in the homes in which they were born, I was sort of a young vagabond, reaping the benefits from one parent while I longed for the other. If only I could find a way to keep my emotions at bay, I would feel less anxious. My interest in music was helping me. I brought our tape player, to Cassis, along with a collection of cassettes, which included songs from dad's collection of 45s and other various albums I owned, for my own personal entertainment. The sounds emanating from the three-inch cassette recorder's speaker was satisfying, but I missed my stereo. I longed for my room and the place of solace it provided. My music was at a stand still since I had no interest in listening to foreign radio stations. AC/DC would grace the covers of local music mags and I would try to read them, as best I could, but the language barrier frustrated me. Mom would eventually pick up AC/DC's latest LP, *For Those About To Rock (We Salute You)*, in New York over the coming holiday, but since we had no record player in the apartment, I had to find someone to tape it for me. Luckily, the Director of the Camargo Foundation, where we lived in Cassis, was pleased to do this for me, but asked me afterwards how I could listen to such loud racket. I shrugged my shoulders and moved on.

As the consumption of my Perrier came to completion and I fell out of my daydream, evening approached the city and the streetlights came alive. The ambient light above us inside the café illuminated the room while snowflakes began to gently fall from the sky outside the café. Not small flakes, but big, wet ones. My parent's conversation changed course from academia to the weather. The snow caused a stir at the table. My stepfather spoke of witnessing a winter's eve, similar to tonight, during one of his first trips to Paris twenty years prior. While we deepened our banter about how the snow reminded us of home, a solemn group of marchers began to parade in front of the café down Rue St. Benoit. They carried banners, held vigil candles and sang as they passed by us. We recognized the parade. It was the same protest group we observed earlier in the day near L'Esplanade des Invalides. Gone were the outbursts. The emotion, permeating the throngs of men and women, was quiet, as if a requiem mass for a fallen soldier was about to commence. The falling snow, at this point, was becoming a special effect as Stefano struggled to interpret the scrawl on the banners, which we could now see with clarity because they were stretched out in front of the marchers approaching us. He thought the word was solidarity, but wasn't sure. We figured out that the crowds were up in arms about something in Poland because we recognized the Polish flags. What was there to demonstrate about, in the middle of December, concerning Poland? We had to find out.

As soon as the masses passed by, life returned to normal on the street and in the café. We paid our bill and exited into the evening towards the restaurant.

"I really want to know what that single word was scrawled on the signs and placards," I said, as I dragged my feet through the soft snow.

"I'm puzzled too, Eric," Stefano replied.

"When we first saw them, I thought they were ravaged soccer fans as they waved their flags while shouting at that building earlier this afternoon," I stated.

"Yes, Gonfalon, they had passion. I'm sure they're not protesting about living in the south of France," he said, trying to bring me into the conversation.

"I'm over that. I guess I enjoy school now," I said with some hint of low-key exhilaration.

"Remember when Eric fell asleep at the table the last time we were at Petit Zinc. The waiter brought over the dessert and tried to wake him?" mom said, as she squeezed my hand tighter.

"Yeah, I had to carry him back to the hotel that night," Stefano interrupted.

"Was that the '74 trip?" mom asked rhetorically.

"Yes, the first time we took him to Paris," he replied. My stepfather had the brain of a sponge and remembered everything. His intellect was off the charts.

In the coming days, we discovered the chaos, that enfolded in front of us near L'Esplanade des Invalides, was a reaction to the Polish government closing the borders to Poland, resisting anyone coming or going from that country. I was a spectator, on

December 13, 1981, to the beginning of the Solidarity Movement marches, the rise of power of Lech Walesa and observing firsthand the basis of the narrative for U2's song, *New Year's Day*. The events I witnessed would eventually become the cornerstone in my interest in the Irish quartet. U2, observant of the Polish Solidarity movement, would be huddled in a studio, completing work on the *War* album, in the coming spring of 1982. Reported accounts said U2 were so moved by the passion of the Polish people that they reworked their existing love song, aptly titled *New Year's Day*, into a political anthem. The narrative of the song doesn't echo, nor mention, the Solidarity Movement of Poland, yet the undertone of the lyrics spoke to a new beginning and a new day. In time, *New Year's Day* would become a hit single for the band, launching Bono, Edge, Larry and Adam onto the world's stage.

5: the summer of introduction

Eight months after witnessing the Solidarity protest in Paris, mom enrolled me into Cascia Hall Preparatory School in Tulsa, Oklahoma in the fall of 1982. I was now a freshman in high school and knew no one in my class except for Kip Stockton. Kip's dad, Avery, sat on the Board of Trustees at Cascia and provided me acceptance into his Alma mater. I now had to wear a uniform to school, consisting of a blue blazer, tie and slacks. Gone was my individualism and showing up at school wearing jeans and a T-shirt. Now, my parents wanted me to have the best education one could receive. However, I didn't buy into the prep school ideals. I craved to keep my individuality among a sea of blue blazer wearing kids as AC/DC was still implanted in my tape deck at home.

Prep school also brought on new challenges. Not only did I have to make new friends, but also had to wear the right clothes when not on campus. The Stockton family assisted me during my adjustment period. Kip's sister Beth, a senior at our sister school Monte Casino, helped me shop for clothes. Since she was a preppy fashionista, Beth contributed her insight into the Cascia lifestyle. Button-fly jeans, top-sider shoes, and button-down shirts were a must in my closet. I had to look the role in an already-established clique. However, I didn't adhere to the ideals of what-to-do and how-to-do it all the time. I found relief from the surreal world of preppiedom by hanging out in my bedroom with my stereo tuned to local FM radio or hijacking my cassette deck with various recordings, both in styles and performers, I collected over the years. Thanks to Kip's influence, my record collection began to expand with the likes of the Stray Cats, The Clash and more Who albums.

While I adjusted to high school, the musical panorama was changing as well. Rock radio was about to become a dinosaur. A new form of radio was invented for cable television. The station was named Music Television, or MTV for short. Over the next seven years, MTV would revolutionize the music industry. We didn't just listen to music. We watched it. Melodies and lyrics were not auditory anymore. Musicians now had to think differently about their promotion, which now included the addition of these music videos. Sometimes, the video would eventually compete with the single itself, as song lyrics came to life, in the tale told through these short films. A perfect example is The Clash's *Rock the Casbah*. Everything mentioned in the lyrical narrative, of the recorded song, was represented on screen: a sheik, a Cadillac, and fighter jets. As the medium moved on and more indie film directors were hired, the videos took on an art house style as well as the introduction of groundbreaking technology. Take, for instance, the band A-HA, who mixed cartoon-like drawings and live action in the video for their hit song, *Take On Me*. What they were doing, in those five minutes of film, was revolutionary. On the flip side, there were videos created from the silliness of the song. You need no examples here because they were a dime a dozen. MTV was the only vehicle playing music videos and had very little competition in their early days.

Sadly, I didn't have MTV. Our house was a no television zone. Mom and Stefano fell in love with BBC television while we were in Reading and threw the boob tube out the window shortly thereafter. They never looked back nor regretted their action. However, during the summer of 1982, thanks to some neighbors in Des Moines, I had been exposed to just enough MTV that I now had to find my fix in Tulsa. Kip was my connection. He was a fellow MTV junkie. We would stretch out on his parent's bed to catch rays from their Zenith television, watching rockers, like The Cars, Van Halen or Peter Gabriel, who became as familiar to us as the families portrayed in the television sitcoms of the day. We were video voyeurs with our hormones raging out of control. If music was the hook, then the gross displays of sexuality, or the over-the-top portrayals of masculinity, were the enticement. While radio produced a handful of Madonna fans, MTV created an army of Madonna wannabes who wore sexually provocative tops, disheveled blonde hair, short skirts and strutted around in torn-fishnet stockings while looking 'oh so coy' over their Ray-Ban sunglasses. The power of the image was the new thing of the 80s. Nothing could compare to the impact MTV was to have on our pop culture and it affected me.

During my high school years, I would land on my father's doorstep for every holiday and therefore, formed two peer groups, one in Des Moines and one in Tulsa. It was hard to make friends in a new school and even harder in a town where I lived for a handful of weeks during the year. I had no social network in Des Moines other than my parents. Dad, however, had the foresight to enroll me into ceramic classes at the Des Moines Art Center each summer. He signed me up for two reasons. The first was to foster the creativity I had inside me. The second was to introduce me to other kids, possibly leading to a friend or two. He was right in both cases.

In my ceramic's classes, I would make friends. Some would stick while others would fall by the wayside. Then there was Chad

Kaperak, whom I met in the summer of 1983, after my freshman year in high school. Chad, four years my junior, was a dirty blonde haired kid who stood out in class with his know-it-all mannerisms. He was advanced for his age, sitting on the potter's wheel throwing bowls out of raw pieces of clay with ease. Some days, when I sauntered into class, I thought he was the teacher by the amount of students standing around him, watching as he effortlessly threw pots. It was Chad's ability to creatively problem solve, his thirst for trying new things and his simply being different that attracted me to him. Also, Chad and I shared the same insatiable appetite for music and movies. His bedroom was a fine example. One step into Chad's room and you were transported to another place as he plastered his bedroom walls with subway movie posters, including *Mad Max* and *The Terminator.* Chad also had a thirst for indie bands such as The Smiths, The Cure, R.E.M. and the list goes on for miles. One of the bands in the mix was U2, an Irish post-punk group who barely made it onto a record label, but would make a big, musical footprint in the coming years.

Inseparable that summer, Chad and I were either at the Kaperak's house after our ceramic's class or on bike riding adventures into Water Works Park. Some afternoons after class, Chad would occasionally cart over his tapes of U2 to my house and we would play them on dad's recently purchased cassette deck. Dad was protective of his Hi-Fi system, which consisted of a tube amplifier, a preamp, a reel-to-reel tape deck and a turntable. The sound, emanating from dad's hand-built speakers, was the richest and most delicate sound one could ever hear. It had just enough bass that when the rhythm section kicked in, it would rumble the floor. Luckily, my upstairs bedroom was hotter than a swamp, which gave Chad and I the excuse to use dad's stereo in the air condition first floor of the house.

On this particular afternoon, I sat in dad's Corbusier chair about arm's length from the volume knob of his stereo while Chad sat on the floor cross-legged next to me. He dug into his backpack for some cassettes as I flipped on the switches, just as dad had taught me, and let the stereo warm up. Chad handed me U2's *Boy* album. While waiting for the stereo to come alive, I put the cassette into the player. When the tubes started to glow, I hit the play button and began to stare at the speakers in anticipation.

The opening track, *I Will Follow*, began with an amateur band count in by the lead singer followed by a repetitive guitar riff. I recognized the instrument, yet the sound, emanating from the speakers, was foreign because I was more familiar with bands crushing a wall of six-string, distorted sound. The guitarists I listened to, Pete Townshend, Angus Young and Ace Frehley, sounded nothing like U2's guitarist, who was using a natural sounding guitar with a little echo. I wasn't buying into Chad's new band just yet. In fact, I wanted to know what attracted him to U2.

Eight bars into *I Will Follow*, the singer's voice appeared, again. Now, he was announcing the name of the tune; an added amateur practice I thought as I waded through another half-dozen or so bars of music before he began to sing. To me, the singer lacked enough guts, or grime, in his intonation to front this huge wall of sound, coming from the drums, guitar and bass, which was being projected from the back of the track. Chad had no album art for reference, just a generic plastic case. I relied on my imagination and conjured up an idea of what the singer looked like. I wasn't granting the dude any lead way as I stopped the tape mid-song. I then swiveled around in the chair and looked at Chad.

"Where's U2 from?" I asked.

"They're out of Ireland," Chad responded. He was a walking U2 encyclopedia.

"Where'd you hear about them?"

"Partly my dad, some friends and MTV." Chad was exactly like me. He got his musical input from his peers and parents.

I turned back to the tape deck. Hit the play button and wallowed in the song some more. I let the tape roll for another minute or two and then hit the stop button. I swiveled the chair back around to Chad.

"What do you find so intriguing about them?" I asked, as I silenced the band.

"Oh, they're awesome. Listen to the drummer."

"Listen to the drummer? How can I listen to the drummer when the singer sounds like a girl?" I was irritated and hoping for something to grasp onto in the tune.

"Girl? The singer? What do ya mean, Shivvers?" Chad looked at me through his double-barreled, shotgun eyes.

"Your lead singer sounds like a fag, Chad, plain and simple," I said. "He doesn't sound like anyone I know in rock music. He ain't no Bon Scott of AC/DC nor does he have the vocal range of Roger Daltrey in The Who."

"Wait. Give'em a chance dude! All you listen to is that metal crap. Okay. I give you credit for listening to The Police but that's it." Chad was now becoming defensive and agitated.

"What about The Who, Chad? What about Elvis? Give me a break. I listen to a lot more than just metal!" I retorted, knowing I wasn't going to get anywhere with him.

"Come on Shivvers, let the tape roll. You've only heard one song you fag!"

"You're calling me a fag. Listen to your singer. He's turning me off," I replied and paused.

Now, I was stuck because I am, and always will be, a visual person who relies on album covers to give me insight into the band I am listening to. In this case, I had no images to refer to, not even a band photo.

"Chad, since we don't have any album art, let's go through the band one member at a time. What's the singer's name?"

"His name is Bono."

"Bono? Like Sonny Bono? What the hell kinda name's that, Chad?"

The vision of U2 fronted by a cross dresser was becoming an ever brighter picture in my imagination. I knew bono was a Latin word for good, but good for what in terms of U2, I didn't know. I turned to start the tape in anticipation of a reply.

"I don't know. It's his stage name. By the way it's Bah-no. Who cares what the fuck his name is anyway," Chad replied. Now twiddling his fingers, Chad sat motionless and stared at the stereo.

"Well, it's your band. You should know how he got such an odd name, right? Not every band has members with stage names. What are Bahhhh-no's bandmate's names?" I stammered.

"Who cares Shivvers! Do you like them or don't you?" he interrogated me.

"Answer my question first. Again, what are his bandmate's names?" I asked with disgust.

"The Edge, Adam and Larry. Edge on guitar,..."

"The Edge?" I interrupted.

"...Adam on bass and Larry playing the drums. You happy?"

"No. Now, I'm even more confused. I got the Larry and Adam part, but now The Edge? Where did he get that name?"

"I dunno. Some name he made up. Like Sex Pistol John Lydon did by calling himself Johnny Rotten," Chad said while deflecting his disgust.

"Seriously Chad, I'm not sure if I'm in on U2 just yet. I know of no band that counts off their songs, on a record, nor do any of my bands announce their song's title at the beginning of the track. A little amateur, if you ask me...Secondly, I'm not sure the music's doing it for me...The singer, BAHHH-NO, is out."

"Fair, but keep listening. You cannot judge them on one song.

Play the next tune on the tape," Chad said. He was now pointing to the tape deck and spurring on the debate.

"Fine, we'll move on," I said, as I leaned backward and blindly hit the play button while staring at Chad. The player head met the acetate tape and the cassette began to roll along once more.

With the contention behind us, Chad and I listened to the rest of the album. Not only was I having problems with the singer's voice, but the lyrics were unfamiliar territory to me as well. The tunes were more ethereal than anything I listened to prior and the idea of singing about the adolescent shift from boyhood to manhood went way over my head. I liked the simplicity of heavy metal. Such genre stayed within a very limited scope of narrative, mostly on sexuality and heightened masculinity. None of that existed here. I couldn't make the connection between the title of the album, *Boy,* and the main thrust behind the collection of songs. Bono, like me, had strife in his life when his mother died, which mirrored my struggles, dealing with my parent's divorce. U2, and Bono, were speaking to me, through the album, and I didn't know it.

By the end of the afternoon, the sun had cut through the golden-rod colored drapes and lit the living room. I was becoming a little less agitated. However, all I could see in the tape deck was the name of the band and album printed on the cassette. The songs were hidden. Again, I had no visual reference of the four members making up the band. At least when I was first introduced to KISS, Blake had an album cover to refer to, but as Chad sang his favorite song, *Shadows and Tall Trees*, which was now emanating from the speakers, I was slowly getting hooked. The song opened with a simple drum tap and an acoustic guitar as Bono sang in a much more acceptable vocal range for me. He lulled me into the tune, captivating me. I didn't want to give into U2 after my harsh criticism. I held onto my feelings, but the song I was listening to was beginning to melt me inside as the guitar and drums danced together without stepping on one another's toes. The lyrics floated above. I was now, for the most part, intrigued.

"Chad, is this the song you sing when you are at the potter's wheel in class?"

The song stayed with Chad and he began to sing the lyric alongside Bono.

"Yeah, it is. You like?"

"I'm interested. Not completely sold but interested."

The song came to an end. The tape ran out of acetate and stopped. The play button popped with finality. I contemplated ejecting the cassette. The interest in the last song was still with me. I wanted to hear it again. I yearned for something in the tune and needed to go back for another listen. I swiveled around in my chair and hit the rewind button. The whirring of the tiny tape reels began. I found the song's beginning and hit play.

6: still unsure

During the summer Chad introduced me to U2, I built a stable of lawn mowing clients, in Des Moines, who I cut grass for between ceramics classes and hanging out with friends other than Kaperak. Thanks to my entrepreneurial spirit, I was able to feed my musical interest from the cash income, which was spent almost bi-weekly at a record store a few blocks away from dad's house and, ironically, right across the street from his architectural firm. Going into the store was a challenge. If dad looked out his office window, while printing specs out on the Kroy lettering machine and saw my bike locked to the street pole, it wasn't going to be a fun dinner conversation that night. Getting caught spending my money on frivolous albums could've landed me in some hot water because dad always preached to me about saving my cash. But this summer, I was on a musical excursion.

As the hot summer heat melted the tar below my bicycle wheels, I cruised down the four-lane main drag of Ingersoll Avenue to The Record House, a record store housed in an old dilapidated building. Upon entry, there was a light smell of must as the window air conditioner blasted a cold breeze from across the room. The lighting wasn't the greatest either, but the air was cool and a welcome relief from the sweltering midday sun while searching for a Ska influenced band, The Police. Given one of their tapes, *Ghost in the Machine*, as a gift when I was in France two summers earlier, I started to gravitate towards them. This afternoon would be no different as I went straight to the P section of the racks and found the Masonite board emblazoned with their name on it. I flipped it forward and stumbled upon the album of theirs I already owned on cassette. I kept flipping and three albums later, I came to *Outlandos d'Amour*, which was recorded at the end of the punk boom in 1978. It contained two hit singles, *Roxanne* and *Can't Stand Losing You*. I grabbed the album, dug out the ten-dollar bill that was squashed into the bottom of my shorts' pocket and went to the cash register to pay. I then exited out the door, with my purchase, into the July afternoon furnace.

Purchasing *Outlandos d'Amour* was a significant milestone in my musical timeline. It marked the beginning of the end of my interest in heavy metal. The transformation didn't come overnight, but definitely aided by AC/DC's *Flick of the Switch* record, a flop of an album released later that summer, which allowed me to cut them loose. My KISS fandom was all but six feet under and the glam rock scene out of Los Angeles wasn't really my bag. Yes, I had a lot of interest in Quiet Riot, but who didn't. They were the first real metal band launched to number one in the charts and became MTV's metal darlings, who pushed the genre toward the main stream, as I was breaking away from it. I felt okay with my decision to move on with other musical genres because I needed more substance.

Summer came to a close quickly in 1983. Before long, it was

time to pack up and leave Des Moines for Tulsa. Chad and I said our good-byes. Unfortunately, our friendship would never be the same. We would hang out in the coming summers, but something was missing. I was now a sophomore in high school and the excitement of being a Catholic Prep school kid was beginning to dull as well. My best friend back in Tulsa, Skip Foster, obtained his driver's license just after football season ended that fall, which helped with access to our social life as it moved off campus. Some nights were spent party chasing. On others, when we weren't looking for the social scene, we'd drop in on any given classmate's house, especially girls from our sister school, Monte Casino.

One night, shortly after Thanksgiving break, we arrived unannounced to the house of my freshman homecoming date, Britney. Our impromptu visits to her home were nothing new with either her or her folks. Her parents knew the two of us well and always granted us entry when we rang the doorbell. As usual, we headed for the couch in the television room, adjacent to the foyer, and made ourselves comfortable.

The Ruskin's lived in a sprawling ranch style house, covering almost the entire corner lot of 42nd and Yorktown Road. In fact, it was so big that Britney's parents would summons her from her room via intercom just to let her know she had guests in the den. On this particular evening, while waiting for our hostess to arrive, we made ourselves comfortable. Foster grabbed the cable box tethered to the television set and went channel surfing. Skip was usually cool, but tonight, was acting like an ass because he knew I still had a thing for Britney.

"I know you're an MTV junkie, Eric," he said, punching the keys of the box.

"Yeah, I confess. I've stayed up many a late night at your place watching it just to get my fix."

"Remind me why you don't have a television at home?" Foster asked with a hint of being an asshole.

I was embarrassed to respond and luckily saved from interrogation when Britney arrived, giving each of us a glass effervescent with Coca-Cola. She was the consummate hostess and always knew what we wanted when we came over. Finally, after saying hello to both of us, she took a seat on the ottoman with her back facing the television, near Foster's feet.

"You know Skip, I can't believe you're in Father Mendez's Algebra two class with Ellen," she started the conversation in mid-thought. "She hates the class. She keeps sending me notes throughout the day, telling me what a prick he is."

I was focused on the television and not the conversation. I took a drink of my soda. The cola-coated ice rattled against the glass when it was tipped away from my lips.

"Yeah, he's a real dick. He'll put a problem on the board that we've yet to see and he expects us to solve it. Kelly's the only one in class who comes close. He's one of Mendez's blow hard ass kissers," Foster replied. He tightened his right hand into a fist and kissed it, mimicking someone kissing ass.

Foster was a year ahead of me in math and science. Instead of Mendez, I had Mr. Tate for geometry, which was enough to bitch about, but I felt I had nothing to add to the conversation. I was transfixed on the television, my eyes became glazed over as one video finished and another began. Like a jukebox that kept on playing 45s, MTV kept rolling out the videos without interruption.

While Foster and Britney became even deeper in conversation, a video came on with a guy, marching in place and dressed in a pair of black jeans and a black T-shirt, introducing the song *Sunday Bloody Sunday*.

"Oh my God!" Britney screamed. She dropped all conversation with Foster and turned toward the television, recognizing the video of U2 playing live at Red Rocks Amphitheater in Colorado. "I gotta tell you a story about this concert!" she exclaimed. "My cousin's a sophomore at the University of Colorado and had tickets to this show. Oh my God!" There was a slight pause so she could catch her breath, again. "Two nights before this show, she got the flu and couldn't go. She called me to see if I could fly out and take her tickets. I begged mom and dad, but they wouldn't let me go," she explained at a rapid pace.

While halfway through his soda, Foster sat back in his chair. He looked blankly at Britney with a conniving smile. "Guess she was shit out of luck," he said, with a hint of sarcasm.

"Oh yeah!" Britney said, with a sound of resentment hanging in the air.

"So, she missed the concert. Who cares?" I retorted, still looking at the television.

"Who cares? Look at me, Eric. This is U2 for God's sake!" Britney shouted. She was now staring at me as though the devil incarnate was running through her veins. Her pale face turned red.

I turned and looked at Britney, then to Foster for help. He shrugged.

"Well, they're not The Police," I fired back.

"The Police? They don't even compare!" she shouted, pointing her finger at me. "The Police just played Norman and lip synched the whole effin show. I was there!"

Lounging comfortably on the couch, I raised my hands in the air and said, "I can name ten more bands better than U2..."

Now, Britney was furious. She turned back to the television to take in a few more frames of the video as I began to rattle off a list of bands using each of my fingers on my right hand to indicate them by number, "Rush, AC/DC, Van Halen, The Who..." I ceased.

Foster flung a coaster at me to shut me up. It was uncool to have interest in a girl and then diss her band.

"Eric, you don't get it. You just don't get it!" Britney said, as she stared at the television.

"Yeah, shut the fuck up, Frog," Foster said to me.

"Hey, Foster, you know I hate that nickname, you ass!" I shouted back.

"Hey, you two, keep it down. My parents are in the other room," Britney scorned Foster and me.

"Ooops. Sorry," Skip said. "But you're are still a frog, Shivvers," he shouted in a loud whisper.

The video for *Sunday Bloody Sunday*, shot at Red Rocks in Colorado, came to an end. Britney blabbered on about seeing the band at the Brady Theater earlier in the summer and how she moved herself up, to the front, near the stage. I knew U2 put out their third album, *War*, a year prior, but I had yet to jump on their bandwagon. Like the song *I Will Follow* from the *Boy* LP, *Sunday Bloody Sunday* wasn't doing it for me either. It was too political. I was still having issues with the band's lyrics and trying to come to grips with the singer. Albeit, I had seen the video for *New Year's Day* and loved the footage of U2 riding horses in the snow while carrying their instruments on their backs. I'm sure Britney had a copy of the *War* LP, along with every other pop band created for MTV at the time, but I didn't ask to borrow it. I had pissed her off enough tonight and retreated in our friendship. However, her passion for U2 stayed with me.

In the coming weeks, I prepared myself for my semester finals, which would be followed by a two-week break for Christmas. Upon my arrival to dad's house that fateful holiday, I dug into his closet, looking for a camera lens. What I found were boxes and bags of unwrapped Christmas gifts. While keeping an ear out for dad, I slowly opened each bag for a peak in. Sadly, I found quite a few pieces of clothing. My heart sank. I didn't find the one fun gift I wanted until I delved into the last bag from Sears. What I uncovered was a Walkman-like personal tape player. For some reason, I knew it had to be for me. There was no question. I was excited as I was finally going to get one. I now had to figure out how to sneak in a question to my father about what I had found and to whom this gift was for in the family. One possible recipient would be my stepmom, Sylvia. My curiosity was getting the best of me. I had to find the right time to ask what he was getting her for Christmas. Several nights later, the opportunity presented itself.

"Dad, what do I do about getting Sylvia a gift?" I asked, as the highway rolled underneath us and the lights on the interstate danced over the car.

"There's no need to buy her anything, Eric. You've got time to make her something," he replied.

"Hmmmm. Make her something? What're you thinkin'? Like a piece of pottery? I've got little time over this vacation to execute anything. Plus, Chad won't let me use his potter's wheel at his house," I said.

"Yeah. Well, you've got time to go down into the wood shop and build something. She'd like that," he said, looking over at me with reassurance.

"Like what, Dad? A pencil holder?? Ah, come on," I replied.

"Hey, no attitude. There's no need to get upset. I've got you covered."

"Well, in that case, what'd you get her?" I asked.

"Well, I bought her a really neat outfit from Casual Corner at Merle Hay Mall which needs to be picked up tomorrow. It's being altered. Plus, I bought a couple books," he said, as he was changing lanes. "Oh, I also got her a personal tape player and some tapes that she can listen to at work or while she's in her office at home."

My stomach tightened. I now knew the truth about the tape

player. It wasn't for me. I always wanted one. I reminisced in my head about those days in Cassis when my friends would come to school with the very first Walkmans. I was so jealous. To hear music so clear and with your own volume, while not bothering others, was really cool. I wanted one, yet couldn't come up with the heavy outlay of cash. They were about a hundred bucks in French Francs and my allowance would come nowhere near that sum of money. Now, Sony didn't have a corner on the market anymore and they were relatively affordable.

"That's great, Dad. I've wanted one of those too. You know I make cassettes of my LPs all the time. I like the portability," I thought out loud.

"Would you like a simple one?" he responded to my verbal spouted thought. I couldn't ask for a better entry to get what I wanted.

"Yeah, that'd be cool. Would you get me one?"

"You've got to give up one of your other gifts. Well, what I mean is, I get to choose what gift you won't receive on Christmas. Instead, you get the cassette player early, on one condition. You don't show it to Sylvia until after she has opened hers," he said in a stern voice.

The following morning was freezing as dad decided to run his errands before noon. I climbed into the car, excited about the prospect of getting a new toy. However, driving all over town, to pick-up architectural plans and then courier them to the blueprint shop with my father, was the price I had to pay in order to get what I wanted. All the while, I was introduced to his cronies. For my father, he was proud to show me off. For me, it was the long day I had to endure in order to get what I wanted. Dad was cool about it. He made sure Service Merchandise was on the way home so we could stop in to make the purchase. The real question was how to explain the deal we struck in the car the night before to Sylvia, but I didn't care. I was on a musical mission, to find out more about this Irish band, U2.

As we exited Service Merchandise with my purchase, I asked dad for one more favor.

"Can we swing by The Record House on Ingersoll? I've got some cash and want to get a cassette for my new player."

"You should save your money," dad said, with an undertone of guilt.

"Awww come on, Dad. I want to buy a cassette that I've been hoping to get for the past couple of months. It'll be a short stop. Plus, I have navigated the whole city of Des Moines with you today."

"Cut the attitude! I've got to get stuff done at home for tomorrow night's open house at the Palmers. Do you know if they have it? The cassette you're looking for? I don't have much time to spare running more frivolous errands with you today."

"Oh, yeah. They'll have it. I'm sure of it."

"Who's it you're looking for?" Dad asked, wanting to know everything, even if he didn't know what, or whom, we were talking about.

"U2, Dad. A band Kaperak introduced me to last summer."

"Can't this wait?"

"No, I'm on a mission. U2's the hottest band at Cascia Hall right now and I am curious about them."

"Why can't you just go buy the album and tape it?"

"Because Dad, I want to take them with me wherever I go. Like when I fly back to Tulsa, hence, me getting the cassette player."

"Fine, I'll do it, but you'd better make it quick," dad retorted.

As soon as we got home from our journey of endless errands, I disappeared into the upper reaches of the house to my make-shift bedroom. I was so excited to listen to U2 that I couldn't open the cassette player box fast enough. The only clink in the plan was I needed batteries. Luckily, I had some double A's, in a penlight flashlight, which had just enough power to get me through the album once, but first, I had to retract the player out of its packaging and then peel off the acetate wrap covering my first U2 cassette, *U2 Live at Red Rocks: Under a Blood Red Sky.*

Once everything was ready, I shoved the tape into the player and hit play. The wheels of the cassette turned. The tape head cut across the plane of the leader and into the recording. All of a sudden, the crowd on the recording came to life. Bono announced the opening track, *Gloria*, while an eerie shimmer of a guitar entered the song. He then counted in the band and I was propelled into the live show. Unlike the U2 studio recording I was exposed to the previous summer, the energy of the band, captured between the reels of my *Under a Blood Red Sky* cassette, was more intoxicating. I forgot how reticent I was of my first criticism of U2 as the flood of crowd noise increased, indicating Bono, Edge, Adam and Larry were on fire. As the recording rolled on, I used my imagination, based on what I saw at Britney's house, of what it was like to be at Red Rocks for this show. The repetitive playing of the cassette over the coming days helped me open my eyes to my newfound band.

7: fanning the fire inside

While home in Des Moines for the Christmas holiday in 1984, my junior year in high school and a year after I purchased *Under a Blood Red Sky*, I was hell bent on buying the new U2 record release, *The Unforgettable Fire*. The first single off the new album was *Pride (In the Name of Love)*. The tune was getting a lot of airplay on local radio in Tulsa. U2's sound changed. The introduction of keyboards, the overlay of falsetto voices and the use of orchestral stringed instruments in order to fill out songs with musical texture was infused by U2's new marriage to producers Brian Eno and writer Daniel Lanois. Brian and Daniel brought the craft of creating richer songs with layering, therefore dampening the rawness of U2's sound housed on previous records. Songs emanating from *The Unforgettable Fire* record were much more ethereal. Gone were the driving beats found in tracks such as *Two Hearts Beat As One* or *A Day Without Me*. Also missing, were the religious overtones such as those embedded in the album *October*. The raw sounds rooted in the *Boy* album were memories long ago. *The Unforgettable Fire* was U2 opening Pandora's box of sonic experimentation. However, the band had issues reining it in. One either loved the album, and the new direction, or hated it. The press arrived at it with hesitation. Hard core fans despised it. I loved it.

As I resorted to my bedroom upstairs at dad's house during winter break, I listened to *The Unforgettable Fire* album frequently. The LP slept with side one face up on my turntable. The sound I found in the record's vinyl grooves sent me places I had never been to sonically. Songs were built to lull you into the strife of heroin addiction, as detailed in the song *Bad*. Another track, *Pride (In the Name of Love)*, emitted a history lesson of fallen civil rights leader Dr. Martin Luther King, Jr. and his impact on the world. I was amused. Funny, it took an Irish band to make such a deep-rooted, political, American story come to lyrical life. For me, I was born on Dr. King's birthday in 1968, the fateful year of his assassination. I was also one of the lucky kids who had the day off from school because the State of Illinois, where I lived, was one of the only states in the country celebrating January 15, Dr. King's actual birthday, as a state holiday. It took the rest of America another decade to find the "pride" to give the man his national day of recognition.

I learned over time that *The Unforgettable Fire* recording session was never quite finished or as polished as it should've been. An impending tour to promote the record was scheduled, which rushed the completion of the work. The same issue would be true for U2's *Pop* album in the 90s, over a decade later, which is important because each album moved in a different direction from its predecessor. For this conversation, it is neither here nor there. What is important, however, is MTV picked the single *Pride (In the Name of Love)* and milked it. Two video versions of the song existed on the channel, one shot in Slane Castle while the band was recording the album and the second took place in an empty music hall with the band performing to no one. MTV and U2 were creating a buzz, a brilliant idea in marketing the band to a wider audience.

Sadly, my classmates dragged their feet on this album. Even Chad was falling off the U2 horse he used to ride while I found gems on the recording, especially the third track, *Wire*. It was one of my favorite tracks. I dropped the needle on the record, at the beginning of the song, just to hear Edge's opening assault of notes. It was his signature style, the arpeggio, the art of picking individual notes from a single chord. He accentuated the arpeggio using his revered guitar effect, the analog delay, which added more depth to the song by turning those singular notes into little echoes. Edge's technique made him part lead guitarist, part rhythm section and total guitar genius. Within twelve bars of the song's beginning, Adam and Larry brought in the rhythm section at full force while Edge kept his guitar riff rolling along and over the top of the track. Adam, who used to finger pick his instrument on the *War* album, now slapped his bass, adding more percussion to U2's new sound. Meanwhile, Bono wasn't left out. In fact, he opened the song with a wordplay, which moved into the deep, narrative abyss about throwing one's life away to heroin. Edge, in turn, gave up the arpeggio when Bono sang the opening verse. The guitar player now emphasized Bono's lyrics by playing full chords with a chukkah-chukkah like sound, which now worked in harmony with the percussion. The band was tight. When the song hit the chorus, Edge kept playing whole chords to build tension. The march of Larry's drums was the glue holding the song together. As the band moved into the second chorus, Edge created a dive-bomb effect balanced with his chukkah-chukkah scratch. The storm of the song didn't look to let up for over four minutes and nineteen-seconds. The wailing of Bono, near the end of the tune, led to a rhythmical rap of lyrics. The band cut out leaving Bono to sing the last line of the song in silence.

When *Wire* ended, you felt out of breath. The following tune, *The Unforgettable Fire*, opened with softness over a heavy subject, nuclear war. While U2 stopped in Chicago on the War Tour, a local DJ, Terri Hemmert, took the band to the Peace Museum to see an exhibition aptly titled, *The Unforgettable Fire*. The survivors of the Hiroshima and Nagasaki nuclear bomb strikes created the works U2 observed in the gallery that afternoon. America, at that time, was in the middle of the Cold War and U2 needed a new theme. They found it.

The title track, *The Unforgettable Fire*, is, in some ways, a political song with no mention of the physical dropping of nuclear bombs except for one, the bomb of love – the ultimate way to move away from war. At the midpoint of the song, arrived a string section. One may see this as the turning point of dropping the love bomb without a lyrical notation. The narrative spoke to the strength of those left behind after the bombing. It was a weighty set of lyrics for side one of the album and duplicated, on the second side of the LP, in the track *Bad*, a lyric influenced by a friend of Bono's, who dove deep into heroin addiction. *Bad* was the heaviest six-minute song in their entire catalog to date and the one song people gravitated towards, as the rest of the second side of the album disappeared into tunes filled with musical ambiance.

After being immersed into *The Unforgettable Fire* album for three months, I began to meander through what was left of my high school years. I could now say U2 was there for me as a band. I eventually joined a monthly mail order record club subscription, which all my friends were into as well, and began to build my record collection at a fairly deep discount. Dad despised the idea because the subscriber had to send back order slips every four weeks, requesting not to take the featured album of the month. Otherwise, the album would arrive on your doorstep and you had to send it back. He said that's how they got you and, in the end, it was more headaches than what it was worth. I, on the other hand, had time on my hands and was responsible for returning the monthly slips promptly.

My initial order included *War*, U2's album preceding *The Unforgettable Fire*, which housed the tracks *Sunday Bloody Sunday*, *New Year's Day*, *Two Hearts Beat As One* and *The Refugee*. *The Refugee*, the one track I was attracted to first as I was already familiar with *Sunday Bloody Sunday* and *New Year's Day*, opened with Larry drumming a simple four-beat intro, which turned into a complicated march tempo. Adam's bass slid in under the beat as Bono belted out the opening verse. Edge refrained from playing his guitar until the end of the first stanza as he dovetailed into Bono's primal scream with a heavily-distorted, chord attack. The guitarist slid up and down the neck of his instrument playing the chords in the song. He followed the slide style with his signature arpeggio, filling in the gaps between the beats of Larry's thunderous, primordial-like march. Edge backed off during the chorus and then unleashed another charge of rhythm at the end of the second verse. It was this all out guitar attack that Edge did with the drummer, which made this one of my favorite U2 tracks to date.

My stable of records now consisted of three U2 recordings and I now considered myself a fan. All I was missing now, was seeing them live in concert. Genesis and Hall & Oates were the live acts I caught my junior year in high school. Fluff bands, at best, passing through my life for a fleeting moment. What I really wanted to catch was U2 playing live. As luck would have it, the band hop scotched over the state of Oklahoma for The

Unforgettable Fire Tour. However, on July 13, in the summer between my junior and senior year's in high school, I had my first opportunity to see U2 live, albeit on a black and white television, in my bedroom in Des Moines. The event was Live Aid. A concert so big that local television stations picked up the show while it was simulcast on a local Des Moines radio station, KGGO. Sadly, I didn't know the schedule of bands, but I knew U2 was on at sometime during the day. I left the television on as I went about my chores and lost track of the show until a voice punched out of the two-inch speaker.

"Up next at Live Aid will be U2," stated the television announcer.

"Holy Shit!" I screamed.

I dived towards my receiver and turned it up. My tape deck was ready, as I just happened to set my levels for optimum recording earlier in the morning and I was all set for the U2 blast off. KGGO was amid a commercial as my cassette was in the Pause/Record mode. I looked back at my television and could see the band still setting up while the announcers chatted about starvation in Central Africa. The radio commercial ended and I hit the record button on the deck. I glanced back at the television. Bono walked to the microphone, wearing his mullet, announcing *Sunday Bloody Sunday*. Larry's marching drumbeat followed. I got up and strutted in step while the band played half a world away. Dad shouted to me from downstairs to turn it down. I didn't care. I was watching my first live U2 show and couldn't believe it.

When the band hit the midpoint of the song, the lead singer strutted across the stage, singing in a call-and-response style while making sure all seventy-thousand fans in attendance felt as though they were in a small venue. Once the band had the audience captured, they settled down and fell into a thirteen-minute version of *Bad*. It was a mesmerizing performance. Bono was so caught up in the moment that he did the unthinkable and jumped off the stage. He proceeded to the front row of the audience and grabbed a woman from the crowd. Security helped her out of the crush and into no-man's land, in front of the stage. Bono and the gal danced cheek-to-cheek while being captured on a live television feed around the world, helping raise money for assistance in the continuing Ethiopian famine. It was the singular performance of any live act partaking in Live Aid that day and subsequently launched U2 into the stratosphere. When *Bad* arrived to its fateful end, U2 was now immortalized in the pantheon of rock 'n' roll. Their lives changed and so did mine.

For the next month, I played the tape of the Live Aid show incessantly, almost wearing the cassette out. Chad and I ran into one another after the broadcast. He said he was impressed. However, U2 was no longer a band he cared about. I could tell we were beginning to drift apart. Gone were the days of cycling and watching the Tour de France together. Gone was our connection behind the potter's wheel. Chad had lost his innocence while I was losing a friend. It began to hurt. We'd been so close two summers ago.

I headed back to Tulsa with some trepidation as my senior year in high school began in 1985. Once again, I had to catch up on what I missed during the summer. Really, nothing had changed over those three months I was gone up north. I asked the same questions. Who was dating whom? Who got fired from their summer job? Who found out about marijuana for the first time? Each summer away caused more separation with my classmates. Anxiety attacks now appeared out of nowhere and would become a repeated life burden. Mom and Stefano were discussing leaving Tulsa for other academic pursuits, which made my life even more unsettling. I liked Tulsa in some ways and in others, I didn't. Apprehension about next moves in life haunted me as college loomed on the horizon. Would I follow in dad's footsteps to the University of Oklahoma or would I go elsewhere? I wasn't sure. I had a few months to ponder the question. I knew one thing was for certain. No matter where I was going in life, U2 would be joining me for the journey.

8: the tree of life

Dad, bare-chested, leaned over the kitchen sink while dressed in his white boxer shorts with his crew socks clinging to his calves. He was amid his nightly ritual of cleaning his architectural drawing pens in the sink as I was summoned to talk to him about my future after graduating from Cascia Hall. I was on spring break, during my senior year in high school, and dad needed some clarification of what I was going to do after graduation. Yes, I was dragging my feet, hoping someone would help shed a light on the decision process.

"So, what're you doing after you graduate in three months?" dad inquired over the drone of water trickling out of the tap.

"I'm going to college but I haven't made up my mind where I want to go," I replied.

"Are you going to college, Eric?" Dad's question stopped when he put the pen tip to his mouth. He forced air into it. All of a sudden, black water spewed out the other end like a fountain.

"Oh, yeah. Why would I not wanna go? I just don't know where. I have applied to Illinois, Tulsa and your Alma mater, Oklahoma."

I stared at the floor hoping the conversation wouldn't become a verbal altercation.

"Let me ask you a question," dad said, as he wiped the ink splatter off the side of the sink.

"What are your mom and Stefano going to do after you graduate from Cascia?"

"They're moving to Miami."

"So, they won't be in Tulsa next year?" dad asked, as he was transfixed on scrubbing the now dirty sink with a green scrubbie that was about as old as me.

"Yeah, they're leaving Tulsa," I replied. My usual irritation with my father began to take hold. He always took on heavy topics while he was doing something else.

"So, where will you call home?"

"I'm not sure," I answered.

"You probably won't move to Miami with your mom. Am I right?"

The conversation paused again.

"Yes," I said very quietly.

"Now then, let's talk about college. Where've you applied?" He was now looking at me.

"As I said, I've applied to the University of Oklahoma, the University of Illinois and the University of Tulsa..."

"Well guess what, Eric! Mom and Stefano will no longer be teaching at Tulsa and therefore, you cannot use their academic benefits. Am I right?" he said, staring at me. My response was to say nothing and look at the floor.

"Also, you're classified as an out of state student for Illinois and it'll be very, very expensive. Sounds like you're not thinking this through," he said just before turning back to inspect the pen tip he had just cleaned.

"What about OU, your Alma mater? I have a driver's license from Oklahoma and I'm considered an in state student."

I had to stay within the boundaries of the conversation as not to be overwhelmed by my father's heavy hand of practicality.

"You could go their son, but it's ten hours away by car from here. If you go to Oklahoma, you'll not see us much, except for the holidays. It's kinda like that now. I'd love for you to go to school at my Alma mater, yet it's not practical," dad said, while inspecting the shell of the pen. He continued, "Sylvia and I've discussed you living here. I'd guess this house would be your home. If that's the case, we need to figure out what works for us." He was now fumbling with another mechanical pen. Then dad, as so often was the case while cleaning his pens nightly, went on his typical tirade and yelled, "God dammit! These fucking pens. Why can't they make them like they used to. They now use cheap plastic shit! Now, I have to go down tomorrow to get a new barrel. Fuck!"

My spine locked. Numbness anchored my stomach. Dad was irritated because I hadn't taken care of my college business. He was pissed off at his pen, yet irritated at my indecision. I shrank inside myself as I leaned against the kitchen door frame.

"Well, I think you need to look at the University of Iowa. I got the application. It's on my desk next to the slide rule and I highly advise you to fill it out right now. You're only going to be down the road. You can live here in the summer and help me out with the workshops. I'll pay for school. However, you'll have to pick up books and pocket money," he said this as he grabbed the sponge.

With dad still leaning over the kitchen sink with his butt pointing towards the back door, I left to get the application.

Upon returning to the kitchen, dad was in the same position I left him in. But now, he was slowly rubbing his hands with soap and digging the ink out from underneath his fingernails. My attitude wasn't the best. The conversation left me defensive. I began to fill out the application, adjacent to dad, with little care. Without hesitation, I declared my major, graphic design and where I would live on campus, Burge Residence Hall. It sounded as though it had prestige. From the map provided in the housing application, Burge looked pretty central on campus. I also requested a "Quiet Floor" to live on because I knew college could be unruly and I needed a place to live where I could get my stuff done. Within fifteen minutes, I turned my application over to my father with zero familiarity of the campus except for the time dad took me to Iowa City to attend a basketball game at Carver-Hawkeye Arena. Kaperak had filled me in on Iowa's Ceramic's Department the previous summer. He did a two-week intensive ceramics study and raved about it. Also, I grew up on the University of Illinois campus where Stefano taught ten years prior so I was familiar with Big Ten schools.

Within weeks of dad sending in my application, I was accepted to Iowa and organized my move out of mom and Stefano's house in Tulsa. Final exams at Cascia Hall would be finished in a few days and while readying myself for another summer with dad, I was trying to fend off my anxieties. I was about to live with my father and the rules would change again. He wasn't used to having me live with him as this was no short-term vacation, but a four-year commitment. We were both going to be challenged. College is a big change in one's life. I was now an adult, yet in dad's mind, I was still a kid. It was awkward, however, I had to make it work.

As I loaded my life into dad's van the day after high school graduation, I came back for one final trip into the house and grabbed the last remaining box. Mom, dressed in a robe, arrived from the bathroom as she heard me come down the hallway. She shadowed me to the front door. Her feet shuffled across the carpet. I stopped and shifted my weight as not to fall over when I turned to look at her. Our lives would change forever. I would no longer be living with her. I put down my box and hugged her good-bye. I could feel her tears dampen my neck. I didn't need to ask. I was off to college to become a man. After the long hug, I picked up my box and exited the front door. She closed it behind me and immediately pulled back the shade for one more look. I could feel her stare as I walked down the steps towards dad's baby blue Ford Econoline cargo van. Cascia Hall, the town of Tulsa and living with mom would all soon be a distant memory as dad and I pulled out of the driveway.

Two and a half months later, I arrived on campus at the University of Iowa with nowhere to live. My late application subjected me to temporary housing until the university could find me a place to live permanently. No one wanted to be in temp housing. Tempers, as we were called, shared an open living space with no less than eight others in a lounge room adjacent to a residence hall floor. We had no closets and very little privacy. Luckily, my temp housing flanked one of the floors where the football team lived. They had first priority when it came to moving out the tempers. Since I chose Burge Residence Hall, on my application the previous spring, that was to be my destiny. Burge had just been named one of the top ten party dorms in the United States as ranked by *Playboy* magazine the previous year. Twenty-four hours of chaos permeated Burge and I was shocked to find out a "Quiet Floor," which one could only find via a maze of back staircases and hallways, existed in the building. Next, was meeting my potluck roommates, Jimmie and Doug.

Jimmie, a typical Southern Californian, had just transferred from San Diego State. Classified as a freshman, Jimmie was waiting for his credits to transfer in order to make him a sophomore. A mix between surfer, lounge lizard and straight-up, smart kid, Jimmie had a love for all things heavy metal. Mötley Crüe, Cinderella, Quiet Riot, Black Sabbath and the list went on as long as the Sunset Strip. Being an AC/DC fan in my youth, I knew the lingo and garnered some respect. MTV, at the time, was keeping the genre alive and well with a show aptly titled *Headbangers Ball*. Jimmie would be more than happy to interrupt his second and third loves, chewing tobacco and dating all of the girls in his rhetoric class, in order to explain the difference between speed metal, heavy metal, and pop metal.

And then, there was Doug, my other roommate. A smart pothead from Palatine, Illinois, Doug was into music as well, yet steered his collection more towards the classics: Pink Floyd, Cream and Led Zeppelin to name a few. He was also our floor fool. Doug always arrived back to our room well after the midnight hour, on Thursday nights, piss drunk from the bars. His favorite trick was to grab the fire extinguisher, out of the hall cabinet, and spray the common floor down with water, which we traipsed through the following mornings on our way to the communal showers. He was the only one among us who had a solid girlfriend, Geo, who attended the University of Illinois. Doug was committed to her and known to mooch last minute bus fare from me as he was running late to get to the station to hop a Greyhound to see her. They would chat all the time on the phone in our room. Jimmie and I would do anything to disrupt the nightly phone calls. Some of our favorite practices would be to fart and then abruptly leave the room; lay on our beds and dry hump our pillows in order to get Doug to laugh; or even better, grab the telephone from his hand and ask Geo how he was in bed. There was no privacy in our abode. We were freshman and it truly was like a small, animal house.

In the grand scheme of things, our "Quiet Floor" was a mixed gang of intellectuals, future pharmacists, trippers, biology majors and soon-to-be college dropouts. The cool thing about where we lived was our proximity to the back of the building. We never had to go through the front of Burge to get to class. Instead, we used the building's fire escape exit as our private entrance. Also, we formed cliques, but they most often melted into one another as the biggest fixation, and most common connection we had, was our varied interest in music. All of us had libraries of CDs or tapes. Just like a free economy, we made them available to others. Daily interactions of exchanging music with others opened my taste to the indie music scene with the likes of The Cure, Depeche Mode, and The Smiths. In those first few weeks of school, I started to make a connection with my neighbor, Clark, who was also exploring the indie scene. Unbeknownst to me, Clark, a quiet tall blonde kid from small town Iowa, was into U2. Far be it from me to pass judgment based on someone's geographical upbringing, but I did. He had never really traveled much out of the state let alone out of the country. Yet, he compiled this vast knowledge of music and was rarely seen on our floor except for around lunch and early afternoon. His girlfriend lived across the river in Hillcrest Residence Hall where he took up a second residence. Whenever I did see him in his room, I made sure to stop in to find out what he was listening too.

I endured those first twelve weeks of college because I was thrown into the freshman soup like everyone else. We were all taking classes that were really forgettable. Mom never told me about academia and the crap classes you had to tolerate in order to move into your major. I felt that it was remedial for me to enroll in a math class when I was going to be a graphic designer. After all, I took calculus in high school and barely survived. Why would I need to relive my high school angst in math? I didn't. However, this was college. The tedium of my fall semester forced me to look forward to winter break when I would hop the Greyhound bus down Interstate 80 to Des Moines without too much to write home about. Well, I had just escaped from failing Rhetoric 101 and since I had very few friends in Des Moines, coming home for winter break was like being sent to the library for a month and forced to read the encyclopedia in its entirety. Seeing my grandparents for the Christmas festivities was the apex of excitement of my holiday trip. Well, Kaperak was around, yet not enough for me. I needed an escape, which came in the form of piling old U2 cassettes into my portable tape player and drifting away. I would daydream and scribble daily in my drawing journal. U2 provided me comfort as I was coming to grips with being a young adult, wading through common freshman distractions while keeping my nose somewhat in the books.

I arrived back on campus in the dead of winter five weeks later and much to my social life relief. Crossing the ice-covered Iowa River on a bridge, two hundred feet in length, to the art school was now my daily endeavor. The scraping of the harsh wind, across my face, meant I had to walk faster. My book bag was now heavier, not from the burden of my art school tools and notebooks, but from my eclectic collection of cassettes, as well as my tape player, that I hauled with me daily. I was listening to various mix tapes from R&B to metal. But, U2's *War* album kept coming back. I could now relate to the anger of the songs as I was struggling with life and getting out from underneath my father's shadow. Since he was paying for college, he dictated what classes I could and couldn't register for. It seemed as though I was going to school to appease him. *Sunday Bloody Sunday* was my battle cry. I wasn't feeling malice towards my father. Sometimes, I became defensive when it came to my education, specifically what classes I was taking. Campus was my vitality and where I lived while dad was trying to keep me on the strait and narrow. He had no idea what it was like having an adult son to take care of. Prior to college, I was only in his home for three-month vacations at maximum, which allowed him to groom his parental skills only so far. He would have to relearn them, upon my next visit, very quickly.

Spring semester is a misnomer at Iowa. The frozen tundra and snow-covered sidewalks weren't defining spring. Between classes, I would duck into one of the many record stores near campus, just to flip through the racks. A great source of information concerning U2, or any other band for that matter, was to hang out in these local independent record stores. Iowa City was the Mecca for them. Yeah, there was Musicland, but who cared about a corporate, over-priced record store encased in a shopping mall. The store was sterile. Trust me. Instead, I scoured the racks of Record Collector, a dinosaur in today's terms of digital music, in order to seek out old classics on tape like Dylan or The Stones. Above the check-out counter in the store was a chalkboard covered with dates of new releases. Most of the bands I had never heard of, yet it was nice to know when things were being released. More importantly, I relied on my neighbor Clark.

Vividly, I remember the day I heard about a new U2 album release by way of running into Clark behind our dorm, on the way to class.

"Shivvers, where're you goin?" he asked, knowing I would stop in his path.

"Off to class. What's in the bag?" I asked.

"I've got the new U2 album!" he responded, as a huge, shit grin came across his face.

"Really? Didn't know they've got a new album out."

"Yeah, it's called "The Joshua Tree." It's bitchin."

""The Joshua Tree?"" I said puzzled.

"Dude, I was in Record Collector where they're playing the album. I stayed and listened to the whole thing, twice. I immediately bought it," he couldn't get his words out fast enough.

"Can I get a copy?" Manners lacking, the words spilled out of me without a thought of politeness.

"Go buy the cassette, dude!"

"Cassette? Who wants a cassette? I'll buy the album later when I'm at home this summer. Stoner Doug, my roommate, doesn't have a turntable. So, there's no need to buy it just yet." I paused and asked, "You don't have access to a turntable, do ya? I'm sure you're goin' to dupe it."

"Yeah, I'm taking it over to a friends to tape it this afternoon. Not sure I'll have the time to record it twice. I can, however, have him make a tape-to-tape copy. Work for you?"

"Hell yeah, that'd be awesome," I replied.

"Got any spare blanks? Eh?" Clark asked.

"Yeah, in my room," I said, as I looked at my watch. I had five minutes to make a ten-minute walk to the ceramics studio. "Shit Clark, I'm gonna' be late for class. Let me go get one."

I then turned and skipped down the concrete steps of the fire escape. Clark was on my heels as I heaved open the door to our floor and headed to my room. Luckily, it was unlocked as Jimmie was lounging between classes with his feet on my desk taking in some random soap opera on TV. Without even thinking, I pushed his feet aside and threw open my top desk drawer where I found an unopened two-pack of Maxell 90 tapes under some clutter. I snapped the cassettes against one another, breaking the seal of the packaging. I turned to Clark, who was now leaning in our doorway, and tossed him one.

"When'll I get this back?" I asked.

Clark thought for a minute knowing I was late for class.

"How about tomorrow? After lunch? You in class?" he asked, while clearing his throat.

"Yeah, that works. How about meeting here at twelve thirty? I got class at two. Work for you?"

"Yeah, done," Clark said, as he pulled out his keys and opened his door adjacent to ours.

I slung my backpack over my shoulder and left out the fire escape door. I was now very late for class and didn't care. I had wiggle room. Studio classes never started on time anyway. Running into Clark and having a chance to listen to the new U2 album was now a priority for me.

Like clockwork, Clark showed up in my room the following day. Excitement and curiosity ran through my body when he tossed me the cassette. Thankfully, he took the time to handwrite out all of the songs on the Maxell paper liner. I mumbled the list of songs at low volume, *Where the Streets Have No Name, I Still Haven't Found What I'm Looking For, With or Without You, Bullet the Blue Sky*...Luckily, I could make out his cursive penmanship. I then looked up at Clark.

"Thanks man! I can't wait to listen to this!" I said.

"Your welcome. Let me know what you think," he replied, as he unlocked his door.

I slid the cassette into the player and shoved it into my backpack. I routed my headphones out of the back of the bag and fumbled for the play button. Once found, I punched it. I had only a few minutes to listen to the tape as I was off to Baroque Art History. The seven-minute walk to class allowed me enough time to get a taste of the first track and a half. The album opened with a low hum, which turned into an Edge arpeggio catapulting me into the opening bars of *Where the Streets Have No Name*. I became entranced. So much so that when I arrived at my class, I didn't stop the tape player until the exact moment lecture began, as I was three songs in and wanting more.

In the coming days, *The Joshua Tree* never left my cassette player. Everything Clark expressed two days prior, on the street behind our dorm, was true. From the opening Edge induced arpeggio of *Where the Streets Have No Name* to the last notes of *Mothers of the Disappeared*, I was captivated. I listened to the album over and over. Some songs came to the forefront like *Red Hill Mining Town* and *In God's Country*, both of which spoke volumes to me. *In God's Country* opened with a two-chord riff strummed with quick intensity. Once the band came in, the song leveled out and Bono began a soulful lyric, depicting an empty landscape bigger than the western skies of Montana. In the chorus, Edge moved to a three-chord play while Bono pushed the religious imagery. I was captivated and understood the narrative. Simple, but complex, Bono had revisited Christianity without beating us over the head. There was a rawness to the minimalism in the song's structure. As I peeled the skin back for a closer look at U2's new masterpiece, I found an almost back to basics album lost in their previous release, *The Unforgettable Fire*.

Once again, U2 looked deeper into politics more than ever before. Tracks like *Bullet the Blue Sky* reflected on El Salvador's Civil War and the bombing ensued by American warplanes in the narrative. The track opened with Larry's marching drum sequence, Edge sat in the background with a haunting vibrato, which emanated from his guitar. Seconds later, he became aggressive, striking full chords on the opening beat of each measure. He then halted his attack as Larry kept moving and Bono came in to tell the story. It was a haunting song and balanced at the end of the record by another one, *Mothers of the Disappeared*. The song was a lullaby like tune, telling the story of the unknown numbers of men, dragged away from their wives during the Pinochet reign in Chile, who never returned home. It was a beautiful, yet disturbing tune to close out the record, typical of a U2 recording. Yes, *The Joshua Tree* album covered the gamut. It was intellectual, spirited, smart and poignant. It hit me like a boxer going for the knock-out punch. I would get back up and take a listen, just to be punched in the gut again.

9: rock's hottest ticket

As fall colors began to decorate Iowa City, a late breeze of summer's warmth floated through campus. It was mid-September, 1987 and the beginning of my sophomore year at Iowa. I lived with U2's *The Joshua Tree* album the previous summer and still had the hunger to listen to it on the way to class that fall. I craved the less radio friendly songs of the album, *Exit*, *One Tree Hill* and *Mothers of the Disappeared*. There was still a fresh sound to the album as modernity arrived into our dorm rooms in the form of cable television. In other words, we got our MTV. I once again became a junkie of the station and basically slept in front of my roommate's twelve-inch television, trying not to miss a bit of excitement. Or, perhaps, I was catching up to what everyone else had watched in their lifetime? To me, it didn't matter. We had MTV, which was a luxury to the sophomore slump that I was about into fall into.

I thought I went to Cascia Hall Preparatory School in order to stave off taking General Education required classes in college. I was wrong. In order to graduate from Iowa, I had to fulfill certain non-degree bearing requirements. With what was being offered, I tried to craft a non-art curriculum as close to my degree as possible. For example, I had to meet two science requirements. So, I took geology because it would help me in ceramics. For the second one, I took astronomy. This was all well and good until I had to take a sociology requirement and looked to Clark's roommate, Dan, for a suggestion. He told me to take Human Geography, which became the bane of my existence because Dan's easy professor took sabbatical leave and his replacement, some high minded visiting professor, made my elective class a living hell.

While my sophomore classes put me on unfamiliar parts of campus, my roommates were at least stable, somewhat, by comparison to the previous year. I met them the prior semester and ironically, both were named Brian. Which was their sole commonality. When it came to their academic pursuits, they were polar opposites. Brian White wasn't the academic type. He did everything, but go to class. I was amused as he was a good-hearted kid from Omaha. In fact, he was the spokesman for the campus. He gave tours to prospective freshman and worked at night checking people's IDs when they entered our residence hall after hours. All the while to raise cash so he could stay in school, though he had no academic pursuits. White's best asset was he knew what was happening on campus well before everyone else.

On one particular day, three weeks after school started, Brian stood outside our room, holding court with some neighbors. The door was propped open as I was lying on the floor in front of our television, sucking in some MTV, just after lunch. I heard him say U2 and Carver-Hawkeye Arena in the same sentence. My ears perked up.

"Are you fuckin' serious? U2, the Irish rock band, is coming to Carver!" I shouted.

Brian heard me and leaned into our room. He looked at me and said, "Keep it down, Shivvers. It's just a rumor for now, but I think it'll happen?"

"Wait a minute. You heard U2 is coming to Carver? Where'd you hear this?"

"Yeah, I did. I was at the Student Events office picking up my mail and ran into a friend of mine, Sonja, who works at SCOPE. You know, the Student Commission on Programming and Entertainment? She told me they're coming. However, she couldn't confirm it."

"What do mean she couldn't confirm it? Either they're coming or not!"

He leaned back into our room and looked at me.

"I don't want to start any rumors. Okay, Shivvers?"

"You just said you heard they were coming."

"Yeah, I know, but you didn't hear it from me."

Now, I was excited and wanted to hear the story of why U2 was coming. I toned down my antagonistic inquest and turned down the television volume.

"White, tell us what's going on? Why would U2 want to play Iowa City?" I inquired as I picked my ass up off the floor.

He now rolled his shoulders against the frame of the door and was glaring at me. "Okay, Shivvers, here's the deal. As I understand it, U2's in conversation with SCOPE about playing at Carver-Hawkeye Arena because the University of Northern Iowa, where they're scheduled to play, won't allow the band to set-up their outdoor stage in the UNI-Dome. It would take days to erect and tear down. U2's looking elsewhere to fill the open date and may choose our campus. That's all I know."

"U2's coming to Carver! U2's coming to Carver! Hell yes!" I

shouted while jumping up and down in our room with glee.

"Shivvers, shut up! I cannot confirm this and it's a rumor. You didn't hear it from me because I don't want to get into trouble starting gossip," Brian replied hastily.

In the coming days, I shared the news with everyone I ran into on campus. I was ecstatic. True or not, in my mind, U2 was coming to Iowa City. It was like the rock gods looked down on us, zapped a lightning bolt onto our campus and said, "By the power invested in us, we've chosen U2 to play Iowa City on the Joshua Tree Tour." I couldn't contain myself. What I didn't realize was I wasn't the only one who was taken by the news. The buzz, of U2 coming to Iowa City, spread around campus like wild fire. I waited for validation. A week later, I grabbed one of three copies of *The Daily Iowan* that lay at the foot of our door. While yawning and trying to wake up on my way to breakfast, I flipped through the paper aimlessly like I did on any other given day. Something caught my eye. There it sat on the corner of the *Metro* page, a display ad. "U2 - One night only at Carver-Hawkeye Arena. Tickets on sale this Saturday at 10 a.m." I couldn't believe my eyes. U2 was really coming to Iowa City. Brian was right. I was in shock.

After breakfast, I headed back to our room with the caffeine shakes. I didn't know what to do. Brian was asleep and I dare not wake him. The band I had always wanted to see was about to arrive on our doorstep while they embarked on one of the hottest concert tours in years. And, thanks to the early morning caffeine rush, my brain went into overdrive with questions. I asked myself, "Who was I going to go with? Where's my ticket connection?" Having a U2 show on campus would be a monumental night in my rock concert life experience. I wanted to make the best of it. I had to think things through. Clark had moved off campus, but I ran into him days after I heard U2 was coming to town. He said all of his eight allotted tickets were spoken for. My current pals, whom I was running around with, weren't into U2. So, I had to embark on a different group of acquaintances to build a strategic battle plan for the acquisition of tickets. I chose my fellow floormates. Unfortunately, due to my naïveté, I discovered we weren't the only ones devising plans to get good seats for the show. Others on campus were working their networks and coming up with their combat plans as well. Brian informed me he was working his connections inside the SCOPE ticket office. However, I wasn't betting on him getting us tickets.

While I trudged through monotonous course work, news about U2 and ticket sales flowed through various channels, mostly by word of mouth. The Iowa Memorial Union, which housed the ticket office, was organizing itself for the worst-case scenario of bedlam on their doorstep the day of ticket sales. SCOPE set-up a time to pick-up line numbers the day before tickets went on sale to the public. We were grateful for their action. It would bring order to chaos. Or, would it? I questioned the motive and found my answer when I got to the Iowa Memorial Union, otherwise known as the IMU, in order to get in line for a number at about two o'clock. A line of some 150 people had already amassed themselves for the same prize. Four o'clock was the magical hour when the doors would open and dispersal began. I didn't expect to be so far back when I arrived. I thought to myself, "Did anyone go to class today?" Several people made a night of slumber on the steps and sleep deprivation was getting the best of them. Fights broke out near the front. Someone cut somebody off and people took sides. The passion to see Bono, Edge, Larry and Adam, at any cost, began to emerge. Where I was standing, a little more order existed.

As the floodgates to the IMU opened to obtain our numeric fate, the mad rush began. People were coming out of the other side of the building ecstatic as though they were clutching a winning lottery number. Someone immediately tried to sell his for a hundred bucks. Maybe it was his need for beer money or a ride home that caused his madness. Or, maybe the taunting fueled his ego and let him feel like big shit on campus. Whatever it was, we didn't care. We had our numbers and more important things to do like finding cash and plenty of it. Taking a risk, that the IMU ATM would have ample supply of funds the following morning, was ludicrous.

As the sun rose the next day, my floormates and I sauntered down the hill behind Burge Residence Hall to the Union, barely dressed for the day. Some of us hadn't showered while others were hauling beer breath from the night before. Who really gave a shit what we looked like as we stood in line for U2 tickets? We didn't care as we hung around on the sidewalk, waiting for the megaphone toting SCOPE representative to call out the next group of numbers. Time passed slowly. The first century of numbers was called and the energy surrounding the initial purchasers subsided as the steps into the building became more desolate. We, Men of Burge as we decided to call our group, were some of the last ones holding slips of paper inscribed with our U2 destiny. Finally, the man with the megaphone called out our numbers.

Anticipation grew, as we were led through the building's foyer to another line in order to wait for one of the two ticket windows to become free. I recalled the image of U2's cover story from *Time Magazine*, the previous spring, aptly titled "Rock's Hottest Ticket." The article was about how the band had written one of the quintessential records of our time, *The Joshua Tree*, and the subsequent tour would be one of the most anticipated after U2's performance at Live Aid two years prior. U2 was the fourth band ever to be featured on the cover, next to icons like

The Beatles, The Band and The Who. When the magazine came out, I bought several copies, knowing full well it would be a collector's item. Now, I was seconds away from obtaining that hot ticket *Time Magazine* wrote about.

When my turn came, I approached the ticket window with excitement. I immediately looked at the seating chart on the counter. My stomach sank. I became anesthetized. Almost the whole arena was marked in red. The show was nearly sold out. I had to get tickets.

"What's left?" I asked the gal behind the counter.

"We've tickets in section H row twenty-two or I have them in F row eighteen," she said, as she pointed to the seats with her red pen.

"Are those behind the stage?"

"Yes."

"Do you have anything in front?"

"I have two in section GG row twenty-four or two in JJ row twenty-one."

The ticket agent took her red pen and pointed to seats in the fifth to last row of section JJ. Yes, the stage would be in front of us, but about two Iowa counties away. I was shaking inside my shoes. I had to make a decision. For now, I didn't care where I sat. It was U2.

"I'll take the JJ tickets," I said, as I pulled out my wallet with the crisp twenties I got from the ATM the night before.

"That'll be thirty-three dollars and fifty cents," she said, waiting for me to hand her my cash.

"Here you go," I said, as I forked over the forty bucks.

"Six dollars and fifty cents is your change. Here are your tickets. Enjoy the show. Next!"

In the days following my ticket purchase, I put my pent up creativity to work. I wanted U2 to know that from the worst seats in the house sat one of their biggest fans. A fleeting idea crossed my mind about buying an Irish flag or creating one. I was sure someone closer to the stage would toss a tricolor to Bono at some point during the show. A poster board sign wouldn't help either, too small to be seen from such a far distance. Since I had been a season basketball ticket holder the previous year, I knew the arena like the back of my hand and well aware of the many support columns throughout the venue. One of which was just behind our seats. A brilliant idea popped into my head, "How about a white bed sheet with U2 emblazoned on it and hang it on the column behind me? It won't block anyone's view and the band would definitely see it."

I had four weeks to execute my idea. Between classes and studying, I went to Ragstock, a local second hand clothing store on campus, to purchase a white bed sheet and then to the student bookstore to get some black acrylic paint. I spread the sheet out on our bathroom floor and taped all four corners down so the cotton would be taught. I began to paint a large U and 2 on it. In order for my creation to dry, Brian allowed me to hang it under his lofted bed. The sheet became a focal point of conversation with whoever visited our room, invited or otherwise. I was inspired by the white flag Bono traipsed around Red Rocks, in the *Sunday Bloody Sunday* video from *U2 Live at Red Rocks*, and ready for the show.

As the days grew closer to the concert, my anxieties worsened. U2 was coming to campus. I couldn't believe it. To help with my stress in school, and with the U2 show, I had my cassette player handy. My headphones blanketed me in comfort as another Parents' Weekend came and went without a visit from my dad. I felt alienated and forgotten. However, the knowledge of a U2 ticket, resting in a secret hiding place in my desk, was helping me hold my shit together.

10: live under a black & gold sky

On the eve of Bono, Larry, Adam and Edge invading Carver-Hawkeye Arena, a fog, like the ones I witnessed in my youth on the moors in Ireland, engulfed me. It was the perfect welcome for the Irish quartet while I traipsed my way back to the dorm for dinner. My stomach began to growl and I quickened my pace as I walked down University Street then cut my own path up the hill of the Pentacrest. All I had to do was cross Jefferson Street and I would be two blocks away from the Burge dining hall. However, something caught my eye before crossing the street. Out of nowhere, and from my left, came a white pick-up truck, at a good rate of speed, blaring U2 tunes out of the passenger cab while two fools were in the bed of the truck waving a white flag. I stopped and watched the red taillights vanish into the fog. As they did, I continued to cross the street. Within a few paces, I passed my old roommate Doug. I stopped and put out my hand in a friendly gesture. It had been a semester since I had last seen him. Gone was my displeasure of his evening, drunken antics.

"Doug! Hey man! What's goin' on?" I said.

"Eric, what's shakin'?" he responded, as he readjusted the backpack slung over his right shoulder.

"Nothin' man. Just excited about tomorrow night," I said with a huge smile covering my face from ear to ear.

"What's tomorrow night?"

"U2 at Carver, man? You goin'?" I fired back at his smug, stoner look.

"Ah, no. I'm not. I don't have any interest in them at all."

"Dude, it's U2. What do ya mean you ain't got no interest?"

"I'm just not into them. They're jack offs to me," he laughed his stoner laugh.

"You don't know what you're missing, man."

"Ah fuck, I seriously could care less about them. You still livin' in Burge?"

"Yeah, with some leftovers from last year and some new guys. Living with White and O'Reilly. Complicated because they're both named Brian, but it works," I countered.

"That place's a shit hole, man. I hated it there. The RA was cool, but some of the guys on our floor were dicks."

"Where're you now?" I asked.

"Off campus. Over by The Sanctuary."

"You still seein' Geo?" I inquired out of courtesy.

"Nah, we split up over the summer." Doug stopped to think about his comment. "It just wasn't workin' out. She's in Champaign. I'm here. Plus..." His voice faded. I realized the moron I'd lived with my freshman year was in my past. I didn't need Doug's downer shit to get in my way as I quickly exited the conversation by blaming my hunger.

Twenty-four hours later, I couldn't sit still. I wanted my pal Ray, a waiter who I worked with in Des Moines during the summers and my 'date' to tonight's concert, to get here fast. I went to dinner, still I couldn't eat. My stomach was in knots. I went back to my room and packed up my banner. I was shaking. A knock at the door broke the silence. It was Ray who just arrived from Des Moines. I must've looked porcelain white as I was amid a severe anxiety attack. Unable to eat dinner in the dining hall, Ray coaxed me to go out for a bite. He was loose and comfortable in his skin. McDonald's was our restaurant of choice since it was near the venue and we could order drive-thru. He suggested I get a shake to soothe my stomach.

"What're you so nervous about, Shivvers? It's just a show," he said, as we parked the car, literally, right next to the front door of the arena while polishing off our grub.

"I've been waiting to see this band for four years. I wasn't into them when they came to Tulsa for the War Tour. They skipped Oklahoma altogether for The Unforgettable Fire Tour and I was one of millions who caught them on television for Live Aid. So, the anticipation is overwhelming. This could easily be the concert of my life," I responded, looking blankly out the front window of the car.

"Dude, don't put so much pressure on this show. Seriously, it's not worth it, man."

Ray was like my older brother. He shared his life with me over the past two summers as he waitered and I bussed tables. Over the clattering of plates, we discussed his dropping out of Iowa. Now, he was putting his life in order.

"It's U2. Okay. I'm a huge fan and we've got the worst seats in the house," I fired back.

"It doesn't matter. You'll see them. Maybe someone'll have binoculars," he calmly replied.

I slurped on my shake still looking out the windshield, observing the ticket takers readying themselves for the onslaught of fans.

"Eric, you're the man. I'm so lucky 'cause you remembered me when I mentioned to you last summer that I wanted to see them on tour," Ray said, using his charm to cheer me up.

"Yeah, I know, but we're the furthest fans away from the stage. If you only saw those cocksuckers, bragging about getting to be number ten in line on the day of the number distribution for the public sale. It's not fair. I'm too much of a goody two-shoes. I should've skipped class. What was I thinking?" I said, trying not to be too childish.

"Eric, man, life's not fair. Think of the guy that can't get here. I'm sure they're a few of those as well. We may not have the best seats, but we've got the best parking spot. Here, finish my fries off and we'll go in," he said, as he turned off the ignition.

I ate the remnants of his fries slowly, one by one, in order to kill time. We were about forty-five minutes early, which was adding to my anxiousness. As I slurped the remainder of my shake, I took one last gasp of air before opening the car door into the chill of the evening. I felt the bed sheet, stuffed under my coat, as we walked those few steps to the arena door. I extracted the tickets out of my billfold and gave them to the ticket taker. My concealed contraband made me feel portly, yet we got into the venue with ease.

As I said, Ray was a student at Iowa, a few years before me, and lasted only a handful of semesters. He never graduated. In fact, the arena wasn't built when he attended Iowa. He reminded me about his seats at the old Field House, which is where he saw basketball games. The building he was speaking of had long since been turned into a gymnasium for PE classes. We began to roam the concourse and reviewed the display cases as if we were at the Louvre rummaging through the halls of antiquities. Ray's reminiscences about his regret of never graduating were beginning to spew from him again. He had a feeling I was in a slump and spoke from his experience while driving home the point, and with good intention, that these are the best years of your life.

We eventually spun by the U2 merch table to see what paraphernalia we would buy. For the umpteenth time, I looked at my watch. We still had thirty minutes until the opening act. The minute hand on my watch couldn't move any quicker. Wandering the concourse helped, but I was feeling the onset of another anxiety attack as I found section JJ and descended to our seats. I sat my ass down first. Ray followed, taking off his coat. I gently slid my U2 banner out from under my jacket onto my lap, then through my legs, and finally, to the floor underneath my seat. I did it in one seamless move. My mind began to wander as I panned the stadium looking for my future basketball seats. In my neurotic state, I pointed them out to Ray. If we were sitting in them tonight, I thought, we would be closer to the stage. My focus then shifted to the banner I was hiding. "When should I make my move?" I asked myself. The column was four rows behind us and the lights in the stadium were now at their brightest. I pre-tied the corners earlier in the afternoon in order to expedite my guerilla move. I never thought about getting caught. I was mentally prepared. I needed a second adrenaline rush to execute my plan as the first was used to get the bed sheet into the building.

I looked over my shoulder towards the concrete structure every two minutes. Ray's conversation became background noise. On my third, or fourth, glance behind us, I didn't see anyone official in the area. I knew I had a chance to hoist the bed sheet, but when. Abruptly, the house lights went out. A huge applause rang throughout the stadium for the opening act, The BoDeans, who entered the stage and kicked into their set. The time was right for my hoisting adventure. I waited for the fifth song to begin before making my move. When it came, I slid out of my seat and slowly climbed the stairs to the concourse behind us, keeping the banner hidden behind my back. No one, coming towards me, could see it. When I got to the last step, I looked both ways. It was safe to make my move. The concourse was now full of fans milling around aimlessly as I turned to face the behemoth of a column. I took an end of the banner and put it up against the curvature of the structure. I then stretched my arms out wide to wrap the naked space. As I did so, a voice of authority from behind me began asking me what I was doing.

"Sir, what're you doing?" I heard from over my shoulder.

While trying to hold up my wilting banner, I looked over my shoulder. My arms were outstretched.

"Tying up a banner for U2," I responded.

"Sir, that's not allowed in this here arena," he said firmly.

I thought quickly and said, "I didn't know. I thought you could attach a banner to the column. It's not obstructing anyone's view."

"No, we don't allow it here in the arena. Please, hand me the sheet and come with me," he said in a stern voice.

"Can't I fold it up? Put it under my seat. Case closed," I replied.

"No, you'll have to come with me to the security office," he stated, as I let the banner fall completely limp.

I turned to face the benevolent dictator. He was a rent-a-cop, dressed in a windbreaker emblazoned with the word SECURITY in yellow type and standing right behind me. He leaned forward, picked up the bed sheet from off the ground and grabbed my left bicep.

"Fuck!" I screamed in my head. "Now I've got to go to the security office where they'll do God knows what with me. I may never see U2!"

The officer flanked me as I was escorted across the concourse to a back office where a grey hair lady awaited me behind a desk.

She was friendly and reminded me of my grandmother. She probably had no clue who U2 was. However, she could tell you about the good old days of Pat Boone or Ray Conniff. Under the watchful eye of the security guard and after he gave the lady my banner, I filled out the necessary paperwork. I was calm. I had a lot to lose. My Cascia Hall schoolboy behavior took over as I thanked the officer. The friendly older woman told me I could retrieve my item after the show. I walked out of the security office and slid my way into the growing crowd with the feeling that I had just been busted for drinking while driving, but let out of the ticket by some divine intervention.

Upon my return, from the internal precinct of Carver-Hawkeye Arena, the house lights returned to their full brightness. I took my seat. Ray inquired about my long absence. I told him that I snuck in a banner, painted with a huge "U2" on it, and tried to hoist it on the column behind us. I went on and said that it was taken away by security for the remainder of the show. He quickly turned around and looked at the naked column. No banner existed. He laughed out loud. I wanted to run away. I stared straight ahead at the stage where there was enormous activity. I had to find an escape. I stood up and excused myself to purchase my U2 schwag. Ray followed me to the top of the stairs of our section. I nodded in the direction of the security officer. Again, he laughed out loud. Humiliation covered me like a warm blanket. My heart was in the right place, but the long arm of the rented law decided to kibosh my communication with my band.

Ray and I became lost in a sea of concert goers trying to make our way to the merch booth with a few "excuse mes" and "sorry, gotta cut throughs." When we finally arrived to the table, there was a vast array of U2 items to choose from. Since we had visited the table upon initial entry into the venue, my mind was already made up. Four different shirts hung in the back of the makeshift booth, two grabbed my eye. I wanted both. I passed on the tour book. However, I pondered the purchase of the hoodie and jean jacket, yet there wasn't enough of a U2 logo on either one for me to validate such an outlay of cash. I pulled out my wallet, bought my articles of clothing and tied them around my waist.

As I turned away from the table, my eye caught the back of a jean jacket, passing in front of me. It was emblazoned, in acrylic paint, with The Misfits' logo. I recognized it and shouted, "Hey, Kaperak!"

Chad turned around in mid-stride. He looked in my direction.

"Hey, dude," he said in his Spicoli like reply. "What's goin' on?"

"What in the hell are you doin' here? Thought you gave up on U2?"

"Yeah, I know. KGGO in Des Moines had a ticket package for the show, including a bus ride with a keg in the back. I decided to buy a spot."

Chad's girlfriend was glued to his side. She was a freshman at Iowa and the main cause for the split in our friendship three summers prior. She knew who I was and, as usual, itchy to pull Chad out of conversations with friends of his she didn't like.

I looked at her and said to Chad, "You must've gotten good seats."

His girlfriend stared through me.

"Fourth row."

"Cool. We're in the fourth row as well."

"Really?"

"Yeah, like fourth row from the back of the arena," Ray chimed in.

Chad laughed and asked, "Didn't you get tickets on the day of the sale?"

"I got in line too late for a decent number the day before

the public sale. We were almost the last in line to get tickets," I replied.

Chad's girlfriend was now tugging on his sleeve and paying attention to the crowd.

"We'll look for you when you get back to your seats," I hastily replied.

Chad was now forced to leave.

"You home over the holidays?" I asked.

While turning into the stream of people, he said over his shoulder, "Yeah. Call me. See ya, dude."

I stood there and watched an old friend become engulfed into the masses. Ray and I cut to our right, through the sea of humanity, and made our way to our seats. Like a dog sensing an earthquake, people began to run through the concourse. The flurry of activity on U2's stage came to a stop. Without warning, the lights went dark. Pandemonium broke out. Fans sitting next to us rushed to the stairs. Ray and I stayed back. Rented security and student workers couldn't retain the river of flesh charging to the arena floor. The base of the arena swelled like the waves of a sea. The backing track to *Where the Streets Have No Name* began. Edge's arpeggio commenced as spotlights flickered on and off, creating more tension. Bono, the last to arrive, wore a cowboy hat and a duster. He shouted, "Hello! Ooooohhhh..........Yeah ....Alright." All of a sudden, the stage was awash in blue-tinted light and there was Bono, tiptoe dancing in his cowboy boots and gyrating to the beat. Edge stood next to him strumming his guitar. Adam swayed with his bass. Larry kept them all in line with his marching drumbeat. The show was on. Bono came to the microphone, launched into the lyric and blew the evening into the stratosphere. I was lucky. Everyone has a favorite band and remembers songs or albums from their college years. To have such a big album, like *The Joshua Tree,* break in the middle of my collegiate years, was very fortunate.

At one hundred eighty feet from the stage, we could still feel the passion. Bono, Edge, Adam and Larry couldn't have cared less where they were playing nor the size of the venue. All U2 cared about was performing to passionate onlookers, observing their stripped-down concert, full of raw energy. It was a far cry from the norm where rock acts at the time relied heavily on special effects. On this night, there were no lasers, pyrotechnics or video screens. Just four guys, on a stark stage, letting their music speak for itself. We couldn't contain our excitement and nor could Bono as his arm had been in a sling for two weeks. Tonight, the arm was free to play the harmonica. "My once broken and now mended arm," he said to us as he introduced *Trip Through Your Wires*. Edge, Larry and Adam stayed in line and let the singer speak for them. The roar of a response from the crowd was their validation to be in the band.

U2 sprinkled the set with classics such as *Sunday Bloody Sunday* and *New Year's Day*, which Ray and I sang to. The song *October* was the deepest cut from their catalog and only used as a lead into *New Year's Day*. *MLK*, *The Unforgettable Fire* and *Bad* were remnants from the previous tour; the band refrained from leaving them behind. *Exit* exuded raw power and *In God's Country*, my favorite tune from *The Joshua Tree*, sounded even purer as the main set came to a close with *Pride (In the Name of Love)*. Bono waved to the crowd and slowly left the stage. We clapped, whistled and shouted for an encore. It seemed like eternity. The band arrived back to a stage drenched in red light. Bono was letting us know that the United States had blood on our hands in *Bullet the Blue Sky*. He entered the song with bravado and ranted a long soliloquy. The following tune was the soft *Running to Stand Still*, which was infused with a dark narrative of the inner reaches of heroin usage plaguing Ireland, leaving a heavy burden on the stage. While Bono moved through the lyrics, he grabbed a hand-painted bed sheet scribbled with "Hawkeyes Love U2" and draped himself in it. U2 held out their biggest hit to date, *With or Without You*. It was not an up-tempo closer, but one that was to leave us with two thoughts, one religious and the other about relationships. In the religious sense, Christ and living with or without Him. And in the meaning of relationships, loving someone by giving whole-heartedly without receiving the same level of love in return. It was a heavy, double-entendre song and a storyline the band would visit quite often in upcoming recordings, including the future hit, *One*.

As the last notes of *With or Without You* hung over the crowd, the stage went dim. We knew we were being led to the end of the performance. The standard show's closer, *40*, began to exude from the speakers. Edge and Adam exchanged instruments. Bono, with the help of us in the audience, sang the song in its entirety and said good-night. Adam, followed by Edge, played a little solo and left the stage leaving Larry as the sole representative of the band onstage. With his thunderous beat, he kept the song alive as the crowd sung in replacement of the lead singer. With the last cymbal crash, five years would pass before I would see them again. The show was everything I thought it would be and then some. U2 played it straight and taught us a thing or two about their impression of America. It was a radiant night and worth every anxiety attack I struggled with prior to the event.

As the lights came up, I got my contraband from security and hit the bars back on campus. Upon entering One Eyed Jakes, I was greeted near the door by a woman draped in a bed sheet. It was the exact one Bono frolicked with onstage. I recognized the gal from my literature class.

"Michelle, no way!" I exclaimed.

"Eric! Did you like the show?" she asked in response.

"Pretty cool. Is this yours?" I inquired, as I tugged on the sheet encasing her body.

"Yeah. Thanks to you, I made one and Bono grabbed it," she replied.

"I didn't see yours. Did you hang it up?"

Ray butted in immediately and said, "Security grabbed it from him as he was hoisting it on the column. They took him and the banner away for a while."

"Eric, I'm so sorry. Did'ya get it back?" Michelle inquired.

"Yeah, I had to retrieve it after the show," I said, as I hung my head in shame. Ray grabbed the waitress as the evening sunk into a stupor of celebration.

In the coming days, I fell into a post-U2 slump. School, and my sophomore skids, kept moving along. All the while, in the back of my mind, there was an image of the guy who got dragged up onstage to play The Impressions' tune, *People Get Ready*, with Bono. I for sure knew him, but wasn't certain until I went to my discussion class for Human Geography. I proceeded to take a seat next to the student in question whom I befriended earlier in the semester.

As class began, I sank into my chair, keeping my eye on the grad student teaching the class. I asked my neighbor in a loud whisper, "I think I saw you at U2 the other night."

"Yeah, you probably did," he said.

"No!" I said, "I mean onstage with them."

"Yeah. That was me playing guitar," he whispered back.

"How was it?" I looked at him.

"Awesome," he replied, beaming from ear to ear.

I queried more, but moved my attention back to the front of the classroom. "How amazing was it to be dragged onstage? Did you really know the chords?"

"Ah, it's an easy song," he replied.

I was in shock. I paid no attention to what was being discussed in class. I slid in the comment, "It would've been great to get a picture of you onstage with the band."

"I have one better," he replied. "I've a videotape of the show."

"No fuckin' way," I replied in a loud whisper unsettling a classmate in front of me.

"Yup. Someone found out my name and sent it to the grocery store I work at," he replied.

I was stupefied. The wheels were spinning.

"Really! Can I come over and watch it?" I bluntly asked.

"Yeah. Let me know and I'll invite you over to the house," he said without any hesitation.

Within days, I was at Colin's frat house watching U2. Albeit, the quality of the video wasn't great, however, it was my first U2 concert and this was just what I needed to get me out of my slump, reliving a night where I saw U2 perform under a black and gold sky.

11: the reinvention

It had been four years since I had seen the Joshua Tree Tour and three years since U2 released the movie *Rattle and Hum*. In that time, I graduated from Iowa and moved on with my life to Chicago. I wanted to be in a big city where the arts thrived and bands played. Chicago was a great choice because everything art related came through the city on its way to either the east or west coast. As daydreams of seeing U2 again manifested inside my head, the frustration of working behind an espresso bar, making coffee drinks for well-heeled suburbanites, was becoming more annoying. What I really wanted to do was move on with my career in graphic design, but the economy wasn't helping me out. So, I spent my days off wisely tromping through the city in search of creative inspiration. I visited museums, went to the movies and yes, mingled in record stores. Two of the best, re-sided in my backyard of Evanston, Rose Records and Evanston Music Exchange.

On a day off from work in the summer of 1991, I cruised

into Evanston Music Exchange, a one-stop music store which sold used and new compact discs. I was a regular customer who would scour the used CD racks. However, on this particular day, I decided to delve a little deeper into the back of the store. I was interested in the glass case, which sat at an angle along the far wall and housed unofficial live recordings on CD. The armoire like structure had a tempting glow about it. Each disc was propped up like jewelry on display, tempting each buyer. Some were shrink-wrapped while others had been noticeably opened. I peered deeper into the brightly illuminated case. My eyes glanced back and forth between the compact discs like a pinball between bumpers. Prince, Grateful Dead, CSN&Y and The Who were just a few of the bands whose discs I found. As I panned the case with greater detail, my eyes caught a picture of all four members of U2. They graced the cover of a disc titled, *U2 Live at the Point Depot.* It sat on the second shelf and was the third disc from the left. The price tag stated it was eighty bucks. I gulped.

I sauntered back to the front counter and asked the clerk if I could take a listen to the disc that I just found in the back case. He obliged by retrieving a set of keys to the armoire from a drawer under the till. He returned with the live album and pointed to a listening station. I put on the sleek pair of headphones and hit the play button. The recording commenced. There was an ambient crowd noise as a voice counted from ten to one. I thought, "This is a New Year's Eve show." The voice then introduced the New Year and U2, just as I thought. The band kicked into *Where the Streets Have No Name.* I was immediately transported back to Carver-Hawkeye Arena in a time machine. My ears were glued to every word. My inner soul was filling with my band as I listened to each track from beginning to end. Familiar with some of the set list, I was shocked to hear songs recorded for the *Rattle and Hum* soundtrack, including *God Part II, Desire* and *All I Want Is You*, played live on this recording. It definitely was New Year's Eve in Dublin at some venue named the Point Depot. I didn't know much more because the liner sheets inside such unofficial releases rarely had much information printed on them other than pretty pictures of the band.

While the music swooned the left side of my brain, the price tag stopped my practical right. No matter what, I couldn't validate the purchase on my retail budget. Luckily, my subconscious recorded the show in its entirety and over the next week or so, when I was relaxed and not keyed up, I could literally replay it from beginning to end in my head. It was like my subconscious could drop the needle in my grey matter, recall a song like *God Part II,* and have my brain play it in its entirety. Therefore, I never had to make the purchase. I lived with the fantasy I created in my head, filling it with images I culled from my concert experience at Carver and the live concert sections from U2's road movie, *Rattle and Hum.*

The brush with the live recording resurrected my flattened U2 pulse with newfound excitement. Now, I needed to know what my band was up to and the only place I could trust to find out this information was around the corner at Rose Records, a Chicago record store chain. Unlike the commercial, megalopolis, Musicland record store anchored across the street from it, Rose was a small, yet hip joint, which had college kids, knowledgeable about music, working behind its counters. I took a deep breath and entered the shop.

While taking a survey of the place, I immediately began to aimlessly flip the CDs in the racks. The crackle of the plastic containers, hitting one another, made a repetitious and annoying noise. I tried to soften the racket by using my fingers as insulation between the cases. In doing so, I observed an African

American gal behind the counter. She was chatty with an intoxicating laugh. Her smile was bright against her Nubian skin tone and she made sure every customer was satisfied. Her body language said she was approachable and before I meandered to the counter, I gave her one last once over. She looked about my age.

"Hello," I said with hesitation.

"Hey! How are you? Anything I can do for you?" she warmly replied while reaching for a pair of scissors.

"I was wondering if you could help me with some information about a band I'm interested in," I said, stuttering to get the words out of my mouth.

"Who might that be?" she asked, as she began cutting into a brand-new box of compact discs.

"U2."

"Ohhhhhh, that baaaaaand," she said, as she looked up from her busy work and smiled.

"Yeah, I'm a fan. I haven't heard much about them recently. They recorded a track for the "Red, Hot + Blue" album last year, but I've heard nothing since."

"Let me grab my release list. There's a rumor they're working on something new," she replied, as she unloaded the box of discs.

"Really? No way. I've been waiting for this news for months!" I shouted. I couldn't believe I hit the possible mother load of U2 information.

"Yeah, I had the new releases information right here, yet cannot find it."

She looked up at me with a smug look that reminded me of a Billy Idol smirk.

"Are you a NU student?" she inquired.

"No."

"You say that with such force."

"I look young and could probably pass as a student, but no I don't go to NU. Actually, I graduated from Iowa a year ago."

"Iowa. Like the University of Iowa?" she inquired, as she stopped her search and looked at me.

"Yeah, the Hawkeyes."

"I'm an alum, too," she said, as she stuck out her tongue and blew a raspberry in the air. "My dad works in student affairs. I graduated from Iowa three years ago. I just finished my Masters at NU and look where that got me, Rose Records!"

She kept digging into her surroundings, which were one step away from being a certified pigsty, and began flipping through piles of papers that buried a counter littered with protective jewel case covers, rolls of tape and a few orphaned pens. She then turned around to the back counter and found what she was looking for.

"A-ha! Here it is, the binder of all that's happening in the industry. Now, if someone put in the updated listings for the fall, we'll be in business," she said, while turning around and aimlessly flipping through the plastic coated sheets.

"Where did you hang?" she asked, while mulling the binder's contents looking for information and keeping up appearances in the conversation.

"Where? Here?"

"No, in Iowa City you dork!" she exclaimed.

"Joe's Place, The Sanctuary. The Deadwood. We stayed away from the Field House."

"Field House, yuck! A jock and slut bar. Love Joes. Studied and drank at The Deadwood," she replied, as she stopped flipping through the pages of the binder and stuck her hand out.

"I'm Jamie."

"Eric. Nice to meet you, Jamie," I replied, as we shook hands. She went back to scanning the new releases sheet and mumbled as her finger passed over the release dates "Garth Brooks, Prince, Public Enemy..." The mumble got softer.

"Got it! Yes, there's mention of a new U2 release, however, no date and no title. I assume later in the fall. Since it's July, I won't get the late fall release dates until the end of August. I would stop in around September," she said, as she slammed the book shut.

"Alright! I can't wait. I saw them at Carver when I was a sophomore. Awesome show," I said, now excited with the news.

"I was there too. The night that Bono got use of his arm back, right?" she asked with a wink just shy of flirting.

"Yeah, 'My once broken and now mended arm,'" I replied, quoting Bono, forcing my Irish accent.

"Where do you live, Eric?"

"South Evanston. Near the Dominicks. I work for Starbucks in Glencoe."

"Cool. Very nice to meet you," she said with charm as she turned her attention to a customer who was in need of being rung up.

"Find everything okay?" she asked.

The registered clicked and the drawer opened. Jamie made change.

I was on U2 overload and ready to leave.

"Eric, great to meet you. Come back soon and I'll have a more set date on the release in about six weeks."

"I will. Thanks Jamie," I said with my back to the door, gently pushing it open.

I was excited. Finding out the information about the impending release of a new U2 album was just what I needed. A certain swagger came back to my step. U2 was now flowing through me. The mid-summer light from the sun, casting itself on me, seamed less harsh. Life was becoming more hopeful as I kept the song *One Tree Hill,* from the Point Depot concert, floating through my skull.

Shortly before my nine-week deadline was up with Jamie, I answered a Siren's song from Evanston Music Exchange. Like on previous visits, I stood in front of the glass case at the back of the shop. This time, after a long inspection, I noticed the Point Depot disc was gone, as I wanted another listen in order to get another jolt of the band. Disappointment must have graced my face. I panned the case again and found a tall box, on the top shelf, green in color and covered in graffiti type. Interspersed were images of U2 throughout the ages. I could hardly make out the title. For sure it was U2. The words, *Achtung Bebei,* graced the cover. I went to the front counter to request a listen.

"Can you help me? I'm interested in the tall box in the back case. It's green with images of U2," I said with conviction to the salesclerk, who was on the phone and staring blankly out the front window into the street.

"Hold on Julia, I have a customer," the clerk said into the phone. He then placed his hand over the receiver and turned to me.

"Yeah, that's U2. We've had that box set in for about two or three weeks. It's a collection of studio outtakes. Don't know much more about it than that, man," he said, shrugging his shoulders.

My mind was ablaze. "Studio outtakes?" I asked myself.

"Can I take it for a spin?" I requested.

"Yeah, lem'me get the keys," he replied. He then dug into the familiar drawer, housing the keys to the case.

He removed his hand from the phone's receiver. "Julia, give me a minute. I gotta listening request," he said and then put the phone down on the counter.

With keys jiggling in hand, he went back to get the box. He

opened the lock, slid the glass door open and retrieved the carton, returning to the counter. Out of the graffiti splattered package came a multi-CD holder. He slid out the first disc and placed it into the player.

"You're all set. You can use station number three," he said, as he picked up the telephone receiver and pointed me to a listening station.

I pressed the play button. From the outset, I could tell I was listening to a true working tape of someone in the studio. Sure enough, Bono's singing voice came to light. It was U2 in the raw, recording their next album. Attentively, I was listening to the lyric. The melody of the guitar was different. I was on the inside listening to my band recording. Bono was shouting at Adam to come around to the front of the amplifier to get a better listen. He was in control, but not frantic. One could tell the lyrics weren't set in stone. I imagined Bono grasping a microphone with one hand and holding onto a sheet of scribbled lyrics with the other. The first four tracks were different takes on the same song. The next tracks were long, winding spews of music immersed with guitar licks and meandering lyrics, going nowhere. It was cool to hear U2 working. One almost never hears the inner workings of a band, especially at the nascence of a record. My brain started to race. None of the tunes I heard on the disc sounded anything like previous U2 recordings. I could tell Edge was trying new effects and Bono was pushing the vocals.

Dizzy from the excitement, I reviewed the tracks a second time in snippets and then put down the headphones. I was curious what the cash outlay would be this time for this three CD box set. I went back to the counter to look at the box. The price tag stated one hundred twenty dollars. I swallowed hard. I felt my credit card stinging me in my back pocket. Guilt was holding me back. The impulse purchase was just wrong. Wrong since it would take a few months before being fully paid for and even more immoral because the recording wasn't official. No money would end up in U2's coffers; therefore, I left it behind.

Since Rose Records was around the block, I had to stop in and see whether Jamie was working. I knew she would have some updated information on U2's new release. My hunch paid off when I entered her store.

"Eric, how are you? I was just thinkin' about you!" she said with her usual smile gracing her face. I was greeted as though the store hadn't had a customer in years.

"Really? It's great to see you too. I had a day off and decided to journey downtown. Didn't know if you would be in," I replied.

"Yeah. I've got really good news about your Irish boys. The new album will be out in the middle of November," she said, stepping out from behind the counter.

"Do you have a title?" I inquired, as she began straightening up the front of the store.

"Something like "Achtung Baby," I want to say."

"Hmmm. Interesting title. Doesn't sound like the norm."

She was now flipping aimlessly through the racks, making sure everything looked all right. She stopped and looked at me.

"Oh, it's different. I've heard some tracks and it's very different. Nothing you would recognize as being U2. Trust me." Then, something caught her eye. "Those bastards! I can't believe it! Again, someone cut off the security tag and stole a disc. Those motherfuckers!" Jamie shouted without seeing who was around her. Luckily no one was in the store to hear her rant. Jamie took the empty plastic security case back to the counter.

"They stole a Billy Joel disc. Who the fuck would steal Billy Joel? Why not Zeppelin? Or The Who? Joel? Seriously!" she said, while obviously talking to herself.

"How often does this happen?" I queried.

"Often enough. It's a college student, I'm sure. They're cheap bastards," she said with angst.

I waited for her to cool her heals. She obviously was distraught. One couldn't tell when the crime took place, but she knew it might have been on her watch. I slipped back into our pre-disruption conversation about U2.

"Did you like it? What you heard from the new disc?" I interrogated a little more.

"Yeah, it has a vibe. It may take time, yet I did like what I heard," Jamie said, as she was now filling out the paperwork for the stolen CD.

"This is awesome news. I can't wait. It's been a while. Anything else new with you?" I said, trying to make the conversation more than just U2.

"Yeah, Garth Brooks is coming to town. Yippee skippy," she said, twirling her fingers in the air as she was still knee-deep in the paperwork and not looking at me. "I have to go to his show at the Horizon next month. I work for his label on my off days."

"What label?"

"Oh, Columbia," she said assertively.

"That's cool. I'm sure you get some great shit."

"Like here, it's a job. No glamor. Trust me," Jamie said then looked up at me with her familiar smirk.

I loved her facial expressions. Jamie was never one to hide how she felt about certain things. She continued scribbling away on the stolen merchandise paperwork, which was now looking like a police report. While doing so, an older woman entered behind the counter. I assumed she was the manager. The woman whispered into Jamie's ear.

"Eric, I have to unpack some boxes. Swing by again and I'll get you the date for the album as we get closer to November."

She ended the statement with a broad smile.

"Great. I'll be in soon," I said, pushing the door open with my back as I exited the store.

Blood rushed through my body. Someone I knew actually heard snippets of the actual album. A warm feeling came across my soul as I walked to the 'L' platform to go home. "Wow! In less than two months I will have a new U2 album in my hands," I said to myself. I could feel the warm autumn sun grace my body. The rays were golden and soft just like the day I stood in line to get tickets to the Carver show outside the IMU. I was now wondering if what I listened to at Evanston Music Exchange would become part of the album. It was hard to tell what would survive. The rough demos I heard were exactly what Bono was speaking of at the end of the Point Depot show. He mentioned the band would go on hiatus to dream it up all over again. I now began to countdown the days to the new release in order to hear what came of their dream.

12: wearing them on my back

Soon after the Joshua Tree Tour passed through Iowa City, I thought of the brief encounter I had with Kaperak that night on the concourse of Carver-Hawkeye Arena. I recalled the artwork on the back of his jacket and how cool it would be for me to create something similar for myself, depicting U2. Since I wasn't taking classes in the art department, I needed a creative outlet and custom painting a jacket would be a great project. So, I grabbed some images of the band and slowly started to edit them down to the one I wanted. During the weeks leading up to Christmas break, I began to craft a simple image of all four members in the desert much like *The Joshua Tree* album cover. It would be strictly black and white piece with a little grey for definition. The trick would be getting the image on the back of the jacket. Needless to say, I asked for an opaque projector for Christmas and got one, making my project easier to execute.

Within the first two weeks of the spring semester at Iowa,

I began my project. My jacket became a work in progress as I would paint it at night and wear it to class the following day. The images of Edge, Larry, Adam and Bono gradually came to life. It was cool to watch the transformation, after every painting session, when I put it on my chair to dry. Like the banner, for the concert three months prior, my jacket was becoming the focal point of our room. Soon, my finished creation would adorn my body in its completed state. Like Chad, I could now be identified from behind because no one else on campus owned a jacket like mine.

When I moved to Chicago two years later, my Aunt Nicole, dad's sister and an artist herself, had an idea.

"Eric. I know you're frustrated with your career and I can relate having been rejected entry into art shows. I too feel my work means nothing," my aunt said, while we were driving to Wicker Park, a hip artist neighborhood in Chicago.

"I'm talented Aunt Nicole, however, I can't make any inroads towards my career. My portfolio is shit. My education means nothing. How do I portray hard work in my book? You know I've got the drive," I replied.

"You've got to give it time, Eric. You can't get everything at once. Being an artist is great, yet painful," she said with her soft, squeaky voice.

"Nicole, I graduated a year ago and I'm still working retail."

"I know. You're trying to get into the most cutthroat business. I know someone from group who has his own agency. He says the days are difficult to face when there's no business coming in," she said, as though she was my mother trying to make everything okay.

"Group? What's that?"

"Group therapy. I've been in it for a couple years. It's helped me grow," she replied, as she opened up to me about her life. I knew Aunt Nicole had a mental breakdown and I'm sure group therapy was prescribed shortly thereafter to keep her on the mend. She always seemed fine to me.

"Got any ideas? I'm at my wit's end," I said. She knew of my jacket depicting Bono, Adam, Larry and Edge in the desert.

"You have the coolest jean jacket with your favorite band custom-painted on the back. What about contacting U2? Send them your idea of custom-painting clothing for them," she said, as she looked at me with a smile while her hands, covered in driving gloves, held the steering wheel at the 10 and 2 positions, just like in the Illinois Driver's Ed book told her to.

"Nicole, you're crazy?" I said with a laugh. I paused. "They'd never go for a little unknown graphic designer from the Midwest."

"Eric, you're now in Chicago. That validates you," she replied and then glanced at me.

"Well, you gotta point. I can read the headlines now," I said, as I began to emphasize each of the following spoken words by underlining them while I spoke the following statement. "Urban artist seeks rejection by world's biggest band!" I exclaimed and finished the headline with an air drawn exclamation point.

"Why Eric, you've got the talent and I'm sure U2 would be more than happy to look at your work."

"Flattered. Thank you very much, but do you really think my jacket's going to possibly open a door with the world's biggest band? I know they're approachable, yet I'm still just an Iowa boy," I replied with a little more terse tone.

"Okay. Think about it. I'll talk to your uncle and throw him the idea. I'm sure he'll give you a suggestion or two," she countered, as she looked over her shoulder, trying to merge onto the expressway.

I looked out the windshield and began to daydream. Nicole had a cool idea. "Why couldn't I at least try?" I asked myself. "What do I have to lose?" I didn't want to get too emotionally involved as I am one to become so engrossed in something that if it didn't go through, I would be very disappointed or even worse, hurt. I couldn't become to enticed by Nicole's idea because it would consume me. I tried to let the idea fade, but I kept thinking how cool it would be to have my work accepted by U2.

A week after Nicole came up with her brilliant approach to the band, the three of us, my Aunt Nicole, my Uncle Vince and me, met up for Sunday night dinner. Giggio's Pizza was our usual end of the weekend hangout. The pizza wasn't the typical Chicago deep dish, but thin crust with just enough sauce. It reminded me of home.

On this particular evening, Uncle Vince started the conversation as we lunged into our slices of wonder.

"Nicole told me that she had an idea for you and U2," he said, as pizza sauce dripped from the edge of his moustache. He wiped it away.

"Yeah, she did. It came out of left field. I'm still mulling it over," I said, as I bit into my first piece of pizza.

"I think its kinda cool. You paint jackets for your favorite band," he said, as he picked up his Diet Coke for a slurp.

"I'm not sure they'd go for it Uncle Vince. I've heard they're approachable, but they've been out of the scene for a while," I said, as I wiped the thin smear of grease from below my lower lip.

"Well, now's the time to get their attention."

"I do know this. They have a new album coming out in November," I stated with confidence.

"Even better, get'em while they're making big decisions."

"I think it's a great idea, Vincent," Nicole chimed in.

"Yeah, honey, it is. It came from you, my artist wife," Vince said, as he looked at my aunt and smiled at her. He rubbed her back validating his agreement.

"Vince, I just don't know how to go about this venture. I'm an artist, not a businessman. I don't know what to do. Should I throw my jacket into an overnight bag with a letter saying, 'What d'ya think of this, Bono?'"

"Eric, that's where I come in. You and Nicole are artists. I'm the business guy. You've got this idea to paint jean jackets," he said and paused. "You want to get Bono. Isn't that his name? To get onboard with your brilliant concept."

"No, short O. Not like Sonny Bono. It is Bah-no. But go ahead," I said, clarifying his pronunciation.

"Okay. I think if we come up with a business model where you're the sole person who can hand-paint limited edition pieces that the band can sell, they might buy in. You want their sign-off so you can acquire their rights. U2's not public domain, so you need to receive permission." Vince was getting methodical.

"How do I convince them when they're across the Atlantic?" I replied, heading for the crust of my pizza.

"You have to create a piece, shoot slides and then send them to the band. It'd be like entering a juried art show only this time, it's a business presentation."

"Uncle Vince! All's well and good, but I don't know what they look like now. I need recent photos so my work can be relevant?"

"You're thinking in micro-terms. You know what I mean?" he said, as he wiped his moustache and thought for a moment. He continued, "Here's what you do. You find an image. Paint it onto a jacket. Doesn't matter what era of the band the image comes from. Then we shoot it onto film. Let me back up. You go get the creative work executed and I'll craft a letter."

"Okay. I need to search out an image. I'm afraid that if I don't send a jacket with a recent image that it may not help me open the door."

"Again, Eric, don't think. Just do. Will two weeks give you enough time?"

"I think so. I need to rummage through some books to find something. I'm sure I can paint a piece in two weeks," I stated, as I looked at Nicole. She smiled. She knew her idea wasn't out in left field anymore. As I began to eat the last half of my second slice of pizza, I contemplated the idea.

"Uncle Vince, are you two nuts?" I sort of stammered. "I mean really you actually think U2's going to hire me? What if it doesn't work out? Then what?"

"You tried," Vince said with paternal calmness. "Think of it this way. Ten thousand people in the world have an idea for U2. One thousand will think it through. Of those thousand, one hundred will act upon their instincts and only ten of them will execute their idea. You're one of those ten. Regardless of the outcome, you're going to present your creative work to your favorite band. You're putting the wheels in motion. I know you get obsessive. You are like your father, but hold on. Let's get the horse and the cart together. In two weeks, we'll meet."

He finished the crust of his second piece of pizza. Silence hovered our table. The creative juices began to flow inside me. I needed to keep up my end.

With a fleeting thought of my work landing in U2's lap thanks to my uncle's pep talk, I thought how cool it would be to send U2 my idea as I purchased a jean jacket, paint and Xeroxed some images. Nightly, after work, I sketched feverishly in preparation. The piece was coming together. I was forcing the creative as I needed to be expeditious with their impending album release on the horizon. I knew once the album hit the shelves, the band would be untouchable as they'd be prepping for the tour and whatever else. I was panicking. I knew I had to meet Vince's deadline so my work could be in Ireland shortly before *Achtung Baby*'s release.

Two weeks to the day we discussed the idea, Uncle Vince arrived on the doorstep of my studio apartment with his 35 millimeter camera and studio lights in tow. He had shot all of Nicole's work and been a bit of a camera junkie. As he began to set-up shop, I brought out the jacket and slung it over a director's chair. He looked at it and raised his eyebrows in acceptance.

"This is the piece?" he asked, as he took off his coat and threw it onto my bed.

"Yeah, I said. It is. You like?" I was looking for validation.

"Very cool. Looks like a Shivvers' painted U2 jacket to me. I like the 'U2' in red on the sleeve. Very hip."

Vince pulled out his Nikon camera with a wide-angle lens, followed by several boxes of film. Adjacent to his photo bag was a briefcase. He unloaded a manila envelope and placed it on my desk. He then tore open a box of film and began to load the camera.

"I brought Tungsten film. We use it all the time when I shoot your aunt's artwork. It works harmoniously with my lamps. I cannot use normal, slide film as it would tend to look yellow," he explained as the lens cap dangled from his mouth.

Not only was I getting schooled in business, but also in photography. Uncle Vince knew a lot about the ins and outs of taking photos. He had a darkroom in Nicole's art apartment, which I used when I visited at Thanksgiving the previous fall during my senior year in college. I took full advantage of the space as I was working on a photo essay called "The Day in the Life at Iowa." The essay was a competition put on by *The Daily Iowan* newspaper, our student newspaper. I wanted to take part just to hone my photo skills. Vince, amused by the work, gave me pointers along the way. He became a father figure for me when I faced issues that needed a neutral perspective. My father would give me a lecture. Vince, on the other hand, would listen and give me suggestions.

Vince set up the tripod and anchored the camera. He reeled off a couple frames to advance the film. He walked over to the chair, hosting my newly minted work, and began to gently turn the chair. He was looking for the right angle. He then retreated behind his camera and looked through the camera lens. He went back to the chair for some final adjustments.

"Now, Eric, take a look. See if that's what you're looking for," he said, as he turned on the tungsten lamps and filled the room with an explosion of light.

I leaned behind the viewfinder to take a look at my jacket. Bono, Edge, Adam and Larry were framed beautifully. The detail of the band would be captured just the way I wanted it to be.

"I think it looks great. Let's take a few different shots at different apertures and then make minor changes in the framing," I said. I was in control of the art direction.

"I agree. While I'm shooting, open that envelope on your desk and read the letter. Let me know what you think."

I went to the desk and slid out the letter. I proceeded to read the U2 manifesto as snaps of the camera's shutter were firing behind me. "Dear Principle Management..." I mumbled the letter as I read it. It was single spaced and dense. Vince covered all of the bases about requesting rights, stage wear and one-of-a-kind pieces.

"I think we need to turn the piece," Vince said from behind me.

"Okay," I muttered without turning around. I was deep into a tome of a letter, which was filled with information.

"Take a look and tell me what you think," Vince said.

I turned around, with the letter grasped in one hand, and looked through the viewfinder.

"Perfect. I think giving the band the whole experience of the piece is the best," I replied. A slight hint of excitement came out of my voice. I moved away from the camera and went back to the letter. I was overwhelmed. I was trying to comprehend a business proposal while art directing the photo shoot.

"Am I crazy," I thought. "Do I really think U2 is going to go for this? I mean seriously. I've very little creative self-esteem right now and I'm putting all of it into this opportunity. I must be nuts. My creative career is in the shitter. I gotta do something here to hang on."

I turned around and observed my uncle move the jacket again and then look through the viewfinder several more times, taking a shot or two along the way. My uncle must have believed in my idea and me. I always looked forward to their visits to Iowa and enduring those hot summer treks to the Iowa State Fair. Always with a camera in tow, Uncle Vince took a ton of shots of my cousins and me.

"I think we got it, Eric," he said, as he shut off all of the lamps and then unscrewed the camera from the tripod. It seemed as though the sun had fallen out of the sky. My room went back to its late autumnal glow.

"You just need to develop the film and you're good to go," he said, while winding the film backwards through the camera. There was a pause at my end as I was rereading the opening paragraph.

"What do you think about the letter?" Uncle Vince asked, as he pulled the pin and flipped the back of the camera open to retrieve the film.

"Uncle Vince, it's a dense document. There are a lot of points in here. The band may read this and give up as they try to decipher our request. It's a little overwhelming," I replied anxiously.

"Yes, Eric, we cover a lot of bases, yet it gives them an idea that we mean business. They may read something and have an 'Ah-ha' moment," he said, as he began to fold up the tripod while waiting for the lamps to cool down.

"Eric, you're an emotional guy. I've known that ever since you were a squirt. It's okay. Look, you're going after a dream here. I'm not sure many people have the guts to create a cool piece of art, photograph it and send it to their favorite band requesting permission to use their likeness," he replied. Again, Uncle Vince was becoming part therapist and part father figure.

"What if they say, 'no, we're not interested,' Vince? I'll be crushed," I countered.

"And what if they say, 'yes?'" he responded as he popped open the plastic film container and dropped in the roll of film containing the images of my jacket.

"Here you go," he said, as he stretched out his hand and put the black plastic container into my chest. "Develop the film. Sign the letter. Send it to Ireland. And then, wait."

"Okay. I will."

A pause came between us. The only security I had in Chicago was looking me in the face and telling me to chase a dream. Reality was in front of me. It was no longer a hare-brained idea by my aunt. I had to go through with it.

Uncle Vince unscrewed the bulbs out of the lamps and gently placed them in a terry cloth towel. I stood there looking at my jacket, slung over the back of the chair and lifeless, with the film container grasped firmly in my hand. I wasn't sure. As the clanking of Vince's equipment became background noise, I thought again to myself, "What do I have to lose? Nothing."

I looked back at my uncle. He was now loaded down with equipment. I went to open the door to my studio apartment to let him out.

"Uncle Vince thanks for doing this. I appreciate it," I said and stared at him.

"No problem. Chase your dream, Eric. No matter what the outcome will be, just chase it. Nicole and I are rooting for you," he replied. He then turned and headed down the hallway to the elevator. He stopped to press the button to go downstairs. A few seconds later, the doors opened. He looked back at me before entering and said, "Let us know the outcome Mr. Rock Star Painter Man." The elevator doors sucked him in.

I went back into my studio and reread the letter ten more times. Pulled out a pen and signed it. In the coming days, my film would be developed. I reviewed the slides and found my favorite three to put in a slide sheet, which I stapled to the letter. I then mailed the package to Ireland. I knew I had done all that I could to chase a silly dream. I was making a simple request. I acted upon an instinct and had to believe that no matter what the outcome, I did it.

13: he turned into "the fly"

On a scale of one to ten, my anticipation for *Achtung Baby*'s release hovered around eleven. The recording would be U2's most ambitious album to date. Like a caterpillar, turning into a butterfly, U2's sound and attitude was a metamorphosis. Bono was about to take on a new persona, The Fly, a leather clad, over-sized sunglasses wearing rocker with more swagger than Frank Sinatra. The video, *The Fly*, would be a World Premiere Video on MTV. Sadly, I owned a hand held black and white television with four channels. Therefore, I had no cable television. I felt as though driving to my aunt and uncle's house in the suburbs was too far for a five-minute video so I worked my address book and found a neighbor, Erin, willing to let me watch the video.

Erin was a red-haired gal, whose mom taught my cousin, Nicholas, private piano lessons back in his hometown of Vinton, Iowa. Nicholas' mom, my Aunt Beverly, introduced her to me the previous spring and we formed a friendship. Erin lived only a stone's throw way from my studio apartment with two other gals. The three of us, plus their on again off again boyfriends, would hang out until the late hours of the night in our post college splendor, during the weekends. Erin and her roommates were a good support system as I coped with life while getting used to living on my own.

Erin too was a fan of U2 and more than willing to let me come over. When I arrived at the gal's pad, I knocked on their back door with my arms laden with beers and a videocassette.

"Hold on, Eric, I'll be there in a minute," I heard Erin say.

"Okay."

I looked at my watch. It was exactly twenty minutes to the debut. I saw her silhouette come to the door.

"Come on in," Erin said with a smile as she pulled the door inward. The kitchen light flooded behind her.

"I brought beer!" I said, as I kicked the door behind me closed.

"Cool! I need to put the wash in the dryer. I'll be back," she replied, as she turned around and headed out of the kitchen to the hallway.

"Is it cold?" she asked, as her voice echoed down the hallway.

"Yeah, I just picked it up."

"Great, put it in the fridge. I'm going to heat up some leftover turkey chili. Want some?"

"No, I ate dinner at home," I said, as I rattled the rental apartment fridge door open. I peered inside. Several dishes of pizza, a leftover Subway sandwich and a half-eaten burrito had to be pushed out of the way in order to make room for my beer.

"Are you excited?" Her voice was louder as she was fighting the background noise of the dryer.

"Yeah, I'm pretty stoked! Couldn't you tell when you said you would let me come over? I brought a videocassette to tape the premiere," I shouted back.

"Great. I'll be there in a minute to show you how to set up the VCR."

Thirty-seconds later, we crossed paths in the hallway, which dumped us into her spacious living room. In the middle of the room, sat a couch and across from it, resting upon a couple milk crates, was the TV. While Erin shoved the videocassette into the VCR, I picked up the remote and reviewed it. She gently pulled it from my hands, changed the channel to MTV and proceeded to walk me through the recording process. I recorded many videocassettes in my life and was familiar with the workings of a VCR, but gave into Erin. I continued to make myself at home by throwing my coat on an adjacent chair and parking my ass on the couch. I looked at the clock on the VCR. If it were programmed right, I had fifteen minutes before the premiere.

"Wanna beer?" Erin asked with a smile.

"Yeah, please."

She walked back to the kitchen.

"Glass or bottle?" she inquired from the kitchen.

"Bottle!"

Upon her return, time ticked closer to seven o'clock, the official hour of the debut of *The Fly* video. I was ready. I had the VCR remote in my right hand and ready to gently press the record button. Erin placed the beer bottle on the coffee table and returned to the kitchen to begin cooking. My eyes were transfixed on the digital time clock on the VCR. I looked back to the television. The last annoying commercial ended, as the clock revealed 7:00 p.m. in its window. I punched the record button just in time to catch MTV's ten-second screen shot "World Premiere Video." When the screen shot vanished, there was Bono, dressed head-to-toe in leather with wrap-around shades, walking out onto a city street and pushing a toy double-decker bus. The next image is Bono, running from a real double-decker bus. He then began to conduct traffic. No one recognized him. People were looking at him strangely not knowing who he was. All of a sudden, the high-pitched falsetto-backing track stopped. Edge's heavy guitar pierced Erin's three-inch television speaker. The visuals became grainy with highly saturated images of the band on a nondescript studio set. Bono, still wearing the oversized fly shades, began to reel off the lyrics. Next, we saw the lead singer roam some city's streets at night, armed with a remote control. His journey was interspersed with the band playing on the soundstage. I was glued. U2 turned gritty, loud and looked tougher than ever. Gone was any reference to their previous decade's image. Bono's locks were chopped off. Adam's hair had grown out. Edge looked rugged in a tank top, sequin dotted pants and a skullcap. Larry wore a Ramones T-shirt while keeping time behind his drum kit. It was the visual version of what Jamie was speaking of weeks earlier.

Erin could hear the tune over her chili's slow, boiling, plop sound in the saucepan on the stove. She asked from the kitchen, "Sounds heavy Eric! Do you like it?"

I said nothing. I was intoxicated and truly overwhelmed. I tried to figure out what the copy said as it scrolled across a background billboard in the shot. It read, "Watch More T.V." What did that mean? U2 set the bar high for cool because they were now a leather-clad band with a funk driven tune. I was interrupted as Erin arrived back in the living room, just as the video ended.

"So, what'd you think?" she asked.

I looked at the screen and hit the stop button on the remote, ending the taping process. The video play head retracted from the cassette. I still said nothing. I hit rewind on the remote.

"Hello? Earth to Eric. I asked you a question," she said, as she waved her hands in front of my glazed look.

I slowly turned and looked at her. She was now taking another long swig of her beer. I could see the liquid rolling in the green bottle.

"Awesome. Totally fuckin' awesome," I said, as I pointed the remote at the VCR and hit rewind, followed by the play button. "Wanna see it?"

"Heck yeah," Erin replied. "Don't you think I'm a fan too? I didn't invite you over for nothing. Let's see it."

She sat back on the couch and put her feet up on the coffee table. The smell of the chili was wandering into the living room. The video began. I started looking for more visual clues in the film – Bono tapping his chest with his fingers, a young looking Larry keeping the beat with his kit and Adam's cigarette, dangling from his mouth. The band was dangerous and looking cool. I was curious about Bono and his new persona. "Would we see this dude in concert?" I asked myself. The answer would be confirmed in a couple of months. As for now, I didn't want to read too much into it as the cassette came to the end of the video. Again, I hit the rewind button and began to play it once more.

"Let me go check dinner," Erin said, as she lifted herself off the couch and ambled towards the kitchen to finish the chili. I watched the video for a third and fourth time. I was ecstatic. The band's new look, and vibe, left me wanting more. Before I overstayed my welcome, I ejected the videocassette, got up off the couch and grabbed my coat. I could hear Erin making a plate of dinner as I grabbed the cassette out of the VCR.

"Erin, thanks so much," I said in a humble manner as I entered the kitchen.

"No problem. Come over anytime. I'm glad you could see your Irish boys."

"Say 'hello' to your roommates for me," I said, as I put my

hand on the doorknob.

"Will do," she replied smiling.

I could feel the handle turn underneath my grip. The door then moved, towards me, almost in a jarring manner. From outside, Marissa, one of Erin's roommates, was getting home.

"Hey!...Hello, Eric," Marissa greeted me.

Marissa, a tiny gal with spiraling, curly red hair was a graphic designer who held a BFA from Southern Illinois. Like me, she was struggling with her creative career. She entered the kitchen.

"Erin, is that turkey chili?"

"Yeah, I heated up the whole batch thinkin' Eric would partake, but he's already eaten."

"Dude, you splittin' already? I just got home, man." Marissa was now looking at me.

"Yeah, I taped the new U2 video and now, I'm headed out," I replied with a smile.

"Stay man. U2? I wanna see the video. Also, I know you don't have a VCR at your joint and you wanna see it again," Marissa said, begging. "Let me throw off this heap of a coat and get some dinner."

Marissa then clopped across the kitchen and down the hall. We heard her kick off her boots as they landed separately on the hardwood floor with a thud. Erin ladled a bowl of chili for herself and asked me again if I wanted a bite, however, I declined. We headed back to the living room where I shoved the videocassette back into the player, tossed my coat on the floor and seated my ass on the same spot of the couch where I was minutes prior. Marissa came to the doorway of the living room.

"I heard a rumor there's a new U2 album coming out. What's the name again?" she asked.

"'Achtung Baby,'" I said with spit hurling out of my mouth.

"That sounds fucked up, Eric," she said. "Wanna beer?"

"Yeah, I could go for another."

"Get me one too!" Erin shouted with a mouthful of chili. She began to wave her hand frantically to cool off her mouth.

Marissa spun around like a pixie and headed towards the kitchen. We could hear her open the fridge when the condiments in the door knocked against one another.

"Grolsch? When'd we get this?" Marissa's muffled voice came from the kitchen.

"Eric brought it over!" Erin shouted, as we heard the fridge door shut with another rattle.

"Bitchin! Upscale beer. Momma likes it."

I heard three bottle caps hit the countertop, along with the opening of cupboards, and the clanking of dishes. Marissa reappeared weighted with three green bottles of brew, each one was nestled individually between each of her fingers on her right hand as she carried her bowl of chili in her left. She slowly walked to the coffee table and unloaded her items. She grabbed one of the beers and then plopped herself down on the adjacent Papasan chair.

"Whew. What a fuckin' day?" Marissa said, as she leaned back and let the beer coat her throat. She threw her feet up on the coffee table.

"God, I hate my job!" she exclaimed. "I'm a designer working for the biggest loser company. Does that make me a loser, too? Don't answer Eric. It's rhetorical." She took another swig of her beer. "Yummy. Good and cold. Just exactly how momma likes her beer," Marissa belched.

"Shall I hit play, Marissa?" I asked.

"Fire it up! How many times have you seen it, Eric?"

"This may be my sixth time tonight."

"Six times?? That's how many times you've replayed it!" Marissa said with astonishment.

"Ah yeah," Erin replied for me.

"Shit, you don't need to see it again, but I do! Roll the fucker because this must be one hellova video. I thought they were creatively dead after Rattle and Scum," Marissa said with her own spin of whacky love for U2's overambitious road movie covering the Joshua Tree Tour.

Marissa took another chug of her brew. She leaned forward and grabbed her bowl of chili. She was about to take a bite and looked at us over the rim of her bowl.

"I like them and all, but in my opinion, a little bit of Bono goes a long way," Marissa said, interrupting herself. "Didn't you say that you were sending them some painted jeans? Slides? Some shit like that?" she asked, as her chili-laden spoon went to her mouth after the question.

"Yeah, I sent'em some slides two weeks ago. I've not heard a thing back. I'm hoping time is on my side," I replied.

"Well, you did a lot of work. I think you are crazy. That's just me," Marissa said, as she spooned another bite of her chili.

"I don't," Erin chimed in.

"Don't what?" Marissa said, as she was waving her hand in front of her mouth frantically trying to cool it.

"I don't think Eric's crazy, Marissa. I think he's following his passion."

"I give him props for going through with it. It'd be cool to paint jeans for U2," Marissa said. She leaned forward and rested the half-empty bowl of soup on the table.

"I've no idea if they're going to go for it. If they do Marissa, I'll hire you to help paint," I said.

"Cool. Maybe I can finally quit my crap job at DRG," she said with a smirk.

"I'd love to have a creative job right now, even if it was production," I said.

"I wouldn't give my worst enemy this job. Trust me. The owners are pains in the asses. Everyone wants to quit," she fired back. "Enough about work. I wanna see this damn video!"

I pointed the remote towards the television and hit play. I could hear the cassette reels begin to move and creak as they were forced to play *The Fly* one more time for our viewing pleasure. All of the visuals began to sink in from the previous viewings. I could now enjoy the montage of film clips strung together for what they were, art. Up to now, including the early ones, the narrative for U2's videos was pretty loose. For *The Fly*, Bono was now taking on a persona, which neither he nor the band had really done in any previous work. What Erin, Marissa and I were witnessing was a creative shift in U2. The three of us, regardless of what Marissa said about *Rattle and Hum*, were fans.

"Dude, check out those shades he's got on," Marissa said with amazement.

"Wonder where you can get them?" Erin projected her question towards the screen of the television.

"Oh, I'm sure they will sell them at the merch table," Marissa said, as she was visiting the last swallow of beer.

"I love the chair on the sidewalk and Bono with the remote," Erin replied knowing exactly where the scene was in the video.

"I cannot believe the change. I mean they're now rockers. Where's Edge's long hair? What the fuck is up with the skull cap?" Marissa was now intently reviewing the band.

After watching the video for the final time, I slugged down the last of my Dutch beer. I grabbed my coat and videocassette, all the while saying good-night. I headed out into the late October night under a moonlight sky. I was excited. Bono, Edge, Larry and Adam were coming back into my life at the right time, much like the way they did when I was in college.

14: along came a baby

With a mouth full of Novocaine, I walked into Rose Records on *Achtung Baby*'s release day, close to mid-afternoon. One side of Jamie's store was plastered in photos of U2 while the other was covered with a displaced Garth Brooks promo poster from an earlier fall release. The wall of U2 graphics was mind blowing. Square images, of highly stylized photographs, covered the space in a mosaic pattern, mimicking the new U2 album cover. The subject of each square, measuring roughly 15 inches by 15 inches, was like a small vignette. One had all four U2 members dressed in drag while another had a profile shot of Bono in black and white with a half-nude woman, standing behind him. I was overwhelmed in the transformation, as the creative team behind brand U2 had left behind their 80s ideals of decorating album covers, except for the *October* album, with a stark black and white image.

"What do ya think of the store, Mr. U2 Man?" Jamie said from behind the counter as she was ringing up a customer.

"I'm in shock! Is this what they look like now?"

I was scraping my dropped jaw off the floor as I reviewed the sixteen images on the wall.

"Yup, it's them all right," Jamie replied.

I was now a little frightened as I walked slowly towards the wall for a closer look. The images became more intimate. A question raged inside me, "Why is the band in drag? What's with the image of the bull, or the one of the fruit stand, doing on the album cover along side images of the band? What's their importance to U2?" I was overloading my brain and took a step back. I went to U2's section, in the racks, which was overflowing with copies of the new album. Two versions existed. One was a typical jewel case in a long box while the other was a Digipak. Just to be different, I grabbed a Digipak and stared into the cover. The questions inside my head returned, "What's up with my band and this cover? Am I going to leave them behind? Am I now going to have to look for a new muse?"

"The album has sold well today," Jamie said, breaking my daydream.

"Really?"

"Yeah, I had about twenty sales in the first hour. What took you so long to get here? I thought you'd be the first one in the door."

"Dentist," I replied, while trying not to drool on the countertop.

"Oh, all day?"

"No, this afternoon. I had to run a couple errands late this morning followed by an hour and a half in the chair," I slurped.

"That sucks. What for?"

"Cosmetic reasons. I'm having my front teeth capped. Six of them," I said, as I dug my wallet out of my ass pocket.

She rang the register. The receipt tape stuttered.

"Seventeen thirty-four. Glad the album was released today,

huh. At least it's not all bad." Jamie took my twenty and scurried the change from the till.

"Yeah, I'm supposed to look beautiful when all of this is done," I said, as I grabbed the two sixty-six from her rough hand.

For a split second, we made eye contact. I could tell she was exhausted from the night before.

"Well, heading home for a listen," I said, as I folded the paper bag around the disc and stuffed it into my coat pocket.

"Hold on. I've got something for you in the back," she said, as she zoomed out from behind the counter. "I have leftover promo stuff. Be right back," she said over her shoulder as she ran to the storage room door in the back of the store. Jamie returned momentarily with a corrugated flat box in her right hand and a poster tube tucked underneath the left.

"Here you go. I saved you some of the panels from the wall and the extra poster. Here's the box they came in from the label. I know you'd want them," she said with her usual broad smile.

"Thanks dear! I can't wait to get these things home."

"You're welcome. Now, get your Novocaine induced ass out of my store and get that U2 on boy!" she exclaimed with a laugh.

"Thanks," I said, as I pushed the door open with my butt and headed into the November afternoon.

I sauntered to the "L" station with my parcels, I thought, "Wow. I could now U2-fy my apartment." When I got to the platform and looked down the rail line, in the distance, I could see the faint glow of the oncoming train's headlights. *Achtung Baby* was finally headed home with me. As the "L" approached, I moved a few steps away from the platform edge. I didn't want any mishaps. I just wanted to get home.

Without turning on a light, I entered my pad and put down my packages. The darkness of the day shrouded my small studio apartment. I pulled the Rose Records' bag out of my coat and placed it on top of the right speaker. I lobbed my lifeless jacket towards my director's chair and turned on the stereo. The ambient light from the CD player immediately lit up and glowed. I sat on my futon and scooted it closer to the stereo cabinet, putting me within arms reach of the buttons. I then tore off the acetate sheathing from the compact disc case and flipped open the Digipak. The scent of the freshly printed booklet, accompanying the disc, hit my nose as I leaned forward to insert the CD into the player. I pushed the CD drawer closed and the whirring of the disc began. The illuminated display revealed the track count. Finally, the time had arrived to hear *Achtung Baby*. I hit the play button.

As I leaned back on my futon to bathe in the opening tune, *Zoo Station*, a clicking noise penetrated from the right speaker, and then the left, followed by a very distorted, repeating, Edge guitar riff answered by Larry's heavy sounding drums. Larry and Edge danced together for a few bars when Adam's distorted bass slowly came in to meet Edge's riff. The three instruments formed a tight community of conversation and took off. Over the primal dialogue among the instruments, Bono entered with a falsetto and then charged into the opening lyric. He revealed that he's prepared to take on what would be the next chapter in U2's career. It's a tongue-in-cheek response to the lead singer's statement during the end of the Point Depot show where he said, "We have to go away and...dream it all up again." *Zoo Station* was the result of the dream. The song was heavy with industrial sound as Adam and Larry kept a tight hold on the rhythm end while Edge skipped over the top with an intoxicating riff. The images Bono conjured up about the transition spoke to me. I too had transformed, from an undergrad to now a full-fledged adult, within the same time period as the band's metamorphosis. It hit so close to home that when the song closed, I wanted more. I leaned forward and skipped back to the beginning of the track, just to soak in the *Zoo Station* bathtub one more time.

Darkness encroached my room as the outside light began to wane. The light projected from the CD player seemed brighter. *Zoo Station* opened up once more. I was now drunk with funk. Before I knew it, I'd fallen into the second track, *Even Better Than the Real Thing*. Edge's guitar was captured in a loop at the opening of the song, underneath was a basic drumbeat. The repetition lulled me in until Edge ripped a chord with a shimmering guitar effect. Larry drummed in on time with Adam behind. Bono began to sing in a higher key than I was used to. Two songs in and the band revealed how comfortable they had become with new technologies. U2's musical topography of the 80s had mutated into something fresh. The influences of The Clash, The Ramones, Bob Dylan and The Beatles were long gone. U2 had now plugged into the Manchester dance sound. Bands, such as the Happy Mondays, The Stone Roses and the like, were shaking up the sound in Europe. U2 was aware of their influences.

The entire rhythmic groove came to a halt when the third track, *One*, crept out of my speakers. The song opened with softened chords sliding up and down Edge's guitar neck while Larry was in the background, keeping a simple tapping of time. Bono opened the lyric as though he was having an open and intimate dialogue with a lover in the middle of the night. The questions were rooted in what would come of the relationship with the arrival of daylight. *One* captured that pure moment of self-doubt. I thought of all of the unanswered questions I dealt with during the late hours of the evening as well. "Did my parents have these late night conversations before it all went south too? If so, who in their relationship was asking the questions Bono was posing?" I asked myself as my mind started to wander. I couldn't answer the questions.

At this point, I was now lying on my futon, on my back and lengthwise, while being parallel to the stereo. *One* called me for a return listen. I hit the back button and began to stare into the starkness of the ceiling above me. As the song played again, thoughts of Jessica, a gal whom I served coffee drinks to daily at my Starbucks store, roamed my brain. She was in the store, like clockwork at eleven twenty-five every morning, and always ordered the same drink, grande skim latte no foam. Most days, I made sure I was behind the espresso machine upon her arrival so I could carry on a conversation with her. Our casual exchanges, which would eventually turn into dating, became more and more lengthy as our friendship began to build. The daydream of her kept going as *One* finished rolling through the speakers a second time. The simplicity of the song was catchy, however, the intensity of the lyric is what drew you in. Soon, it would be revealed that the song was dealing, not only with love, but the blight of AIDS and would be a radio single with the proceeds going to AIDS foundations. It was U2 being U2 again, aware of what was going on in the world.

I was now getting anxious and wanted to move deeper into the album. I flopped my arm towards the CD player and skipped to *The Fly*. Already familiar with the video, I now wanted to hear the tune without the bombardment of the visuals. The song opened with a pulsating riff by Edge followed by Larry's drums, filling in the gaps. They danced together for a few bars until Adam rolled in underneath them with a low, thumping progression. For the next four bars, they grooved together and let Bono in on the fun. He sang in an almost spoken word style about the secrets of life. As the verse ended, and the band ventured to the chorus, a backing track entered with Bono singing falsetto. It was a new style for the lead singer.

Once out of the chorus, Edge, Adam and Larry went full

speed ahead with the funk arsenal. It was heavy and followed by an equally weighty lyric in the second verse that almost knocked me out of my seat. Bono sang of creative types seeking a muse, squashing it and crooning to the anguish of what they've done. It spoke to me. I grew up in a house of academics, artists and writers who always sought some sort of divine intervention when it came to being creative. I'm sure Bono was speaking the truths as he too had hit the creative wall many times himself, but not on this track. He got it right and I was hooked. I'm sure my neighbors could tell I was intoxicated with the tune as I laid on my back gyrating to the explosion of sound coming out of my speakers. The wooden frame of the futon below me squeaked against the floor with my sudden jerks. Finally, I had the band back in my veins.

In the weeks following *Achtung Baby*'s release, I was readying myself for the announcement of concert dates. Chicago had to be on the list as *Achtung Baby*'s aptly titled tour, Zoo TV Indoor Broadcast, would be one of the most anticipated tours since The Rolling Stones' Steel Wheels Tour. The four-year U2 tour drought on American soil was about to come to an end. Within two months, of the album's release, the American dates were announced and yes, Chicago was included on the cross-country jaunt. And unlike previous tours, U2 handled the ticket process differently by declining to sell tickets through the traditional storefront outlets, which meant no camping out or standing in line. Instead, the band decided to sell them by phone and at night. It was a way for them to skirt scalping but a pain for me, as I had to schedule my life around the call. Fortunately, the night and time worked for me. I stayed late after our store closed and dialed the Ticketmaster number about twenty times. I received the same error message, "All circuits are busy, please try your call again later." On my twenty-first attempt, the phone line went completely dead. The culprit was a heavy blanket of snow, which had fallen during the afternoon. As the clock in the back office now displayed seven-thirty, I faced a dilemma, wait for the phone line to come back or run to the train, which would take me home. Disheartened, I chose the train and never got tickets to the show.

15: a tough decision

With a cup of coffee in my right hand, I pushed open the heavy, steel door into a cold, February day. I was trying to escape from my retail job, briefly, as a gray sky hovered above me with the heaviness of winter. I took a seat on the back staircase, just a few steps from the store, using my apron as a little insulation from the cold step for my ten-minute afternoon break. I stared into the alley reflecting on life and how I took a chance when I moved to Chicago a year and a half earlier. I kept telling myself I left the confines of my parent's place in Iowa for all the right reasons. While harnessed with a bachelor's degree in graphic design, working in retail wasn't the challenge I bargained for, yet I needed relief from the suffocation of home. Chicago provided me a fresh, new start on life.

As I stared into the java and saw a pale reflection of me, Shannon, my coworker, came outside with her arms filled with broken-down, corrugated-cardboard boxes and was headed to the recycling dumpster. Upon her return, she saw me.

"Eric, takin' a break?" she asked.

"Yeah, for a moment. I've a few minutes before your shift is over. Then I can start the closing process with Sarah. Anne will be in shortly," I replied and then took a deep gulp of warm brew.

"I've got something for you. Something you've been wanting for a while," she said in a singsong style as she walked toward the foot of the steps I was sitting on.

"What???" I asked in annoyance.

"I've a friend who has a friend who resells tickets. I called my connection and asked about U2. He said he's got a couple left for the upcoming Rosemont Horizon show you've been talking about."

"Interesting," I said, showing no emotion at all as I looked blankly in return. Shannon didn't know how much I despised scalpers.

"He said he has tickets for a hundred and twenty-five dollars and I know you want to go."

"Where're the seats?"

"In the twenty-fifth row, section 110, behind the stage," she replied, as she pulled a pack of Marlboro Lights from her coat pocket.

"Behind the stage? For one twenty-five? Are you crazy? That's four times the amount of face. For that sum, we should be closer or at least on the side." I was annoyed.

"Dude, you don't have three hundred bucks," she said, as she pulled out her lighter, cupped her hand and lit a cigarette. She blew the initial drag into the air.

"Three hundred for what?" I inquired.

"In front of the stage."

"Fuck! I can't believe it! I've got to pay for scalped tickets to see my band. For that kind of money, and on my budget, we should be seeing Bono's ass!"

"And that's not a good thing?"

"If you're gay, Shannon!"

"I told you I have a ticket connection and these are the cheapest he has," she said, as she took another drag from her cigarette and shifted her hips from side to side to stay warm.

"How long will he hold them for us?"

"Until tomorrow afternoon. We can buy them together after your shift."

"What am I going to tell Jessica?" I inquired, as I looked at Shannon over the rim of my coffee mug.

"Pfffffht. Your older Jewish girlfriend? Whom I smile at every morning and chat with when she comes in to order her grande skim latte?" she asked laughingly.

"Don't rub it in. Yes, Jessica."

I wore my heart on a sleeve, which made it easy for Shannon to enter my personal life.

"Tell her the truth. I've a ticket connection and got you tickets," she said, as a quick smirk came across her face.

"Oh, that'll help my cause. Jessica knows how much I want to take her to the show." I then took another sip of my coffee as a rage of fire brewed in my loving heart.

"Sadly, you want to go. You don't have tickets. I do. So, let me chat with her. I can explain everything. I'm making my ticket connection available to you."

"No! Let me handle this. I don't need you moving in between me and my girlfriend!"

Shannon looked at me. She knew she had me right where she wanted me. Like a seductress, she was singing to me with temptation, but I didn't want to budge. The tickets, the show, and U2 were now creating a whirlwind around me. She took another drag off her cigarette. Held the smoke in her lungs. Then exhaled.

"Eric, relax," Shannon said, as she crouched on her knees in front of me. "You're going to see U2."

"Ah, this isn't how I wanted to go."

I was frustrated. First by buying scalped tickets and then to go with Shannon whom I had no attraction to whatsoever.

"Maybe it is a good thing. From what you've told me, it sounds like Jessica may not want to go."

"Oh, how the fuck do you know?"

"I am a woman. I can tell by the signals she's sending you," Shannon replied.

"She is my girlfriend."

"Older girlfriend. And Jewish no less."

"So…"

"Face it. She may not want to go."

"Of course she does. It's U2 for crying out loud!" I yelled.

"Eric, she really isn't a girlfriend. How can I soften what I'm about to say? It's a fling."

"Fling, what the fuck do you know at twenty and still a virgin might I add? What do you know about our relationship?"

"Everything because you've confided in me, Eric. Three dinner dates, and a few shack ups, are closer to a fling. On top of that, you have told me several times you're frustrated with the communication between the two of you. You give everything to her. What are you getting in return? Nothing. Therefore, by definition, it's a fling," Shannon said, while squashing out her cigarette into the concrete sidewalk.

"She's my girlfriend!" I shouted in defense.

"Bullshit. You know it's not that deep," she replied with honesty.

"Shannon, like you know."

"Like I know? I can figure it out. You're hopelessly in love with an older woman and you're married to U2. Isn't that the truth?"

She smiled. Her oversized red lips and chubby face reminded me of everything I didn't like about her. I wanted to hide as I had let Shannon know too much about me. I stood up and tossed out what was left of my coffee into the alley. I was fully aware that I had run out of options trying to get tickets to the show. Sometimes, you have to ride into the casino with lady luck, no matter how you feel about her.

"Okay. Let's get the tickets," I said with confidence.

Shannon's shift was over soon. The conversation from the stoop began to haunt me. The pain was obvious. I thought I knew how to protect my heart after my parent's divorce. I guess I was wrong. I was looking for love, desperately, and worried too much about where the relationship, with Jessica, was going while not enjoying it for what it really was.

Shannon might have been right. I was realizing U2 was more than a band to me. They were my therapist, my guidance and inspiration. The tunes of *Achtung Baby* contemplated the fragility of relationships and the difficulty of making them work. I was on my own and looking for a relationship with happiness while unaware, at the time, how delicate the bond of love could be between two people.

On the following night, as the ATM spit out my money for the scalped ticket, excitement came to mind as I had a chance to see U2's Zoo TV Indoor Broadcast concert in Chicago. I knew I was paying a heavy price to go to the show, both monetarily and financially, but didn't care. What I did care about was buying legit U2 product and upon our arrival to Shannon's connection's office, I carefully inspected the tickets. I held them to the light in order to see the reflective sparkles embedded in the ink that told me they were legit and not counterfeit. I felt that we had the real deal. Shannon and I handed over our cash. She put both tickets into her purse and held onto them for safekeeping. I broke the news to Jessica in the coming week. The reaction was zero, just as Shannon had predicted. I'm not sure which hurt worse, buying tickets from a scalper or Jessica's flat lined reaction. It didn't matter. What bothered me more was Shannon's insertion into my life, via U2, which made me become more despondent even though she granted me one of my favorite joys in life, seeing U2 play live.

16: a circus called Zoo TV

Six weeks after Shannon persuaded me to buy tickets from her ticket broker, U2's Zoo TV Inside Broadcast Tour landed in Chicago. Shannon's excitement was on the level of extreme euphoria. Her spouts of exhilaration about going to the show were constant reminders we were going together, which rattled me daily. Even up to the moment we were in line outside the Rosemont Horizon, where Shannon regurgitated everything she knew about the band, the bombardment didn't cease. Thank God we ran into a friend of hers in line. It was a much needed distraction as we stood in the shadow of the stadium while the sun set on the other side. A chill of winter was in the March evening air as we watched the doors to the venue open and close several times, expecting our granted entrance. The wait seemed prolonged, as security wouldn't let us go back to our cars to get warm. Sadly, we had to stand in line wearing whatever we had on. When the doors finally opened, a good half an hour later than promised, I was relieved of the pain of having to listen to

Shannon talk incessantly about my beloved band.

To escape, I headed directly to the merchandise table filled with posters, T-shirts, pins and tour programs, covering the back wall behind the vendors. As I panned over the U2 items, I knew it was impossible to buy one of everything. I began to edit down the shirts. One had the band behind the wheel of the East German Trabant car, using surreal lighting to spotlight them. Another displayed icons from the album, stacked vertically on the front, with tour dates on the back. The one that caught my eye, and eventually took my hard earned cash, was a shirt with all four-band members together in a posterized image. Beneath them were my favorite lyrics from *The Fly*. It spoke to me. Shannon, standing behind me during my review of all of the Zoo TV tour schwag, agreed it was the best one to buy. I also had to keep my cousin Nicholas, or Nick for short, in mind because he too was a fan, living on a farm in small town Iowa and unable to see the tour, except for the snippets on MTV News. Nicholas' passion for U2 could be squarely blamed on me. I'm not sure how my fandom stretched to the middle of Iowa. I think we had that kindred spirit about us because he too was a product of a divorce and an only child as well. Whatever I was into, he wanted to be into as well.

Once finished eyeballing all of the merch, we found the stairwell leading to the balcony section. The Horizon was familiar to me. I had seen Billy Joel and INXS here in the past two years. The venue was known for great shows, specifically for U2. The band played here on A Conspiracy of Hope tour, a six night concert tour across America, celebrating Amnesty International's 25th Anniversary. On that particular night, The Police, who had not toured in two years, closed out the show. U2 performed in the slot right before them. When the Irish lads finished their set, half of the audience left due to their command performance.

The other great U2 moment in Rosemont Horizon history was on the first leg of the Joshua Tree Tour. An annoying concert goer whistled at Bono during the show. The lead singer collected his thoughts and, while amid a lull during songs, fired back telling the attendee that they were not The Beatles, but U2. These two incidents made tonight's stop on the Zoo TV Indoor Broadcast Tour very special. I had a feeling we were in for a treat.

When we arrived to our seats, we were eighty feet up from the back of the stage and dead center behind Larry Mullen's drum kit. Perched like two birds on a wire, we had a fantastic view of the sea of humanity in the venue. Zoo TV Indoor Broadcast was a performance space like no other I had seen before. Video monitors, of all sizes, littered the performance space. Willie Williams, U2's set designer, left no one out of the viewing pleasure as groupings of several smaller televisions faced us as well. Plus, flanking both sides of the stage were bigger video monitors that would eventually swivel and give us a view of what everyone else was seeing from the front of the stage. Above the stage, Willie hung the little East German Trabant cars, or Trabis, painted with urban scrawl and used their head lamps as spotlights. These cars were affordable to anyone who lived in East Germany, where U2 recorded *Achtung Baby*. Added to all of the effects was a crooked leg of a stage, plunging out into the arena. It would become a "B" stage where Bono and the boys would eventually take up residence, during the middle of the show, for a few acoustic numbers. Long gone was the simplicity of the stage set-up for the Joshua Tree Tour. Now, brand U2 was about overindulgence and it worked.

Between the Pixies, who opened the show, and U2, BP Fallon, a Euro DJ, came out to the "B" stage to an awaiting Trabi, which was lowered from the rafters and decorated with fragments of mirror, giving it that mirror-ball effect. BP climbed into the roofless car and began to spin records. We weren't quite sure what to make of this. The world created inside the Rosemont Horizon was so surreal and unfamiliar that adding a DJ, who was dressed in a cape and a funked up cowboy hat, put the night over the top even before U2 hit the stage. BP played classic funk, soul, rock and punk tunes while he gyrated to the beat. I felt as though this wasn't a "zoo," but a circus, as I wanted the band to get onstage to tell me what all of this was about. I had been to many concerts, and even stage plays, but nothing came close to what I was about to witness tonight. I knew we were a TV culture, yet this took the idea to a whole new level. As BP exited his Trabi and left the stage, the house lights stayed on and the crew finished prepping the performance space. Excitement filled the arena. It was now show time.

Within seconds of the last roadie leaving the stage, and due to our vantage point, we could see the band enter into the venue from backstage. They waited as Bono slowly sauntered onstage solo, smoking a cigarillo and began to sing an unfamiliar Irish anthem. The rest of the band was now in place as the video screens lit up and so did Edge on guitar. The house lights dropped and we were catapulted into *Zoo Station*, the first song off *Achtung Baby*. I was intoxicated, watching every move of Bono's stage swagger from behind. He prowled the stage, looking for victims in the audience. Scores of fans in the front row began to fawn over his new rocker image, The Fly. Greg Kot, a local reporter for the *Chicago Tribune*, noted Bono's transformation as he raved about the show, quoting the lead singer from the night, "Somebody's got to play the rock star!"

The second song in the set list was *The Fly*. The tune was just as heavy live as it was on the album. The television screens became animated again with video spouting phrases so quick it was hard to keep up. "Taste is the enemy of art" was interspersed with words like "Racist, Bomb, Whore, Now" and my favorite "Believe." Willie Williams took the word and dropped out the first two and last two letters to reveal the word "Lie." It was brilliant. The show marched on and revealed more tracks from *Achtung Baby* with reckless abandon. *One* became the standout song of the first half of the show. The images of wild buffaloes, roaming the countryside, during the song were set beautifully to the heart wrenching lyrics. Willie had once again streamed words onto the screens. The type was softer and less bombastic than that which flowed through them for *The Fly*. He translated the word "one" into various languages and layered them on top of the buffaloes, using beautifully crafted typefaces.

U2 was diminishing their stage energy as they readied us for the up-tempo blast, *Until the End of the World*, where Judas spoke to Jesus in the afterlife about his guilt of betrayal. The onslaught of new material at the beginning of the Zoo TV show revealed that the band wasn't going to rely on songs from early albums. U2 was on a mission, to get back on top of the touring world and pulling no punches. By the mid-point of the show, Bono led the band out to the "B" stage where they would work themselves into their back catalog of music. *Angel of Harlem* and a Lou Reed cover, *Satellite of Love*, spilled off the "B" stage magnificently. The band knew that they had to reach the older fans, like myself, and were eventually going to have to drag out the old warhorses in order to get everyone into a frenzy. Although missing were the tour staples like *I Will Follow, Sunday Bloody Sunday, Bad* and *New Year's Day*, U2 relied on more recent standards such as *Pride (In the Name of Love)*, *Bullet the Blue Sky* and *Where the Streets Have No Name*. All of which kept us wanting more. As the Irishmen departed the main stage, we were euphoric. The Horizon began to rumble. Minutes later, U2 reappeared onstage for an encore. Bono arrived onstage wearing a silver lame suit and carrying a mirror.

"You know something. You're fuckin' beautiful," he screamed at himself in the mirror. Edge launched into *Desire*. The debauchery of pornography, gambling and excess filled the video walls. Bono came around to the back of the stage. Shannon grabbed my custom-painted jacket off my seat and hoisted it above our heads as though it was a banner for the home team. Bono pointed to us.

"He saw your jacket!!!" she screamed at me.

"No. He was pointing to the crowd, Shannon."

"I'm sure he saw it. Why do ya think he pointed at us?"

Worked into the evening's emotional experience, of love gained and love lost, was the song *With or Without You* followed by *Love is Blindness*, which became the last song of the night. Abandoned was the long standing closer, *40*. It was missed, but the band was all about change and with the last drumbeat hit by Larry Mullen, the band exited the stage for the evening. When the houselights came up, I had fully accepted the new sound and vibe of U2.

Jessica asked me to give her a call after the show. It wasn't too late as she was in Palm Springs on vacation with her mother. The time difference worked in my favor.

"Jessica," I said into the phone.

"Yes," she answered half-asleep.

"I just saw U2 at Rosemont," I said.

"How was it?"

"Oh, my God. Amazing. I cannot tell you how cool it was. Ten times better than the Joshua Tree Tour," I said, holding back my excitement.

"Sounds like you had fun. Listen, I'm half-asleep. Mom's already out. Can we talk about this when I get back from California? Good-night."

The phone went silent. We split three weeks later.

17: it's all in the jeans

In the summer of 1993, U2 released *Zooropa*. The ten tracks on the album were the exact distraction my emotional core needed as I, yet again, crashed and burned at romance. Her name was Marybeth. We were fellow baristas at my Starbucks. Getting involved with a coworker was wrong and now, I understood why. If something went south with us, as it did, we still had to work together while keeping our emotions at bay. The sting from the break-up pushed me into a sleepless state. I began fighting the dreaded family disease known as depression. Even U2 couldn't pull me out of the funk.

As the summer reached mid-August, I struggled not to show my disdain for what happened between Marybeth and myself. Yet, I found my revenge on *Zooropa*. One track, aptly titled *Daddy's Gonna Pay for Your Crashed Car*, was perfect for her. The lyric was a fitting tribute to the daddy's girl, who just let me go. Marybeth was looking for love, but unwilling to move beyond her financial dependence on her father. It didn't cross my mind to be her sole provider, something I wasn't about to do nor could I afford financially. Emotionally, maybe? *Daddy's Gonna Pay for Your Crashed Car* was played incessantly in my apartment during those warm summer days. I got lost in the weighty groove of Adam's bass instead of dwelling inside my discarded relationship. Ironically, *Some Days Are Better Than Others* followed the track, *Daddy's Gonna Pay for Your Crashed Car*. In the coming weeks, after our split, Bono was right. I would have good days and bad.

U2 had always been my moral and psychological support, whether they knew it or not, but as my depression progressed, I knew their music and lyrics couldn't help me out of my post-relationship blues I had with Marybeth. Therefore, I sought out professional help for the third time in my life. I knew I needed it. The first time I saw a therapist was right after college when I was moving out of dad's house and on with my life. It helped me greatly, but as I struggled to make it in Chicago, I needed counseling again. The second round, of therapy results, wasn't great as I rehashed everything from the first round and really got nowhere in the sessions. I knew the central issue. It was my relationship with my father. The dad I needed didn't support my move to Chicago. He felt betrayed as I packed up my life and left him for the big city, just like mom did after the divorce. Mom, on the other hand, was supportive of my move to the Windy City. In fact, she gave me starter money of a thousand dollars and told me I would make it someday. Added to this was my search for love. I desired to be in that relationship both my parents found the second time. I was good at the chivalry game, but it scared everyone away. My parent's divorce hung over me like a lover's omen and with Marybeth that omen reappeared as depression.

To this day, none of my parents knew I was on the brink of falling apart in the summer of 1993. I never really let them in on my private world because I was afraid to. I had to keep up appearances as I struggled with being a career retail employee for three years now and not moving forward in my desired profession of graphic design. I didn't want to fail. Therapy was my only option as I approached the fall months deepening into insomnia and unable to function. Within weeks of reentry into counseling, I became medicated, which helped me even though the issues were still there. Only my very closest friends were allowed access to my internal turmoil. Dad probably would understand what I was going through but if I called home, I would not get the parental ear I needed. Mom was too far away to be the emotional mediator. Luckily, I found someone to confide in, one of my dearest friends, Joshua.

Josh, a Jewish dude from Highland Park and an aspiring chef, worked as a fishmonger across the street from the Starbucks where I worked. We instantly bonded. During our down time, we made our way to the movies or lunch or picked up a concert at a local venue. Our spirits became kindred as neither one of us had brothers. Plus, he was a U2 fan as well. He'd seen the four Irishmen the previous fall at the World Music Theater and was taken aback by their mental, mind-blowing Zoo TV concert. It was his first and he became hooked too, but not as passionately as I.

When Josh and I bonded, U2 were in the midst of the summer outdoor version of Zoo TV Tour in Europe supporting the *Zooropa* release. The tour's final stop was at the R.D.S. Arena in Dublin, a perfect ending to a great spectacle, covering two years on the road. The band decided to broadcast its home show to the world. As the concert approached, something hit me in the gut, telling me the band would be off for a few weeks or months. Finally, I could get my creative work in front of them again as the previous proposal, of slides and a business letter, fell upon deaf ears. This time, I took a pair of jeans, painted with a hodge-podge of U2 graphics, and threw them into a FedEx bag addressed to The Edge at Principle Management in Dublin. Unlike my previous venture, I decided to get up the nerve to call U2's front office once I knew my parcel arrived. Also, I had to time it right. There was a six-hour difference between Chicago and Dublin. The telephones were running on the old technology. You would talk, wait for the delayed comment and respond. I was also a poor retail employee who could ill afford a lengthy, international phone call so I had to be direct and efficient.

"Hello, Principle Management," the voice answered in an Irish accent.

"Yes," I said, shivering in my robe. "This is Eric Shivvers. I'm following up a package of painted jeans I sent to The Edge last week."

"Hold on," the voice said. "I'll get Ita DeLuca on the line."

The long pause seemed like eternity. I was eager and anxious simultaneously. I didn't know what to say or ask. "Holy fuck! I was on the phone with U2's management!" I screamed in my head. A split second later, another Irish voice came on the phone.

"Hello, Eric? Ita DeLuca here."

"Hello Ita."

"Yes. We received your jeans. You should contact Edwin Taylor in London. He oversees our merchandise at Winterland. Let me get his number for you. Hold on."

"I'm in!" I screamed again, inside my head. Euphoria was becoming a deafening roar and my mouth dropped open.

"Eric, here's the number. Zero one zero four four five six three two seven seven zero."

There was a pause.

I mumbled the phone number. Then I repeated it.

"So, Zero one zero four four five six three two seven seven zero?"

"You got it. He's looking forward to your call. Cheers, Eric," Ita replied and I hung up the phone.

"Now what do I do? Should I call?" I queried myself. I was sitting in my robe at my tiny desk built from old shelves, which Starbucks disposed of when they did a store redesign. I leaned back in my director's chair. My nerves were on edge. I looked at the scribbled number. I didn't know what to do. It was as if I were playing the board game Risk and overthinking my next move. I looked at the clock. I realized I had an hour before departing for my shift. I thought for another moment. The first hurdle calling Dublin was easy. Now, I sent my nerves even further into the stratosphere. I picked up the phone and dialed the number Ita had given me.

"Hello, Winterland," the receptionist said.

"Yes, Edwin Taylor please."

"May I ask who is calling?"

"This is Eric Shivvers. I spoke with Ita DeLuca at Principle Management in Dublin and she asked me to give Edwin a call."

"Just a minute," she said, as she put me on hold. Another long wait ensued. My phone call was being pushed through to Edwin.

"Hello, Eric," a voice answered in a heavy English drawl.

"Hello, Edwin? I was asked by Ita DeLuca at Principle Management to give you a call. I sent a pair of jeans to Edge last week. I'm interested in creating some custom-painted pieces for U2's stage wear."

"I know about your idea. Right, the band's on a break and headed to the South Pacific to end the tour in the coming months. Can you send me your materials?"

"You mean a painted pair of jeans?"

"Yes, something I could show the entire band," Edwin replied. He was all business.

"When do you need my work?"

"Send them to me before the end of November. I've upcoming meetings with them concerning the Australia concerts, but I won't have time to pitch your concept until they return from the end of the tour in December."

"What's your address?" I asked, as the discussion was buttoning up, for now.

"822 Tottenham Court Road, London, W12," he replied.

"Great, I will get them to you in six weeks."

"Perfect. Cheers, Eric!" he said, as he hung up the phone.

I got into the shower and couldn't believe what had just transpired. Who was I going to call first? Should it be mom or would it be Aunt Nicole and Uncle Vince? Vindictive, I thought I should call Marybeth and stick it to her. How about Shannon? No, I had to be calm because I was about to paint jeans that would be presented to the band. Staying focused was key as I had a ton of U2 graphics to choose from, including tour programs, shirts, and of course, images from *Achtung Baby*, and I wanted the final work to look as though they could fit in with all of the band's other merchandise. I was anxious and digesting what I had just done ten minutes ago. It was the perfect example of my ambition. My go get'em attitude. What did I have to lose? Nothing. Uncle Vince was right. No one will open the door for you. When you see the handle, turn it. You never know what is on the other side until you make the first move. I had done just that.

Days passed as I feverishly painted the jeans and jacket. My concepts were coming along, as I was more manic in my creativity, focusing on the details of the work. On one particular night during the process, I came home and saw my answering machine light blinking. I knew damn well the message was from Marybeth, trying to get back together. I couldn't be disturbed from my thought process, as I had to keep forging on. To my surprise, I had passed on an invitation by Joshua to see *Wayne's World*. I couldn't be bothered as I was restless trying to finish the work in a timely manner.

The end of October came and I shipped my work off to London. U2 was about to promote the greatest tour, ever undertaken by a band, in Sydney, Australia with a pay-per-view event. Uncle Vince heard about it and graciously asked me to house sit over Thanksgiving weekend so I could take in the show. It had been almost a year since I last saw the band live onstage. My work was about to be in their hands as they took the stage Down Under. Seeing the Zoo TV Outdoor Broadcast show from Australia was like going to a family reunion. I tried to restrain my excitement, as I wanted to see what changed in the set list as well as the welcoming video opening the show. Gone was the intro-montage, mocking George Bush going to war with Iraq, which welcomed us when the show was touring the United States. Instead, Willie Williams opened the show with clips from *Triumph of the Will* and *Olympia*, Nazi propaganda films directed by Leni Riefenstahl, which were followed by menagerie of well-known video clips culled from pop-culture. Bono, as usual, came onstage as his alter ego, The Fly, which was still going strong in the two years since the inception of the Zoo TV Tour. Songs from the album *Zooropa* made their way into the show. Edge's rap song *Numb* bumped *Who's Going To Ride Your Wild Horses* out of the set list. Since I had seen the show four times in various incarnations, beginning with indoor arenas and then outdoor stadiums, I found the song *Numb* to be clunky and out of sorts. U2 tried to make it work. The biggest change was the encore when they displaced the song *Desire*, the most prominent in the Zoo TV set list, with *Daddy's Gonna Pay for Your Crashed Car*. Although Bono's MacPhisto character introduced the song, much like he did with *Desire*, I felt that *Daddy's Gonna Pay for Your Crashed Car* didn't have the same fire and brimstone power as the song it replaced. The band moved on to *Lemon* then *With or Without You* and eventually closed the show out with *Can't Help Falling In Love*. Not the most spectacular ending, yet it worked.

December closed in on me as the days became cold and grey. Time had run out on the world trek of U2's Zoo TV Tour. It was all over. It seemed like another eternity before I heard from London about my custom-painted jean idea. I received a phone message from Edwin a week before Christmas. There was no hint of progress, just a request to call him back.

"Edwin. It's Eric Shivvers. I'm calling you about my proposed project with U2."

"Yes, Eric. How are you?"

"I'm well. I got your phone message yesterday and I'm returning your call."

"Eric, the band's not interested in your idea. However, they suggest you sell your wares through their fan magazine *Propaganda*. Are you aware of the 'Grapevine' section in the back of the publication? It's a place for fans to interact with one another."

"Yes, I'm a subscriber to the fan club and get the magazine."

"Good. So you know the publication," Edwin replied. "Contact the fan club. Have them run something about your work. I will ship everything back to you just after the new year. Cheers, Eric."

There was a click and the line went dead. My heart sank. Yeah, I got my work in front of U2, but something happened in the communication lines and it didn't work out. I ran Edwin's suggestion through my head and felt putting my work into the "Grapevine" section of U2's fanzine, *Propaganda*, was a cop out because the section was a place where subscribers could find pen pals. To me, this wasn't the right space for selling my work. Nevertheless, I knew my accomplishment of getting in the door to U2, with an idea of custom-painted jeans, would mean more to me than any award a designer could achieve because I followed my passion. And yes, I made shit happen.

18: "pop" and circumstance

It was July 1994, a full year since U2 released *Zooropa*. Mom arrived, in Chicago, a few days before Bastille Day for a handful of book signings. Her biography on Edith Wharton, *No Gifts from Chance*, had just hit the bookshelves. During those first days of her visit, we made a valiant attempt to visit every bookstore possible so she could sign copies of her work. We were successful, but mom was concerned. We kept calling Stefano, who was at their summer home in Egremont, Massachusetts. Sadly, our phone calls weren't being returned. It was an odd behavior. Finally, I demanded that she call her closest neighbor to check-up on him. She did, from a pay phone in a downtown hotel. When we returned to my apartment a short while later, the phone was ringing. I answered and gave it to mom. A split second later, she turned white as she learned that Stefano had died of a heart attack. Her twenty-year love affair with a fellow academic had come to an end. It stunned everyone, including his Joycean colleagues, who just saw him a month prior at the James Joyce Symposium.

The following two years would be the hardest and the most trying. Dealing with the death of my stepfather, I moved in with Josh whose spirit helped me lift myself from the pain as I struggled with my mother being a widow. She was such a champion of mine and now, due to the circumstances of my stepfather's death, I was now taking over some parental part of our relationship. Once again, I found solace in Bono's lyrics. I dug deep into U2's body of work. Luckily, I unearthed what I needed in the song *Stay (Faraway, So Close!)*, which was a beautifully angelic song that lifted my spirit.

Almost lullaby like, the song mentions a list of cities in the middle of the lyric, which caught my attention. Each of them was a place where my stepfather had lived in or spoke about in passing conversations. Even more ear catching was the narrative of the tune. It focused on the other side of life and angels. Bono sung about how angels could see, hear and feel what us mortals were going through, yet they couldn't respond. I was comforted in the lyric as I thought my stepfather was with those angels, but his leaving suddenly, without notice, still hurt. As U2 closed out the song *Stay (Faraway, So Close!)*, there's a cymbal crash in the background representing an angel falling from the sky. It gave me hope that my stepfather would come back to me in some angelic terms. He told my mother every morning about his dreams. Mom remembered one of his last when he said he was coming back as a flower. I have been looking for his bloom for some time.

As I struggled with the loss in my life, I watched Josh, five years younger than me, become a man. In the two short years we knew one another, we grew very close and decided to get an apartment together as he pursued a degree in culinary arts at Kendall College, in Evanston. Moving in with Josh was an easy transition for me and a comfortable living situation for him.

Josh promised to take care of me gastronomically. Yet, when he found out how time-consuming class was, and taking on a gig cooking on a restaurant line, the false promise faded. It didn't matter because it was his friendship, and his love for life, that meant the most to me.

One of Joshua's greatest assets was his voracious appetite for music. He liked U2, but he also had his own love for Peter Gabriel, INXS, R.E.M. and a ton of others. Music filled our apartment regularly. We even displayed the *Achtung Baby* promotional pieces Jamie had given me several years earlier. On nights where we would sink into several bottles of red wine, Josh and I would joke with one another about what we'd do if we did run into the four Irish lads. Bono's quotes filled the air while we recreated his stage antics around the apartment, aimlessly careening off the walls down our hallway, dancing like his Fly character. Josh had heard Edwin Taylor's voice on my answering machine and would imitate it at loud, drunken volume.

"Eric, Edwin Taylor. I got the Fly here on conference. 'Fly, what do you have to say about Mr. Shivvers' jeans?'" Josh would exclaim and then burst into laughter, shedding tears. I knew Josh well enough not to take it too personally.

Sadly, after two years, Josh and I parted ways. I decided to stay in Evanston while Joshua moved to the city where his career was flourishing. I was crushed and again lonely, but that would come to pass as news that Bono and company were finishing up the long awaited album to follow-up *Achtung Baby*, aptly titled *Pop*. I was excited, as it would be U2's most ambitious and misunderstood albums to date.

U2 moved from the Lanois/Eno production team and hired outside producer, Howie B, who pushed the band into techno grooves and pulsating beats. Rumors flooded the Internet about what was on the horizon and on February 3, 1997, we got a first listen when the band released *Discothèque*. It was an over the top dance track opening with this roto-sound like Edge guitar effect, which dropped into a throbbing beat. The song, to me, was too bubble gum. I couldn't get my head around the new direction. Added to the pain of listening to the new U2 sensation was watching the accompanying video, which included the band mimicking The Village People at the end. It was too much and I had to turn away.

At the midnight release of U2's *Pop* album, mayhem was in full swing at Borders' bookstore in downtown Evanston. I longed for the days Jamie worked at Rose Records, saving me her extra promotional schwag. On this night, I had no one reserving me these specialty items. Instead, I had to enter a drawing for the leftover posters, inflatables and stickers. My heart sunk as we filled out the slips of paper for the giveaway. What hurt even more was the thought that these kids were going to plaster the posters on their dorm room walls and rip them down at the end of the semester. I, on the other hand, would have had them framed or better yet, dry mounted at least. As the winners were announced, it ate at me. Most of the victors dropped their names in the hat at the last minute. With thirteen years under my belt, and probably the longest running fan in attendance of the midnight sale, I came away with zilch for promo material, but I got the new album. I was ready for the next incarnation of U2.

With my copy of *Pop* in my coat, I exited into the empty streets of Evanston. My desire was to get home quickly, waiting on public transportation would only delay my listening pleasure. Instead, I found a taxi at a nearby hotel and jumped in. Once I gave the driver directions to my apartment, I scraped off the plastic wrap and extracted my portable CD player out of my messenger bag. I dropped in the newly minted U2 disc. Like with *Achtung Baby*, I skipped through the tracks as we drove through the dark, Evanston night. I began listening to the album, in short spurts, which was typical of me as I always searched any new U2 record for the heavy and hard tunes like *God Part II, Desire, The Fly* and *Zoo Station. Mofo*, the third track on *Pop*, did just that for me. The lyrics were a reflection of Bono's life as he questioned his own existence of being a rock 'n' roll success while becoming a father. The narrative was heavy and became even weightier when he spoke to his mother through the song, looking for acceptance for what he had done with his life. I could relate to Bono's soliloquy because I was always looking for approval from my parents. I felt growing up, in a divorced household, I could never do anything right. Everything I did in front of mom was a reminder of dad and vice versa. The only person who accepted me was me. Yet again, I found a new battle cry in *Mofo*, just as *Sunday Bloody Sunday* did in college.

In the coming days, I peeled away the skin of *Pop* to find its roots, a reflection on all of humanity. Most of the album was in the same lyrical vein captured previously in the U2 catalog, yet different. The melodies were flooded with transcendental beats, techno rhythms and even heavier, industrial-sounding loops. Tracks like *Gone* had the new-fangled U2 sound as Edge incorporated his signature simple arpeggio, without the enhancement of any effects, laid on top of a mirroring arpeggio pushed through an analog synthesizer. All the while, Bono lamented about being in a band, on the road and departed from his family for lengths of time. It worked brilliantly. The song was nestled among less mechanized induced gems, such as *If God Will Send His Angels* and *If You Wear That Velvet Dress*, which were written, and performed, in the same melodic vein as previous tracks like *One* or *With or Without You.*

The brilliance of *Pop* was how U2 tied up the whole album into a nice, religious induced bow at the end with the track *Wake*

Up Dead Man. In the stanzas, Bono called to Jesus to let him know that he felt alone and hopeless in the world. *Wake Up Dead Man* harkens back to the days of their religious and spiritual journeys found on albums such as *October* and provided a calmness to finalize the record as the new change in U2's sound pushed the creative envelope a little too far. Over time, I championed the recording even though it's the hardest U2 album to comprehend because it's so not U2 in sound. However, it housed some of the greatest risks Larry, Adam, Edge and Bono have ever undertaken in their career.

During the waning months of the Zoo TV Tour, Nick, my cousin, and I became part of the U2 fan club, Propaganda. We readied ourselves for the next tour. Days before the video release of *Discothèque,* the band celebrated the announcement of PopMart, the tour supporting the *Pop* album, at a K-Mart store in downtown New York. It was a tongue-in-cheek way for them to use a consumer tie-in without asking K-Mart to sponsor the tour. Before the band took questions, they performed a B-side song, *Holy Joe,* and then danced around the questions about stage design, songs that may be in the set list and what to expect of the coming record. Some in the audience knew of the massive LED screen the band was rolling out for this tour, however, the members weren't giving away any tour secrets. PopMart, like the recording *Pop,* was going to be the most bold and difficult U2 outing to digest to date.

When the PopMart Tour landed in Chicago in June later that year, so did my cousin Nick and Aunt Beverly. We'd waited for almost five months for its arrival and on the eve of the show, we ventured down to Soldier Field where the band would play the following night. The stadium was a glow as the stage was being erected. We could see the top of the arch, as it hovered the rim of Soldier Field, with its phosphorescent yellow coating. We also counted eighteen trucks lining the stadium's outer drive. Seeing the arch looming in the Chicago dusk brought butterflies to my stomach. Excitement ran through us as U2 was in Chicago for a three-night stand. Nick and I had tickets to two of those nights. The stumbles in Vegas on opening night, which we saw via a nationally televised broadcast, weren't going to bother us. We knew the *Pop* album would be a challenge to replicate live due to the band's venture into techno sounds. The reliance of loops for the album was going to have to transfer to backing tracks on tour, which all had to sync to Larry's drumming. If the songs failed live, we wouldn't mind because Nick and I weren't going to give up on our band.

The following day after our review of the PopMart structure being built, we ventured to Water Tower Place where a man dressed in fatigues was getting into a limo in the distance.

"That's where the band stays when they're in town, Nick," I said, pointing to an adjacent building.

"Eric, that's Bono. Holy shit!" Nick shouted as he took up the chase after the Lincoln Continental limousine. I ran behind him, at a slower pace, while keeping my camera strap from choking me. Nick was a track star at Vinton High School and could easily sprint on a dime, but this time, the car was moving too quickly for him to catch it.

"Fuck! If we were here only a few minutes earlier," Nick said after we'd caught up with one another. Curiosity got the best of us as we noticed a crowd across the street breaking up. We now had to know what was going on and found a fan coveting an album behind folded arms. We inquired.

"I assume that was Bono," I asked in a quiet voice as we were now in the midst of fans, reviewing their precious autographs.

"Ah, yeah, you just missed him," a gal replied.

"Does he usually come out and sign?" Nick asked excitedly.

"Yeah, at three-thirty," she said, unwillingly. She didn't want the word to spread. It's a fear among fans.

"Do any others come out and sign?" Nick questioned with rapid fire.

"No, not on this stop. They come out of the hotel and climb into waiting limousines. However, they will wave from across the street," her friend said, interrupting our conversation.

"So, three-thirty...here...tomorrow afternoon?" Nick affirmed.

"Yes," said our contact who then turned and walked away.

I spun around, grabbed Nick by the shirt and pulled him towards me. I looked into his eyes.

"We are here tomorrow afternoon at two. Your ass's going to get an autograph," I said fervently as I wasn't going to let an opportunity slip by.

"Dude, let go of my shirt you fuck!"

I released his T-shirt slowly and pushed him away.

"Okay, you ass! No sleeping in. Nothing past noon," I said, pointing at him as Aunt Beverly encroached us.

"Was that him, Nick?" she asked.

"Hell yeah. It was Bono, mom. If we were here a couple minutes sooner, I could've met him," he said with disdain.

"Remember, you wanted to go to FAO Schwarz!" I rubbed it in.

"Fuck off, Eric."

"I'm just reminding you that I had a hunch this was their hotel. Can I now say, 'I told you so,'" I said with sarcasm.

The event we had just witnessed was discussed through dinner. Joshua joined us along the way and we shared with him our limo-chasing escapade. Every time we saw one in the parking lot, as we made our way to the venue, we teased Nicholas.

"Nick? Isn't that the one Bono got into?" Josh asked, jokingly and then looked at me. We burst out in laughter.

"Cool it you two," Bev said, as she grabbed my right shoulder from behind. She was sort of stern, but probably laughing on the inside as well.

Joshua and I had to tone it down as we stopped at every trailer outside the venue, hawking official merchandise, just so Nick could gawk. It was tiresome, yet humorous. I just wanted to get inside the venue and see what all the excitement was about with the arch and the huge screen. So did Josh. But, when we entered the hallowed halls of Soldier Field, Nick ditched us again for another merch table. Josh and I were fed up and we marched on to our seats, on the west side of the stadium, at the 50-yard line.

When we arrived, I basked in the visual display of the stage that sprawled out in front of us. The indirect sunlight, coming from behind our seats, reflected off the massive structure. The huge PopMart arch, at the north end of Soldier Field, appeared to be something out of the futuristic space cartoon, *The Jetsons*. I wanted George Jetson, to fly over the stadium with his family in tow, and dock his flying saucer above the stage. Instead, Nick came back with another bag load of schwag. He took a seat in the middle of our group. I pounced with curiosity.

"Did you get the program, Nick?" I asked.

He reached into the bag to reveal the shiny program, designed with a reflective paper stock, mimicking a disco ball.

"Shit! Look at how crinkled the cover is," Nick said, as he inspected it.

"Let me see," I replied.

Nick held up the cover. It was blinding. I reached for it, knowing exactly what the problem was with the printed piece. U2's print vendor used a heavy, laminated cardstock, which had been die cut.

"Nick, I think it's a printing error. They're pushing too heavy of a stock through the press."

"Should I return it?" he asked.

"Up to you," I replied. "I would go now before they forget who you are and the band comes on stage?"

"Forget him? He's shopper of the month. How could they forget him?" Joshua said, laughingly.

"Hurry up, Nick. Show's about to begin," I said.

"If you see Bee-oh-en-oh on the concourse, tell him to break a leg!" Joshua shouted, getting another jab in about Nick's obsession.

Nick scurried off and returned within ten minutes. The stadium lights went dark. The giant Lite-Brite screen lit up. The 80s hit *Pop Muzik* began to play. A spotlight pointed just below us at midfield and was anchored on the band as they entered the stadium. Adam entered first, wearing a face mask. I wasn't sure what Larry was supposed to be when he arrived next. Edge followed dressed as a cowboy. Lastly, Bono entered into the venue behind his bandmates, wearing a satin robe while shadow boxing. We came to our feet. The band slowly walked towards the stage, eventually taking their instruments, leaving the lead singer by himself at the dog-leg end of the stage, which jutted out into the crowd just as it did for the Zoo TV Tour.

"Moooooooooofo! Moooooofo! Chicagooooooo! Mofo!" Bono screamed, as he jumped up and down, readying himself for the prizefight, singing the night's opener, *Mofo*. The spotlight, focused on Bono, dimmed. The PopMart Tour arch became illuminated. Edge and Adam came alive on the Lite-Brite screen in purples, blues, greens and reds. The band was transformed into video art, much like the animation of Roy Lichtenstein, Keith Haring and Andy Warhol's pop-art paintings would be later on in the show. It was visually stunning and overwhelming at the same time as both the screen and the arch dwarfed the members of the band. Nick thought otherwise, as it was his first concert.

He was like a kid at the circus, pointing out the obvious to all of us. His enthusiasm could hardly be contained as he watched Bono strut under an umbrella for *Bullet the Blue Sky*. To me, I didn't get it. However, I did appreciate the songs chosen from the *Pop* album, *Last Night on Earth*, *Staring at the Sun* and *Please*, were brilliantly captured.

After the main set came to a close with *Where the Streets Have No Name*, an anticipated hush covered the crowd as the LED screen lit up with a belly dancer, swinging to a techno mix of the song *Lemon*, which echoed through the PA. We waited anxiously for the encore to begin. Slowly, on the far side of the stadium, a giant, mirror-ball lemon crept its way down the stage and almost into the audience. With pomp and circumstance, it lifted open and the band stood there in defiance. Whether we wanted them to or not, they were going to perform *Discothèque*, the one song that's so not U2. Harsh for me to say it because I actually like the song now, when I need that groove, but on this night, it wasn't for me. Bono and the band were trying to make the 60,000 seat stadium into an actual disco club. I couldn't catch their vibe. However, the one song in the encore that made the night extraordinary was *Hold Me, Thrill Me, Kiss Me, Kill Me*, a tune they wrote for the *Batman Forever* movie. It was tough like *Zoo Station*, had the ambition of *The Fly* and was the only song in the entire set list that could take on the PopMart arch while depleting the sourness, in my mouth, left behind by the lemon, which I visually devoured moments earlier in the show.

19: the first autograph

"Nick, I'll meet you at the bridge under Lake Shore Drive," I said, as we were being crushed by waves of fans exiting our section. Nick was toting three bags full of PopMart paraphernalia and wasn't finished purchasing more U2 schwag. His intention was to hit the two kiosks outside the venue because God knows what would happen if he didn't get everything branded with U2 on it. My cousin's buying spree interested Josh, so he tagged along with him as I went on my merry way.

"Joshua, you know where I'll be? Don't let them get lost."

"Yeah, Eric, by the 18th Street bridge."

"Exactly, see you in fifteen minutes. Good luck!"

"I'm not sure what I'm in for, but watching your cousin personally handle every trinket and spend money is hilarious," Josh said with a laugh.

"Hey, see if Nick has room on his credit card for you. He may buy you something, Josh."

"I'm just a chaperon. Well, spectator too."

Josh's voice trailed off behind me as I headed towards the nearest gate to gain relief from the crush of spectators exiting Soldier Field. I was happy to have my tour program and my token shirt. They're all I needed to satisfy my own U2 product craving, for now. It was, however, Nick's first U2 show and he had to have everything. I, on the other hand, needed some space in order to ponder what I just witnessed. Inside me, I felt the band lacked fluidity. Staccato was the musical term that best described the show that I had just witnessed. From the opening of *Mofo* to *I Will Follow* to *Even Better Than the Real Thing*, U2 uncorked a concert with huge leaps through their catalog. Not in all of my live experiences with the band, had I witnessed them nosedive so quickly into old songs. I felt as though they lacked confidence in the new material. I mean they're professionals, aren't they? Did they not set-up a CD player and listen to the songs in sequential order as to get an idea of the musical flow? Something had to give. The old warhorse song, *Where the Streets Have No Name*, used the same shtick from the Joshua Tree Tour with a stage flooded in red. Add Edge's mid-concert sing-a-long to *Sweet Caroline* and I was now beginning to be disenchanted as my band, felt to me, a little karaoke.

My concentration came back to reality when I arrived at our meeting spot. Ten minutes had passed since I had last seen Nick, Josh and my Aunt Bev. I parked my butt against the wall of the bridge and stared back at the glow of the field lights hovering Soldier Field, with the tip of the PopMart arch reaching towards the heavens. Throngs of fans passed by me as I stood my ground waiting. Suddenly, I heard recognizable laughter approaching me. I had to put my hand over my eyes to fight the glare.

"Josh! Over here!" I shouted.

Joshua arrived at my feet' crying from laughter.

"What's so funny, Josh?" I asked with a smirk.

"Your cousin, Niiiiick."

"Nick what?" I asked. I was concerned, but Josh was laughing so hard he couldn't speak.

"Your cousin….whew," he said, trying to catch his breath. A pause followed by more laughter.

"Nick purchased his last U2 item from the stand outside the venue. Remember, the one we passed on the way into the stadium?" he asked, pointing blindly over his shoulder towards Soldier Field.

"Yeah, I remember."

"We got about 30 feet beyond the booth when Nick noticed some dude hocking shirts along the edge of the pedway. As we know, your cousin wants everything U2, whether legit or not, right? Without seeing the shirt, he headed over and inquired about the price. 'Ten bucks,' the guy replied. Nick gave the dude his money. As the guy was unloading Nick's shirt out from underneath his jacket, two undercover cops bum rushed the bootlegger," Joshua said. He paused, caught is breath and continued, "The cops then pushed Nick away mid-transaction as they cuffed the dude. Your cousin began to plead with them. Nick told them that the guy had his ten bucks and he wanted his money back. The cops turned to Nick and said, 'Tough luck. This man is under arrest for bootlegging.' Nick just stood there arguing. I had to drag his ass away before they cuffed him, too."

I looked at Nick, who arrived mid-conversation, and burst out laughing. He was visibly distressed and pissed that he lost his ten bucks. Never mind the gross amount of money he spent tonight on legitimate U2 merchandise, which could have fed a small, third world country.

"Those fuckers wouldn't give me my ten bucks back. It's not fair!" Nick exclaimed. My Aunt Bev held her son's shoulder in comfort.

"You didn't need to buy everything with your lightning bug

money, Nick," I said, as I looked at my cousin.

"Lightning bug money? What the hell's that all about?" Josh inquired, as he escaped one humorous moment and headed to another.

"When Nick was on the family farm growing up, he collected lightning bugs and sold them," I explained.

"I made one hundred fifty bucks. Assholes!" Nick retorted.

"So, I tease him, Josh, because during the same summer, I busted my ass schlepping dirty dishes while he was chasing lightning bugs."

"That's enough, Eric. Don't dampen the evening for your cousin," Beverly said, as she shot her eyes at me.

Silence fell on us, but every now and then Joshua would smirk. I would explode into spontaneous laughter. The two "older brothers" were picking on their youngest in tow while his mom was by his side for protection. We were a family as we crossed the bridge to 18th Street with the dwindling masses. My car was parked a few blocks away as Lake Shore Drive awaited for the drive home. Along the way, Nick and Beverly would pause in their conversation about the show so I could get a word in edgewise. Josh just stared out the window. I could tell he was exhausted from his chef gig and was happy to be home when we dropped him off. I was too and upon entering my apartment, I announced to Nick and Bev that I was retiring to my bedroom for the evening.

"Nicholas, get some shut eye. We're not sleeping into the afternoon tomorrow. If your ass wants to meet Bono, you need to be out of bed by noon. Understood?" I said, as I closed the door to my bedroom.

When I awoke the following morning, I curled up on the couch with my aunt and talked about life. I knew Nick didn't go to bed when I left him the night before. He was a college night owl spurred on by the giddied excitement of his first U2 show. Bev told me they were up until three in the morning looking at all of his shirts and paraphernalia. I looked at the clock on my VCR. The witching hour was getting ever so close to noon. Nick had yet to rise. He was sleeping in my office, on my futon, adjacent to the kitchen. I walked in and nudged my foot into his back.

"What? I'm awake!" he shouted from underneath his pillow.

"Awake, maybe. Out of bed, no. Its past noon, Nickster," I growled.

"So, give me five more minutes," his muffled voice replied.

"Five will turn into fifteen. I know you. Get your butt up. Bono doesn't wait for your ass to get out of bed."

He rolled over and chucked his pillow at me as I left the room. Fifteen minutes later the bathroom door shut. I heard the shower turn on. Twenty minutes passed and Nick had yet to shut off the shower. I stuck my head into the bathroom. My glasses fogged up as I shouted at the white, tiled wall.

"Come on Nicholas! Put a foot on it. I don't have any fresh film nor Sharpie pens. And because I don't have these things, our asses have to stop at Walgreens on the way into the city."

"I'm almost done!"

"I hope you didn't forget to wash behind those big ears of yours!"

"Fuck you!" he replied, as he shut off the water to the shower. "Can you get off my ass, Eric?"

"Nick, you want to meet Bono and we need to get a spot in line. What if he comes out early? I don't need to be dragging your pissed off ass around all night long. Let's get a move on."

"Okay! Give me a chance to dry off and get ready?"

My plan was to run the one errand to Walgreens and then park the car in a Northwestern hospital lot two blocks away from U2's hotel. There was nothing to screw-up except my cousin dragging his feet. Finally, Nick exited from the bathroom half dressed and went to the kitchen to make himself breakfast. Upon his return to the living room, he was carrying a bowl of cereal and began to eat while I collected my camera bag and some back-up batteries. My patience was being pushed to the limit because I wasn't just doing this for Nick, I was doing it for me as well. I watched Nick eat, hoping he would devour his breakfast faster. I was wrong. He took his time and when he was finished eating, a sigh of relief escaped me as he went to the kitchen to deposit his bowl in the sink. En route back to the living room, he made a detour to the bathroom.

"You ready?" I asked, as Nick returned to the living room brushing his teeth.

He nodded. With a mouth full of toothpaste, he cocked his head back as not to spit a fluoride spray all over me when he spoke and said, "Gotta do my hair."

"Hair? What the fuck Nick? It's nearly one o'clock. We gotta get goin'."

I placed my camera bag over my shoulder and headed to the door. I waited and turned around while my hand rested on the doorknob.

"You're just like your father, Eric," Beverly said, as she sat on my faux leather couch dressed, acting like she was ready to join us. She wasn't. She was waiting for my mom to arrive. "We're cut from the same cloth, dear. When I want to go, I want to go. Nick's on a different time clock all together," she explained.

Nick came out of my office, pulling a shirt over his head that he purchased the night before. He thought he was Adonis and loved to display his six-pack abs.

"How do I look, mom?"

"Great. Now make sure you take some Kleenex for your nose," the ever-Jewish mother said.

I sighed.

"One more interruption and we're screwed," I said sternly.

Nick collected his wallet and camera while stuffing Kleenex into the front pocket of his shorts. He then leaned over and kissed his mother good-bye. As I shut the door behind us and exited out the front of my apartment building, Aunt Bev screamed, "Give my love to Bono!" Her voice echoed into the courtyard via an open window from my pad.

Nick and I were now riding lady luck while pushing our own luck. We hit Walgreens, jumped Lake Shore Drive and parked the car. As I opened my camera to load the film, Nick smothered himself in sunscreen. I looked at the clock in the car's dashboard. It read one thirty. Nick and I had two hours of standing on a sidewalk ahead of us. We didn't care, as the two of us were about to meet Bono. But first, knowing we weren't coming back until after our encounter, I double checked my bag and made sure I had all of my photo paraphernalia, including water. I then locked up the car and ambled out of the garage into the welcoming sunshine with Nick.

For June, the warmth of the day wasn't overwhelming as we strolled our way to the hotel where a crowd was gathering. We fell in line and stood across the street from the hotel patiently waiting. I leaned into Nick's ear and said, "Just look like you know what you're doing here."

"I know," he replied and nodded his head in acknowledgement.

From underneath my sunglasses, I observed hotel employees and security working the entrance across the street. Every time a limo pulled up, we rubber necked to see who was coming out of the hotel while we overheard reviews about the show the night before from our fellow fans. They were positive, for the most part, since the median age of the group we were standing with hovered around twenty-three and this was probably their first tour if not second. I didn't want to interfere and spill my U2 tour history onto them. I wanted to keep it tight to the chest. There was no reason to one-up anyone around us as I took in the banter trying to see whether those around us understood what we saw the night before. Boredom and stoppage of conversation with our neighbors were intermittent throughout the wait.

While we waited patiently, we noticed several aggressive fans, with the intention of flanking the front door of the hotel for a better place, dismissed from their spots by hotel security. Slowly the band's entourage drifted out of the hotel as waiting limousines drove up and devoured them. We knew the Bono hour was coming ever closer and we were getting itchy. The crowd had grown and due to the crush of people from behind us, we were now barely on the curb. Any movement from the hotel doors across the street, caused a tremble of excitement within our ever-growing mass of fans. Adam came out with his blonde hair and he waved to us from across the street before he entered the back of one of the limos. Edge exited shortly thereafter and waved as well with no intention of coming towards us. He entered the back of his own car with its rear windows lowered. Nick took off chasing the vehicle and stuck his hand into the back window.

"Edge! Thank you man. Have a great show!" he shouted into the rear window and returned out of breath. Sweat was now beading at his brow line.

"I saw that dumb ass! You almost got rolled over. Contain your enthusiasm. What if Bono was on Edge's heels, you fucking moron?"

"I just shook Edge's hand, asswipe!" Nick retorted.

Suddenly, a scream came from the vicinity of the hotel. We stopped and looked. Bono suddenly appeared under the hotel's canopy. He was shorter than I had thought. Two security guards flanked him as he walked across the street towards us. Our group of waiting fans slowly crept toward him. We were a moving wall of humanity. As Bono approached, we engulfed him. I was just behind Bono's right shoulder, monitoring the chaos while Nick was in front of him. Bono signed a girl's shirt as she cried while standing in front of the musical Messiah. Nick saw an opening and put his hand on the singer's shoulder like they were good friends. He greeted the rocker with his other.

"Hi Bono. I'm Nick Jensen. I'm a big fan of yours," Nicholas said, while he pulled on his T-shirt, giving the U2 front man a flat place to autograph. Bono took Nick's pen and began to draw on his shirt. While doing so, Nick asked, "Why didn't you extend "With or Without You" last night with the extra verse like you usually do when you sing it live?"

"Eh, thanks for reminding me. Eh, we forgot. We'll add it tonight," Bono replied, as he began to move onto the next fan.

Once the crowd heard Nick's request, others barked out a request list of songs.

"Why don't you play "Lady With The Spinning Head?"" someone shouted in retort to Nick's request.

"My head is spinning," Bono replied, as he kept signing.

I kept shooting frames. I already had the shot of Nick, talking to Bono, as he got his first autograph. My selfish sense subsided. In time, I knew I would get my own from the rocker. Now was Nick's shining moment and what a first autograph experience it was. Security returned to flank Bono on both sides and began to escort the singer away to his waiting vehicle.

"We have to leave. No more autographs," one of them said.

Some blonde chick pursued the singer, who was dwarfed by his protectors. She ambled to the waiting limo with the lead singer holding conversation as I stood in the middle of the street capturing the last frames of the camouflage-wearing rocker entering his car. I could feel the closeness of a taxi bumper against the back of my legs. I wasn't letting the aggressive driver get the best of me. We had too many witnesses standing nearby for anything to happen. The horn honked and I turned around. I threw my hands up in the air with disgust and stared at the driver through his windshield. Nick grabbed my arm and dragged me away.

As we walked back to the car, we were excited. Nick and I got what we wanted. Now, we had to share the news so we used the mobile phone, in the car, to call home and break the news. As the phone began to ring, I put the call on speakerphone.

"Hello? Shivvers," answered the voice at the other end of the phone.

"Bev?"

"Yes?"

"We got Bono's autograph," I said loudly. There was a pause.

"You're shittin' me. You didn't. Really?"

"Yup, mom, cousin Eric has it all on film," Nick jumped in.

"Really? Let me sit down. I cannot believe you."

"Yeah, everything worked like clock work, Aunt Beverly," I said, as I was rewinding the film in my camera.

"Nick, what does he look like up close?" Bev was now curious.

"He's short and looks like Bono, mom," Nick said with a laugh.

"No, I'm serious. He's short?"

"He is your height, Bev," I chimed in.

"Eric, come on. You two are pulling my leg. Did you get a chance to talk to him, Nick?"

"Yup, I put out my hand to shake his and introduced myself. I gave him a Sharpie pen and he signed my shirt. I told him I liked the show and asked him why they didn't extend "With or Without You" last night."

Bev was forwarding the story onto my mom, who had arrived after Nick and I left for the city.

"Really!" mom shouted from the background.

"No, Sharon it's the boys. They just met Bono of U2," Aunt Bev said to my mom.

"Eric, before I go, I just cannot believe you made it happen.

I'm so excited for you. You know the city, knew where to park and when to be at the hotel. I'm in awe. Now, you boys have fun tonight and get home safely. Here's your mom, Eric."

"Helloooooo," mom said. I could recognize her voice anywhere and through any device.

"Hey mom. We just met Bono!"

"I heard. Was it fun?"

"Hi Aunt Sharon. It's Nick."

"Nick, how are you?"

"Great. We're on our way to the second U2 show. We just got Bono's autograph," Nick replied.

"Tons of fun. Nicholas, am I going to see you?"

"Yeah, we should be home tonight about eleven-thirty."

"Okay. Great! We'll see you guys tonight!"

"Bye mom," I said.

As my mother hung up the phone, I turned on the ignition and backed the car out of our parking place. Nick and I were hungry and decided to hit McDonald's for a bite. Amazement still graced our faces as we ate. We felt tonight's show could be better than the previous for the simple reason we met Bono on the street and it would be just that more exciting. But, that all came to an end when we got to the stadium and found out that our U2 fan club tickets were the crappiest tickets money could buy. Our seats had us looking straight into the side of the stage, barely seeing the band, and no way of seeing the giant LED backdrop. In fact, we saw a good sum of the support structure, holding up the giant video wall and arch. Sadly, there must have been a mistake. To say the least, we were pissed. How could this have happened to us U2 fan club members? We had the worst seats in the house.

"Nick, I bought some tickets for a friend. They're on the east side at the twenty-yard line. Let's take those until we get kicked out. We can only try."

"Deal. Anything has to be better than here," Nick responded with disgust.

Quickly, we made our way to the other side of the stadium and sacked the seats. Once we arrived, no one asked to see our tickets nor did anyone ask us to move the whole night. It was a textbook cool move. Once again, the rock gods looked down on us or maybe it was the luck of having a stepfather upstairs talking to them. Or, was it meeting Bono on the street, which gave us the luck? Who knows? Tonight, unlike the previous evening, we were on Adam's side of the stage and in clear view of the LED screen, the PopMart arch and much closer to the mirror-ball lemon.

As the sun sank in front of us, across the rim of the stadium, a warm breeze pushed through the venue. The lights dropped and U2 entered the floor of the stadium on cue. Bono, again, shadow-boxed his way onto the stage for another night in the Windy City as the Lite-Brite stage seemed more powerful from our new vantage point. With one night of PopMart under our belts, I knew what to expect until the band changed the set list adding *New Year's Day*, a song I had last heard live on the Joshua Tree Tour ten years earlier. The insertion of this *War* album gem brought excitement to the crowd, but for me, it returned memories of being with my step-father that day in Paris, seeing the Solidarity marchers. The song was such a juxtaposition to the consumerism theme being pushed through the PopMart Tour. However, I welcomed its return though the package it came in still confused me.

20: taking my spirit away

The Internet rumbled with rumors during the summer of 2000 about a new U2 album release. Finally, excitement filled the atmosphere circling me again. The air felt fresher as I drove with Monica, my girlfriend at the time, back from Evanston in the late summer. The windows were rolled down as we were listening to U2's *The Million Dollar Hotel* sound track through the stereo. The tune *Stateless* blew around the swirl-of-a-breeze inside the car. I caught the lyric and fell into a trance. I sang the chorus while Monica looked at me in disgust.

"Does your whole life revolve around this band?" she asked.

"Well, whenever I need them, they're there for me," I replied, as I hit the gas to make the oncoming green light.

"No really, Eric, it's a sickness," she said, while walking on thin ice. I looked over at her in the passenger seat.

"Sickness? What's so sick about listening to a band?"

"With you, it's always U2." Her Long Island accent was beginning to take over.

"No, Monica, it's not U2 all the time. I listen to a bevy of other bands. Depeche Mode, Midnight Oil, The Beatles to list a few."

"Whenever we're in the car, you throw in something and it's always U2. I don't get it."

"Wait. Is this about me or the band?" I asked.

"It's about your fascination with U2's. I don't think it's healthy."

"Don't go there!" I shouted in my head as I could hear the proverbial ice crack under her feet. I was watching the traffic in front of me while holding court in a discussion, which was pushing the argument boundary.

"Drinking heavily isn't healthy. Smoking isn't healthy. Eating fatty foods isn't healthy. In my mind, being a fan and supporting a band that gives a shit about the world we live in is invariably quite healthy."

"Explain to me why you're so passionate about them?"

"Passion, passion, passion! Is that all you are concerned about is passion, Monica?" I was answering her curiosity with a question.

"It's a passion you have. I want to know how you got it?"

"It just came to me."

"How?"

"I don't know Monica. My friends introduced me to them and I drank the water," I said sarcastically.

"So, you're passionate about U2 because...you like the music?" she inquired, as she looked at me.

"It goes deeper than that. To me, they're more than a rock band. It's hard to explain, but when I need some inspiration or solace, they're a tune, or two, away from taking me to a place where I need to be. Also, they believe in a better world and stand behind their convictions," I answered and then collected my thoughts. "Do you think that my passion for Bono trumps you?"

"Sometimes, I feel as though you're closer to them than you are to me. That's all," she replied.

"Music is my passion. Marry me. Marry my passion. I'm not going to change. By the way, you find your passion as it mutually finds you. You cannot get it from overturning stones and looking underneath them."

Our relationship was waning. I'd been on the skids emotionally with Monica for a month and this was just the type of discussion needed to cut the ties, as I wasn't leaving my band for her. The conversation began our emotional separation. But, we continued dating into the fall and things continued to feel forced with her. I had become a "yes" man too many times to appease her. My workspace was becoming my sanctuary. I began to drive my cube partner crazy with Monica's issues as I yearned to find myself. I hungered for some Irish reckoning and it arrived when my cousin, Nick, flew into Chicago for a long visit while on retreat from Harvard Law.

Nick wanted to share the excitement for the newest U2 release, *All That You Can't Leave Behind*, which was going on sale in the coming days. He also got the chance to meet Monica over dinner where we conversed, with fervor, about our album pre-sale experiences and meeting Bono. Monica couldn't keep up with the banter and a hint of disgust came through in her comments. Nick and I were fueling her notion about the U2 sickness we both had. She thought we both needed to go to a U2 rehab hospital to get sober. We laughed. The comment revealed her insecurities as well as her desire to change me. Nick found Monica passionless and lacking self-esteem. He didn't want to expend anymore time in her company and decided to call around Chicago, seeking record stores hosting a midnight sale of the new release. He ended up empty, as record stores were less inclined to market midnight events because interest, in those events, was beginning to wane. We were witnessing the slow death of the national record store as the Internet was slowly taking over music distribution and with it, went the touchy-feely browsing days we loved.

On the night of what would have been the midnight sale of the long awaited U2 release, Nick and I decided to hit an Irish bar, Tommy Nevin's. It was a place where no televisions existed and the conversation flowed.

"What'll ya have?" asked the waitress.

"A pint of Guinness," Nick immediately replied.

"One for me as well," I chimed in.

When our beers arrived a few minutes later, the brew tops looked creamy like coffee ice cream. I knew the taste well before the glass hit my lips. I lifted my pint and clinked it with Nick's. We toasted the first gulp to the band.

"This pisses me off. No midnight sale," Nick said, watching the horizon.

I began to sing, "This is the end..."

"Funny."

"I think that "Pop" did our band in, Nick."

"Yeah, I remember an interview on VH-1 where Larry said he was out if they had another crap, expensive tour."

"I'm sure a lot of fans left them after the PopMart Tour. I, on the contrary, like 'Pop.'"

"I call it Poppie. Like "Pop," but Poppie," Nick laughed. He said it again, "Poppie."

I interrupted, "You know the new song, "Beautiful Day?" It's gotta be a way back into the hearts and minds of those turned off by "Pop" or a way to get a hold of new, younger fans in order to build back the U2 base. I find it too radio friendly. And from the album title, I wonder what they cannot leave behind?"

"Ahhhhh, I know what you can leave behind. Without question, Monica," Nick said, as he picked up his menu.

"Oh, yeah?" I said before taking a hard, swig of my beverage.

"I'm not impressed with her. Seriously, Eric, she asked you about giving up U2," Nick said to me blindly as he was perusing the menu.

"Yeah, may have to give up my religion too. Can't give up the boys though."

"Wait! She wants you to convert, too?" Nick asked in amazement as he let his menu go limp. He looked at me and continued, "Ahhhh, this ain't right. She's not worth giving up your band and your religion. Seriously, I don't mind your marrying someone of another faith, yet to give into her this much and she's not meeting you halfway is way too much compromise on your side."

I motioned for the waitress.

"Another round?" I requested.

Our waitress picked up Nick's empty glass as I guzzled what was left in mine.

"Would you like to order dinner?" the waitress asked.

"Yeah. What comes with the burgers besides fries?" Nick inquired.

"Either coleslaw or beans."

Nick then proceeded to rattle off his order. I said I would have the same and we went back to our discussion while Nick did the once over on our waitress as she stepped away into the darkness of the room.

"How can Monica not like U2? She's going to take your spirit away. I can see it," Nick said and was now being the protective, younger brother.

"All you can see is our waitress's behind," I interjected.

"Ha. Funny. You caught me," he laughed. "Back to your love woes."

"Come on. Do we have to?"

"Yes, dump her. She's no good."

"How do you know after only meeting her once?" I asked, as our second round of beers arrived.

"Eric, I'm your cousin and protector. Trust me. Within five minutes, I knew she wasn't right for you. In fact, I think she's jealous of me and I don't know why. It's my gut reaction."

I was listening intently as I pulled the newly poured beverage to my lips.

"One question, Nick. Got an exit strategy?" I asked, as I tipped the pint glass for my first sip.

"Yeah, get the fuck out. Just get up, leave and don't let this go on forever. The back and forth shit ain't the best. Nip it in the bud I'd say." He then took a drink of his beer.

"It's not that easy," I said, as I retracted the glass from my lips.

Nick swallowed hard and collected his thoughts.

"I know, however, you are eight months in and emotionally about six feet under. Do you have stuff at her place? Do you have a key?"

"Yes to both."

"Then pick an afternoon and move the fuck out!" Nick roared.

He wiped the Guinness mustache off his face. He smirked, but he was right. Although he was eight years younger than me, Nick did have a solid grasp on the world. He made me realize that you should never change for someone. Once you do, you become a shell of yourself and lose the special attributes people like about you. It was a hard pill to swallow but in this case, I had to.

The next day, I bought *All That You Can't Leave Behind*. The album spoke to me immediately, even before a note was played. Gracing the cover was Bono, Edge, Adam and Larry standing in an airport preparing to go to a destination unknown. I projected myself into the image and felt as though I was right there with them as my emotional being was at a turning point as well. Again, the band was returning at the right time in my life.

As I slipped the shiny compact disc into my portable player, I put on my headphones and took a deep breath. I hit the play button, letting the album unfold in front of me as I looked out my office window down Michigan Avenue. The first track, *Beautiful Day*, was released weeks earlier as a single. The new musical direction, I felt, wasn't going to be groundbreaking. However, *Beautiful Day* was crafted with one of the best melodic themes since *With or Without You*. Bono pontificated about life in the first stanza, being trapped and not able to progress. The symbolism was an easy transfer to my life. Monica and I were in an emotional traffic jam and I couldn't get out of the car. The doors were locked and all I did was pay for gas, with my soul.

As U2 sucker punched me with *Beautiful Day*, I had to keep diving deeper into the album. I was curious. Was there more to this album that I could hang my hat on? The second track, *Stuck in a Moment You Can't Get Out Of*, opened and I continued to stare out into the clear blue sky, hovering the skyline while a wisp of clouds floated in the distance. What I was looking into was the perfect backdrop for daydreaming. Now, I was getting spooked. U2 was hitting two for two in connecting with my internal strife. I couldn't believe it. All I needed was a little more push in order to get me out of my relationship nightmare. The band gave it to me two tracks later in the song, *Walk On*. It put my inner discord over the top. The gentle entry of Bono, speaking metaphorically about the perils of relationships becoming a suitcase brimming with emotions, which one had to decide to leave behind or not, hit home. Actually, the song was written about Aung San Suu Kyi who was fighting for freedom from house arrest in Burma.

The lyric was so profound that I bent it my direction, like I had done it a million times before, but this time it cut extremely close to my emotional core.

A few days after Nick left, I finally got up my nerve to pull the plug on my relationship with Monica. I didn't want confrontation. Without thinking twice, I went to her place right after work. I slipped my key into the lock and turned it gently. I waited a minute to hear her voice. No one was home. I gathered as much as I could clutch in my arms – a suit, a drill, some shoes plus odds and ends. Tears streamed down my face as I dropped my 'Dear Monica' letter on the floor shortly before closing her apartment door. It hurt, yet I had to move on with my life. Before doing so, I had to collect my mountain bike I named *Bertha the Red Beast*. It sat in the building's bike locker, which meant one more stop before going home.

When I got to the basement, barely able to stay upright while holding onto all of my belongings, I dumped my possessions into a lifeless pile and rescued my prized ride. Freedom was coming over me. As soon as I opened the back door to the building, I was greeted by sunlight and warmth. I hailed a cab and shoved my retrieved possessions into the trunk of the taxi. I knew the wrath I would face from Monica for pulling the carpet out from underneath her, but I didn't care. I just wanted my life back and in time, my heart to mend.

21: the heart of the matter

A simple envelope, with the return address from New York, mingled with a consortium of junk mail and bills. I knew exactly what was inside, my U2 ticket pre-sale paperwork from Propaganda for the upcoming tour supporting *All That You Can't Leave Behind*. Naturally, I opened the envelope, before the bills, and scanned the ticket order form for the Chicago dates. My fan club membership allowed me first right of refusal for concert tickets. I grabbed a pen and filled out my request for general admission tickets, a new option, making each show an "intimate club feel" by eliminating physical seats on the arena floor and allowing everyone to have an opportunity to be in the front row. I recalled the disaster from my childhood, in the late seventies, when The Who tried a similar ticket idea in Cincinnati. Eleven fans were crushed to death. I had to have some belief U2 wouldn't repeat the same mistake. I took the risk and ordered a pair of what would become the golden tickets to the upcoming U2 tour aptly titled Elevation.

Nicholas, in the throws of finishing law school in Boston, received the same envelope, but didn't succumb to the general admission idea. His preference was to be higher up in the stands. Neither Nick nor I rested upon our Propaganda laurels. Thanks to our PopMart Tour fiasco, we both knew we needed to go to the public sale just to be safe. Over the coming days, we chatted strategy via e-mail and once we heard the public sale dates, we put our separate plans into action. Mine was to go stand in line at our local grocery store at eight o'clock in the morning. Unlike the old days of buying tickets for shows, the spot where you stood in line today didn't determine your ticket fate. Instead, the new way was to get a line number, upon arrival, and wait. Half an hour before tickets went on sale, a random number was drawn by the store manager. Said number would represent the first person in line and everyone else would have to fall behind. As always, my luck would again relegate me to the back of the procession. By the time I got to the ticket machine, my only options were scattered seats in the nosebleed sections. Without hesitation, I took what I could get.

Shortly after my purchase, U2's first show sold out. An announcement of a second show followed soon after. I shuffled back in line and bought tickets to the added show, lower and closer to the stage. Before the end of the hour, U2 had sold out four nights at the United Center. I had tickets to three of them. It sounds selfish, yet I really wanted to see my band on multiple nights because I blew off the third night of PopMart at Soldier Field to see Lyle Lovett at Ravinia with mom. This time, I had an opportunity to see U2 for the full stand. It was expensive, but I had no worries, the charges for these tickets were on my credit card and the bill wouldn't arrive for another month.

After waging the ticket sale war on limited sleep and a lot of caffeine, I collapsed on my couch and dialed Nicholas in Boston.

"Nick? It's Eric."

"Oh, hey, mom's on the other line. Let me say good-bye to her," he said. There was a click. I waited. A minute later, Nick came back on the line.

"What did you score for Boston?" I asked.

"Well, I got seats in the Mezzanine section at half court opening night. On the second night, I'm in the 20th row and the third night, I'm behind the stage. Plus, whatever Propaganda sends me."

"Really? You didn't get any floor seats?"

"No, I'm not interested in them."

"Why not?"

"They just don't appeal to me. I hate standing at shows."

"You'll be standing no matter where you have seats in the arena you moron," I said, laughingly.

"I'll at least have a seat to park my ass on if I need to fart knocker," he fired back and laughed.

"Well cool. Looks like we're going to see the boys ten days apart in our fair cities."

"Yeah, it'll be cool, but you won't believe this, Eric." A long pause came from the other end of the phone. "My mom got us tickets to opening night in Fort Lauderdale!" Nick shouted through the phone.

"Nick, you're shittin' me. Opening night of the Elevation Tour in America? In Fort Lauderdale? Tell me you're pulling my leg?"

Nick then proceeded to tell me the story about how his mother, my Aunt Bev, was on the phone with Ticketmaster. She immediately got through for the Fort Lauderdale show, but was put on hold for forty minutes. When a sales rep finally returned to the call, she asked why Bev was still on the phone. My aunt replied by explaining that she was waiting for the confirmation number, but the woman never came back. Ticketmaster double-checked the credit card and seats. Sure enough, the order was in a hold state and never processed. The sales lady reprocessed the tickets. I was shocked.

"Fuck yes!!!!!! We're seeing U2 on opening fucking night!" I shouted with the phone away from my mouth and sinking into my couch while scissor kicking in the air like a little girl. I came back to the line. "That my friend is incredible. I can't believe your mom had the will to stay on the phone for forty minutes, waiting for someone to answer."

"Yeah, can you believe it?" Nick asked with excitement.

"I'm shitting bricks. This cannot be true," I replied.

"It's true. Trust me. Mom called about ten minutes after I got home from the sale at Tower Records with the news."

"Dude!! This is so cool because my mom, your Aunt Sharon, lives in Miami. Even better, mom's best friend Emily lives about twenty minutes away from the arena in Fort Lauderdale. I'm very sure Emily will let us stay with her and her husband on the night of the show."

"No shit! Amazing. Cannot believe our luck."

"Yeah this is going to rock. I'll call mom and let her know we are coming. Oh, and make flight arrangements. When's the last time you saw my mom, Nick?"

"Aunt Sharon? Wow, I think it was grandpa's eightieth birthday. No, it was the summer of PopMart in '97. So, four years ago."

"Been a while. Well listen, I'm going to call her but first, I'll ring your mom. Will you be out on spring break when we meet up in Miami?"

"Hell yeah! The show lands on the second weekend of break!"

"Awesome, I cannot believe we are going to opening night."

"Listen, I gotta split. Homework beckons me! Love you!" Nick replied.

"Love you too. Let's stay in touch via e-mail."

I called my aunt to confirm Nick's story. She told me the account in exact detail, including what music was playing in the background and how many times the recorded message of upgrading her Tickmaster account was played.

"Drove me nuts, however, I had to stay on the line, Eric. I had given them everything they needed and then they left me," Aunt Bev said.

"I cannot believe they didn't come back to the phone with the confirmation number."

"Can you believe it? Christ! They gave me your seat information and said, 'be right back with the confirmation number.'"

"You have the patience of a saint. Did you ever fear the line would go dead?"

"Yeah, it crossed my mine, shit."

"So, the wait was how long?"

"Forty-minutes or so. Poor girl got on as sweet as can be to help me. Here's little old Beverly from Vinton, Iowa left out in the cold. I wasn't going to give up on my boys for U2. No way."

"I'm so shocked you took the time to try to get us tickets. Now, I need to ring my mom," I said, as my hand was covering my yawn.

"She's going to be so excited to see the two of you. Cryin' out loud, I think it's been five years since she's seen Nick."

"Actually, it's been four years and I think you're right, mom will love seeing us boys."

"Well say hello to her. I love her dearly. So great to see her that summer Nick and I came for that U2 concert in Chicago. Hopefully, you two can come to the farm sometime. Love ya, Love ya, Love ya!"

I hung up the phone.

Five weeks after the public sale and a few days ahead of Nicholas, I landed at the Miami International Airport. I was on vacation and euphoric. A week off from the office, to see my mom, my cousin and our favorite band, was a much-needed break from programming in HTML and meeting production deadlines. Those few days before Nick's arrival was important to me. I needed to reconnect with mom after Monica and I split five months prior. Mom watched my relationship with Monica begin and then fall apart as she was on sabbatical, in Rogers Park, just a stone's throw from my apartment the previous year. She met Monica several times, knowing we had issues, yet played it neutral.

In fact, one of the greatest memories I have with my mom, on her sabbatical leave, was a conversation we had in her car after a matinee movie shortly before her departure back to Miami. For two hours, we sat in her car outside my apartment and talked about life. She spoke freely about all of her relationships, including those with dad, Stefano and her current boyfriend. She understood the trials and tribulations I was going through and knew I was going to have to end the relationship with Monica. Mom wasn't one to directly interfere with my life, but stayed on the sidelines with suggestions. She knew I was hurting and left it up to me to make the decision to cut it off. It was the greatest mom and I time I ever had.

Upon Nick's arrival at Miami International, we picked up a convertible and headed to South Beach blaring *Mysterious Ways* out of our rented car's speakers. Nick had never been to Miami before and you could tell as his eyeballs feasted on all of the hotties down on spring break. It was great to be together in the Florida sun and away from the cold climates we had escaped from. Nick and I slowly made our way to the beach where we unrolled our towels. Next to us were four middle-aged married men drinking beer and hitting on the college girls surrounding us in all directions, only to be busted by one of their daughters later when she arrived back from the surf. It was hilarious and just the comedy Nick and I needed to bond for the weekend.

While we took in beach life, we steeped ourselves in conversations about life. Nick was headed from Harvard Law to a clerkship in Minnesota. He was a studious undergrad at Iowa, however, with grad school coming to a close, he was at a cross roads in a newfound relationship with a gal he met on a flight back from Chicago a semester prior. He knew it wouldn't last past the U2 shows in Boston because she had no intention of moving with him from the safety of her city, Boston. As the conversation was about relationships, Nick was right, I needed to move on from Monica. Hanging out on the beach together, and seeing U2 opening night, validated my departure from the relationship he witnessed several months back.

When I woke up the following morning, ready for the coming evening with U2, Mom made a simple breakfast of toast, coffee and fruit for us. It was typical for Nick to rise later. I, however, took in the Florida morning with mom on the patio. The grass was still wet with dew as the radio blared NPR from the open kitchen window. It was comfortable as summer's humidity had yet to blanket South Florida. When Nick rose, he made himself a bowl of cereal and packed his bag for the next leg of our journey to Fort Lauderdale where I would introduce him to Emily, one of mom's old grad students, and her husband Horace, our gracious hosts for the night.

Emily, like my mom, was an English professor and collaborated with mom on several published pieces. Horace taught film theory and knew of our U2 obsession while still willing to open his doors to us. It had been a few years since I had last seen them. Horace and Emily heard a lot of things about my cousin, Nick, including his love for the *Star Wars* films. Nick hit it off with them during our porch-side introduction, as the halo of excitement around us was intoxicating. Our "inn keepers" basked in our enthusiasm. After our introductions, we soon departed for the National Car Rental Center where the concert was happening.

As the venue loomed in front of us, the air was heavy with excitement. It was U2. It was South Florida. It was opening night of the Elevation Tour! As we slowly moved into our parking spot and closed the roof of our convertible, we absorbed the spectacle. Our neighbor's SUV was cranking various U2 tunes. The buzz engulfed us, which encouraged Nick to purchase one hundred fifty dollars worth of U2 merch before we sat down in our second level seats. I waited. The need to buy my U2 schwag before the show was never my modus operandi. Instead, I wanted to get seated as I hungered to see the new stage with the center cut out. Nick wasn't concerned. He was still reviewing the merch he wanted to buy while figuring out how to pack all of it into his suitcase. I bought a beer to calm my nerves.

"Nick, you're going to see them in Boston. You don't need to buy everything here," I said, as I swigged my beer.

"I know. I'm just taking stock. I want to get a poster in case they run out after the show."

"Understandable, but really, do you need every shirt and trinket like you did on PopMart?"

"Yeah, I'm sure I'll buy all of them."

"When you get old, will you have a U2 shrine in your house, along with all of your "Star Wars" shit, and charge me an entry fee?" I laughed.

"Hell yeah. Well, you're family so I may give you the senior, family discount."

"Oh, thanks, fucker."

A few moments later, we finally arrived to our seats. The stage was pretty simple. The band had given up on the media explosion of Zoo TV. Also, missing from the stage was any ode to an arch, a mirrored lemon or neon from PopMart. What was in front of us was a stripped down performance space, just like I remembered on the Joshua Tree Tour, but something new was added, a sizable, heart-shaped ramp which projected outward from the stage into the arena floor, creating a glorified walkway into the throngs of fans who purchased general admission tickets. It looked like a huge swimming pool filled with people, which I couldn't wait to jump into when the tour got to Chicago. Nick took notice, yet he was still sure he made the better choice for his Boston shows being up in the stands. At this point, it didn't matter as we killed time between the opening act and chatting with our neighbors. During the conversation, it was revealed to us that some had come all the way from Europe. What we had created, in our seating section, was a small United Nations. It was so U2.

Suddenly, all conversations halted when we heard a roar from the crowd near the far corner of the stage. Adam walked onstage first followed by Larry then Edge, who wore a Miami Dolphins T-shirt. Last, but not least, was Bono. The house lights were still up. Edge kicked into the opening riff of *Elevation*, from which the tour got its name, and the show began. When the band hit the third verse, the stadium lights dropped and the heart-shaped stage lit up like a Christmas tree. Long forgotten were those cold days standing in line for tickets in Chicago and Boston. Vanished were our worries of daily life as we relished in the excitement of opening night not knowing what song was next on the set list. I lived for the anticipation. Hearing the first notes of *Sunday Bloody Sunday*, or watching Edge move to the keyboards, hoping he might play *Running To Stand Still*, was thrilling. The buzz of the night would only be comparable to waiting for Bono outside his hotel for that one glimpse.

When the band moved into *Beautiful Day*, the arena sang back the chorus, almost drowning out the boys of Ireland. Bono was taken aback by the love in the big room. Nicholas could tell from the band's reaction that the Irishmen were where they loved to be, playing live and onstage. As the euphoria came to a head, Edge began the distorted wailing of the opening notes of *Until the End of the World*. Bono's excitement rushed to a fevered pitch as he strutted around the heart-shaped catwalk, protruding into the arena. He sang the first verse and headed for the chorus. Drunk with excitement, he fell off the four-foot high walkway. We lost him in the darkness and a hush came over the stadium. The band played on. Security shoved the lead singer back up onto the catwalk without missing a beat. He caught the lyric and ran with it. The spectacle didn't end the show. It was a hiccup of passion.

The opening piano riff of *New Year's Day* came next. A visit to the back catalog was exciting as I was on edge. What I really wanted to know was what songs were they going to pull from *Pop* in this strip down show. I was sure it wouldn't be *Mofo*, too powerful and very techno. *Staring at the Sun* was a safe bet, but its tempo would slow down the show. My answer would arrive a few songs later with *Gone*, an excellent choice but like on the PopMart Tour, it impeded the flow of the show. *Gone* fit like a puzzle piece that was just a little too tight and brought the crowd to a halt. The band marched on to *Discothèque*, another *Pop* tune, which seemed to clunk along as well and nothing could save it. U2 had to move on before they lost the converted. Familiar territory followed with the warhorse tracks, including *I Will Follow*, *Sunday Bloody Sunday*, *Bad*, and *Where the Streets Have No Name*. Sprinkled among them were new tour gems *Sweetest Thing*, a B-side track from the *Where the Streets Have No Name* single release, and *The Ground Beneath Her Feet* from the *Million Dollar*

Hotel soundtrack. *Bad* made its long awaited return after being dormant for eight years. The song was never one of my favorites and I had all, but forgotten it until this night. Willie Williams, U2's set designer, decorated the stage with a few barrel-like lanterns. Each of them had cutouts of various shapes, allowing the inner ambient light to project outwards. The lanterns rotated slowly as the lyric dived into the addiction of heroin. It was a haunting effect that worked well.

Eventually, the stage went dark as a video wall appeared, on cue behind Larry's drum kit, and flooded the crowd in red light. It was time for *Where the Streets Have No Name*. Willie, nor the band, was never tired of this stage effect as the show closed with *The Fly*. At the end of the song, Bono jumped off stage, into the general admission area, and made his exit to the back of the arena. The rest of the band said good-night and left. The stage went dark except for the lights hovering over Larry's kit. They were lit ever so softly and then turned off. Members of the road crew scurried about resetting microphones and putting out guitars. Anticipation of the encore was building.

I had an idea for one song U2 could possibly play. The other two, guessing it would be a three-song encore, would be anybody's game. Nick, on the other hand, was running through a mini-set list. The video wall reappeared with National Rifle Association President, Charlton Heston, answering questions about guns. The band dropped into *Bullet the Blue Sky*. Once again, we rose to our feet in order to soak it all in. I was still in shock it was opening night. The show was moving too fast for me. The band closed out the night with *Walk On*. It hit me like an eighteen-wheeler. I reflected on what Monica and I had been through. I would be fine. In fact, I was fine. Bono's singing the song live was the validation I needed.

As the show slowly tapered off into the night and the band

said their final farewell, the house lights gradually turned on. Nick and I high-fived one another, knowing tonight was special. We exited our section and fought the masses at the merch table where I came away with a program, a shirt and impulsively bought a knit hat, similar to the one Edge wears, emblazoned with the Elevation Tour logo. Nick was now at four bags worth of U2 shit as we exited into the moist night of South Florida. On our drive home, we went over every minute detail of the show.

"Can you believe he fell off the stage, Nick?" I asked.

"Unbelievable, Eric. Unfuckingbelievable. I thought it was over!"

"I think he was drunk on excitement."

"I would love to hear what Edge was thinking when he took the spill?"

"I know! 'Oh fuck, tour's over. Lost the singer on opening night,'" I replied.

"Yeah, Larry, Adam and Edge would now have to create a jazz trio and orchestrate the whole tour without Bono," Nick said laughing.

"It would've sucked if that incident went south, Nick," I said, as I looked over at my cousin while the dashboard lights illuminated my face.

"Oh, I'm sure if he had to, he would sing from a wheelchair. Trust me. Bono would've made it work," Nick replied as we both laughed, knowing full well the tour was on as we readied ourselves for another year of U2 on the road, reading stories daily, on their official site, about their escapades crisscrossing the states.

22: elevate me

"Lisa, it's Eric," I said into my speakerphone at my office.

"Hey Eric. What's new in Chicago?" Lisa asked. She was always cheery. "Clint's so looking forward to this trip to see you and U2. He's in need of a boy's weekend away from the kids," she laughed.

"I still cannot believe he's a dad. So hilarious."

"Yeah, he's the third kid in the house."

"Lisa, I'm calling 'cause I think Clint and I may be going to U2's hotel after the show Saturday night."

"Really!" she shouted.

"Yeah, I gotta hunch where they're staying in the city. My cousin got an autograph on the last tour. I'm hoping to get my first one this time around."

"That'd be so awesome! Let me see if I can't get rid of the kids for the weekend and join y'al," she laughed again.

"The hotel's a swanky joint. I know Clint likes to wear his cowboy boots and duds. I'm wondering if we can dress him up a bit? He needs to look presentable."

"Oh, no problem. Suit jacket?"

"No, just slacks and a dress shirt. I'm sure he'll wear his boots."

"Can't take the Texan outta him, Eric! I'll make sure he has a pair of khakis and a dress shirt. He'll be excited to see them. By the way, come back to Corpus again. Great to see you this past spring."

Lisa's charm beamed through the phone.

"I will. Corpus Christi's right up there on my travel list along with Paris and Milan!" I laughed, as we said good-bye.

Clint, my tall, Texan cousin, arrived on my doorstep two days later. He hinted at the excitement of seeing U2 when we chatted in February. Whenever I saw Clint's sister, Julie, during the holidays, she always reminded me about her Joshua Tree Tour experience when she was in college at the University of Texas. Clint, on the other hand, had never seen them and been curious. Or, maybe, it was the free tickets. Either way, it didn't matter. He had a front row seat to watch my U2 fandom in full swing.

As we headed out the door for the first of two nights of U2 at the United Center, the phone rang. I decided to answer it.

"Eric, it's Jessica."

"Hey. What's going on?" I looked at Clint and drew a heart in the air.

"I wanted to let you know I'm going to see your Irish boys tonight with Daniel."

"Who's Daniel?" I asked, pointing at the phone and looking at Clint.

"A friend. I didn't want to make things uncomfortable if we crossed paths at the United Center."

I covered the phone and spoke to Clint in a loud whisper. "The girl I'm now dating is calling me at the last minute to tell me that she's been invited to go to see U2 tonight with some guy. How brazen!"

"Dude, Eric, she's playin' you, man!" he whispered loudly back at me.

"Eric?" Jessica asked.

"Yeah, sorry. I'm here."

"We're going to Scoozi first with some friends of his and then onto the concert."

"Okay," I said. There was a pause. "I guess I may see you with Daniel."

"See you babe. Enjoy the show. We'll chat tomorrow if we don't cross paths tonight."

"Sounds good to me," I said with forced enthusiasm as my heart sank.

I put the phone on the cradle. My knees went weak. I was already unsteady about the relationship with Jessica. We had only been dating, if you could call it that, for a few weeks, but I already knew there was something special about her. She was a cute, Midwestern gal who, unlike Monica, had a zest for life. When we initially met, we spoke of our childhood, travel and the things we liked to eat, a nice connection from the start.

As Clint and I headed out the door to the "L," he knew something was up. He saw it in my face and began inquiring, in an obnoxious manner, about Jessica, during our walk to the station. I was deep in thought as I replayed the phone call in my head in an attempt to drown out his banter.

"Seriously, Clint. Why would she've called?" I asked when we hit the "L" station.

"Ah, she's got you. How much for the "L" ride?" Clint asked.

"A buck seventy-five. What're you saying?"

"She's screwing with you, boy," Clint said, flipping his shades down from his forehead as we reached the platform awash in the glaring sunlight of mid-afternoon.

"Red Line to ninety-fifth pulling into the station. Making all stops to ninety-fifth," the loudspeaker said above us.

"Dude, she called you to tell her she's going out with another guy," he said.

"Really, I figured as much," I said in a pissed off manner.

"That wasn't smart to pick-up the phone."

"Clint, quit fuckin' with me! Her name came up on the caller ID box."

"Yeah, but you didn't have to pick it up."

"I had to. I wanted to see what she was calling me about. Seriously, why do ya think she called?" I asked, seeing my reflection in his shades.

"I just answered that question."

"Come on. I'm interested in her. Give me some insight, man."

"Women love to screw with men. Why do you think I married Lisa? So she would stop playing these mind games," he said, chuckling.

The Red Line train's doors opened in front of us. I hung my hanging bag up on a bar next to the door and swung into the adjacent seat. Clint took one facing me.

"Eric, she's telling you she's going to the show so she doesn't get caught."

"Get caught? Am I thinkin' what you're thinkin'?"

"Yeah, she probably likes you. She is sending a message that she's with her 'friend,'" he said with air quotes.

"Why did you have to be such an ass in order to make your point?"

"I like fuckin' with you. You're so whipped," Clint said, as he leaned forward and slapped my chest.

"By the way, who cares? I'm in Chicago. What's the plan for the afternoon U2 fan man."

"We'll dump our clothes off at my office. Saunter down to the hotel and see if we can't catch the band for some autographs before they go to sound check."

"Coolio. Mr. U2 man." He began to snicker.

The train rolled on. Clint and I finally arrived at my office. We unloaded the hanging bag and picked up a much-needed Sharpie pen. Clint holstered his camera to his belt while making sure his cell phone was charged. I placed our clothes in the closet adjacent to my office. Turnaround tonight, after the show, would have to be quick. I was hoping we had no glitches as I turned off the lights in my office and signed us out at the security desk.

Clint and I walked down the Mag Mile at a brisk pace. The sun was out and so were the tourists. It was the first warm weekend we had since early April. Clint was taking in the sites while melting in with the other out of towners. A fellow art director tipped me off where U2 was staying. I thought she was screwing with me, but I took the insider information.

As we turned off Michigan Avenue, I discovered about fifteen people milling about the hotel. My insider information was right. Some were hugging issues of *Rolling Stone* with the Irishmen on the cover while others had cameras, dangling from their wrists. I asked one of them under my breath if this is where the band was staying. A nod, noting "yes," was the reply. Clint and I hit the hotel jackpot. The mother load of all U2 finds was at our feet. I was wearing the custom-painted jacket that I had sent to Edwin Taylor eight years earlier and had to find out if Bono really saw it. While my anxieties grew to meet the band, I started to look for my Sharpie pen. I searched through all of my pockets and came up empty. Somewhere, along Michigan Avenue, I lost it.

Twenty minutes later, U2's security greeted us with the rules. We had to be patient; otherwise, he'd throw all four-band members into the limo and be gone. The next five minutes dragged on. Without notice, Adam walked out. As he approached the waiting autograph line, someone near the front of the line loaned him a pen. When he got to me, I found a white spot on the back of the custom-painted jacket. He signed it without question. Next out of the hotel was Larry. He stood taller than the rest of the band members and as he approached the fans in front of me, I panicked. All I could find, as I dug into my pockets, was a ballpoint pen. Fans around me were unwilling to give up their pens knowing good and well how hard his autograph was to acquire. I looked at Larry and waved him on. Crushed, I didn't have my Sharpie. All I could do now was look down in shame at his platform shoes, which made him quite tall.

When I looked up from the ground, the sonic brain of the band, The Edge, stopped to sign next to me. I found another open spot for him to autograph with a borrowed pen. As he did so, I asked him whether he remembered getting a custom-painted pair of jeans. He shrugged off the question and moved on down the line. We waited for the fourth member of the band, Bono. Within minutes of Edge, the lead singer came out in a blaze of glory and was almost mauled immediately. When he got to me, I put my jacket in front of him to autograph. He grabbed the coat from me and raised it to the sky. He wanted to see what he was signing.

"Do you remember receiving this jacket about eight years ago?" I asked.

Bono looked at me through his blue shades and replied, "Yeah, I do."

I was in shock. He took the pen and wrote in big letters — "Bono on your back 2001." I put out my hand and shook his. "Thanks man!" I said with exuberance.

"Oh, my God, he remembered my work," I screamed inside

my head. At least, for an instant, I made a connection. If it were a lie, on Bono's part, it was a good one. No matter what, I was elated as I got three of the four band members to sign my jacket.

"Bro, did you get the pics?" I asked Clint.

"All I got were the back of heads. Your pictures are gonna suck, dude!"

"Quit screwing around. Did you get me with the band or not?"

"I'm sure I got something. There was a really hot chick behind you. Probably got a picture or two of her with that Bono guy," he replied and laughed. "Let's go celebrate. Beer?"

"Do you need to ask? There's a bar down the street."

"Let's go Bono-man fan."

Within minutes, we had downed a pint of beer each. I wanted to wallow in the afterglow. I looked at the bottom of my empty beer glass and began to comprehend the excitement Nick had when he got his first Bono autograph. I glanced at my watch and realized we had time to kill.

"Clint, we've got a lot of time before the show."

"The first ale tasted great. Want another?" he asked just as he tilted his head back in order to take in the last drops of brew.

"No, I got an idea. I'm hungry. Shall we go to Scoozi for a pre-show bite?" I said, as I belched a Neanderthalic explosion from my chest.

"Sure. Isn't that where your chick is? Man, you are whipped!"

Eleven minutes later, we entered Scoozi trying to own the joint. Wearing my now autographed, custom-painted U2 jacket with pride, we found bar stools and ordered beers. After placing our order, I turned around, putting my back against the wooden bar rail and looked out into the restaurant. I panned the crowd and caught Jessica's face. Clint gave me my beer and I took one gulp. I thought for a split second not to interrupt her party, but proceeded to the table adjacent to hers anyway. I sat down and in doing so, I knocked her table and spilled her champagne. My entry wasn't graceful. My cousin parked his ass across from me and crossed his legs, revealing his Texas-sized, Ostrich skin, cowboy boots.

"Jessica, Clint Shivvers. I'm Eric's cousin," Clint said, as he could hardly hold back the twang in his introduction.

"Hello," Jessica replied and turned to stare at me. Fury was now rolling through her eyes.

She leaned over and inquired, "Why are you two here?"

"How did y'all meet?" Clint inquired, swilling back a drink of his beer.

"You told me this was where you were going to be before the show. I thought we'd show up and say hello," I replied in a hushed voice.

"Eric and I met on Match dot com, Clint," she said, as she forced a smile in his direction.

"Oh," Clint said, as he stuck a toothpick between his teeth.

"Unannounced, Eric? I'm with Daniel and others I don't know. You knock over my champagne...And you are drunk. Eric, what are you thinking?" she shouted at me in a loud whisper as not to let the other guests hear what was happening at her end of the table.

"One beer, Jessica. And, I'm not drunk. We just met U2, outside of their hotel, and they signed my jacket. We went to celebrate and then decided to come here."

Before she could say anything, I got up to show her the jacket I was wearing and knocked the table a second time. Now, I spilled her water. She was even more stunned. Her 'date,' Daniel, rolled his eyes at me while the others at the table weren't sure what was happening. The chivalrous man Jessica met a few weeks earlier in me was gone. So much so that when her salad arrived, I grabbed a fork and dived in, eating right off her plate. The scene was quickly going from bad to worse.

"You and your cousin had better leave. You're making a scene," she said sternly.

"Why?" I asked.

"Eric, leave. And take him with you," she said under her breath and then turned to Clint. "You paid up, Clint?" she asked my cousin.

"Yeah, we're cool," he countered.

"You should be getting to the show, shouldn't you?" She stated the question to the two of us, hinting that we should leave the restaurant.

I nodded to Clint that we should get going as he was downing the last of his beer. I put on my jacket in defiance. We left Jessica's table and hit the bathroom. Within minutes, Clint and I exited the restaurant and were surprisingly right behind Jessica and Daniel, who valeted their car. Without hesitation, Clint and I jumped into the back of Daniel's BMW. Jessica couldn't believe it. Daniel played it cool and enjoyed the company. He kept the conversation light as he talked to Clint about his jewelry business. The air in the car was now suffocating.

When we arrived to the venue's parking lot, Daniel took Jessica's arm in protection, hoping not to see us again. Clint wasn't fazed as we headed into the venue to find the next beer vendor and then climbed to the crow's nest of the stadium for our seats. From our vantage point in the third balcony, behind the stage, we could see every movement of who was coming and going onstage. The heart was slowly filling up. Clint began to ask me how one gained entry into the small space.

"You need a general admission ticket. We got'em for tomorrow night baby. We're gonna' be down there with them."

"You're shittin' me?" Clint replied.

"Nope, wouldn't do that to ya. I'm a U2 fan club member and got us primo seats. Like tonight and meeting the band after the show, I've a strategy for us to get in the front row on the outside of that heart walkway. Stick with me dude. We're going to have a blast," I said and then took another long gulp of my beer.

"I cannot believe this! You've got this all worked out."

Clint tipped his beer cup to get the last swallow in.

"You thought you're just going to a concert and that was it," I laughed.

"Okay. You're a U2 sick individual, yet in a good way."

As he spoke, the crowd began to roar. We looked below. Larry and Edge were entering a holding pen in the back of the arena followed by Bono and Adam. Just like opening night in Fort Lauderdale, the house lights stayed on as each band member found his way to the stage on-by-one. We rose up with excitement. I was wearing my jacket on a warm, May night with my band in front of me. Nothing could be more exciting. The show was the same as opening night. U2 played to the third verse of the opening tune, *Elevation*, with the house lights on and then dropped them. Clint grabbed me and shook my shoulders.

"Dude, this rocks. I cannot believe I'm here."

"Aren't you glad you came?"

"Hell yeah, this is better than Summerfest in Corpus!"

As the band ventured out into the arena, to the tip of the heart, a fan held up a sign stating he could play the song *Stay (Faraway, So Close!)* on the piano. Bono and Edge granted an invitation while security plucked him out of the sea of fans. I couldn't believe it. I longed to hear the song live. *Stay (Faraway, So Close!)* was the tune, which I found consolation in after my stepfather passed away. For me to revisit the lyrics this night, seven years later, was like having an old friend knock on your door.

As the show was coming to a close, I grabbed Clint's arm and tugged on it. It was time to put our plan in motion as we exited our section. We quickened our pace to the exit and flew down the stairwell, jumping the last four stairs, in each section, as not to lose any time. We then exploded out the doors onto Madison Street, out of breath and without a cab in sight. Quickly, we thought on our feet.

"Clint, let's catch a ride with Daniel and Jessica. I remember where their car is parked."

"That'll work," he replied without hesitation.

We walked west into oncoming traffic and hooked a right into the parking lot. There sat Daniel's BMW. Our escorts to the show arrived minutes later and not happy to see us. Once again, using my charm, I broke the ice and asked if they liked the show. Jessica said the box seats they sat in were great as the bubbly flowed. We had a laugh about drinking champagne at a U2 show. Luckily, we were granted a lift while continuing to push our fate. We kept the conversation on the concert as we slinked our way through the parking lot, in Daniel's car, and onto Washington Street. Traffic was gridlocked and tension naturally became an inhabitant of the vehicle. I could tell Jessica was inflamed by her lack of interest in our conversation. I kept it cool and kicked Clint to keep the Texas rowdiness down. I knew what we had done, spoiled Jessica and Daniel's evening. Daniel, on the other hand, was cordial and asked for directions to my office as he kept a level head. He wanted Clint and me to have a final exit for the evening, which we did. Upon arrival at my office building, we politely said good-night, possibly, for the last time with Jessica.

Clint and I high tailed it up the elevator in order to transform our wardrobe into something more respectable. Within a few minutes, we returned to the lobby. Clint and I were putting the final touches on our look, tucking in our shirts and tightening our belts as I signed us out. We headed outside to the street to hail a cab. It had been almost fifty minutes since the end of the show and we had to hustle.

When our cab approached the hotel, the doorman opened Clint's door as I paid the cabbie. We entered the lobby and turned right towards the elevator. I tugged on Clint's coat.

"Clint, we need to be on our best Catholic schoolboy behavior," I said under my breath.

He acknowledged with a nod. The elevator doors opened and we hung a left, sliding past the Maître de and into the bar. I found us one of the last remaining seats on a couch, facing the entrance to the bar.

"What's your poison, Eric?" Clint asked me with a little swagger as I let my overcoat slide off and onto the leather sofa. A server came by and hung it up on the wall adjacent to me.

"Scotch…on the rocks. It's a night to celebrate," I said.

"I'll open a tab on my card," Clint replied while digging through his wallet.

"Thanks."

I turned and sat down. My eyes were transfixed on the doorway as I sank into the welcoming leather. I waited in anticipation to see which band member would be coming through the door next. I crossed my legs and tried to look comfortable as I observed my cousin, moving his way to the bar. He had to tap a tall blonde guy on the shoulder to get to the bartender. I thought to myself, "That's Sting. No, it can't be." My eyes, like a pinball, were now bouncing between the doorway and the bar. Clint came back several minutes later with our libations. He sat down.

"What a crowd at the bar, huh, Clint?"

"Yeah, I know. I had to tap that blonde haired guy on the shoulder in order to get him to move out of the way," he said, pointing into his chest, in the direction of the bar.

"You mean..." I said losing my words.

"Sting?"

"Yeah!'

"That's him."

"No shit. I thought so."

I took a sip of my molten, caramel-colored beverage while keeping an eye on our surroundings. Moments later, a man entered the room wearing jeans, a collared shirt and a well-worn pair of Converse shoes. It was The Edge, making his way to the restaurant. Shortly after his arrival, a portly gentleman, no taller than Edge, donning a beret came in. "Shit me if that's not Billy Joel," I said, in my head, when he headed in the same direction as the guitarist. What a sighting! Clint and I had a few more rounds before the bar slowly closed.

While some of the lesser-known U2 entourage was leaving the restaurant adjacent to the bar, a woman seated near us caught wind of Sting eating in the private dining room. She quickly took up the lotus position on the floor and began exclaiming the singer's name, along with her desire to meet him. Her yoga position held for about four minutes until security arrived. Clint and I felt that we had seen enough and didn't want to be escorted out as well. We paid our bill, headed to the street for a cab home and crashed into slumber.

23: the spectacle

The following afternoon, after our bar escapade, Clint and I found the end of the line to the general admission gate, outside the United Center, for the night's show. Clint stood guard of our spot while I walked ahead and counted how far back we were. I knew we had to be in the first three hundred people in order to get into the inner sanctum of the heart-shaped stage. My count put us at four-hundred-fiftieth in line, which meant that we wouldn't get into that sacred space, closer to the band. Instead, we had a shot at the rail when the doors opened two hours later.

After four tours, eight shows and some of the crappiest seats one could have, tonight might possibly be the closest I would ever come to being in the front row. I couldn't contain my excitement. Upon entering the venue, Clint and I got our wristbands and were told to walk slowly onto the venue's floor. While doing so, I looked ahead and saw the inner sanctum of the heart was filled, but we had a clear chance of getting a good spot, along the rail, close to the catwalk, projecting outwards into the stadium. I decided to skip down the stairs and onto the arena floor, headed to the far side. When we arrived, there was one person in front of us holding onto the rail. We were basically in the front row and exactly where I predicted we would be the night before, on Adam's side of the stage and on the outside of the catwalk.

Our vantage point gave us a clear view of everything. Above us hung the sound system and the lights. Across from us, at an angle, was the entrance to where Dallas Schoo, Edge's guitar tech, housed all of the guitarist's instruments. In the center of the stage, sat Bono's microphone stand with Larry's drum kit directly behind it. What was even cooler was looking up into the stands, knowing we might possibly be the center of attention tonight if Bono stopped to sing in front of us.

"I gotta tell ya. This is cool shit man," Clint said, as he hovered over me, from behind, protecting me from the future crush of fans.

"What did I say last night? We would be on the rail and near Adam Clayton. And guess what, we're here!"

"Yeah, but this is really close. It's incredible. I have to say I have never seen Rush this close up and personal. You got these tickets through the fan club you said?"

"Yeah, we get first priority. I get a form about four weeks before the public sale. I knew I wouldn't be able to get these through normal means."

"What do you mean?"

"Oh, I had to have been at least the tenth person in line at the public sale to get these and with my luck, I wasn't betting on it."

"Man, I wonder what they are going for out there on the street?"

"About a grand."

"No shit."

After the opening act was being swept off the stage and U2's crew was readying for the headliners, Clint and I bantered on about other U2 shows I had attended. Meanwhile, Dallas Schoo, Edge's guitar tech, walked in front of us up on the catwalk and stopped to check Edge's guitar's wireless system. We all exclaimed in unison, "Schoooooooooo!" He smiled, knowing we were fans of his as well. Meanwhile, Larry's tech was testing the drummer's microphones while others were milling about placing set lists, setting out bottles of water while making sure all of the band's other needs were met before the show began. The anticipation was overwhelming, as being so close only ramped up the excitement. I remembered how far back Ray and I sat at Carver fourteen years ago. Since that night, I had come quite a ways forward. What U2 meant to me was a lot. I had stuck with them as they provided me some of the greatest joys of my life. Tonight would not disappoint.

As the stage was cleared of crew, the intro music began. I knew it was time for the main event. It was U2's casual entry, onto the concert stage that blew me away. No ceremony or theatrics were involved, just four men, taking their places with the house lights on. It was a reflection of how they were in real life and growing more graceful with age. I did miss Bono's incarnation's of The Fly, MacPhisto and whatever personification he took up during PopMart. It was theater and he played it well but now, it was all about going back to simplicity and letting the songs become the rock star. Nothing had changed from the night before. When Bono got to the third verse of *Elevation*, and the house lights dropped, the show was on. The energy around us was infectious. We started to pogo to the beat. It was that club feel U2 wanted and we had it.

Clint and I stood there blurry eyed, as the band would occasionally walk in front of us. Fans pushed against our backs, trying to get a hand out towards them. Clint was relentless in holding his ground behind me and kept me from getting crushed. He was my protector, letting the night be a special one. Especially when Bono came towards us scat singing like Frank Sinatra during *New York* only feet away. Those around me enveloped me, trying to touch the singer. I too reached out. I knew I could never touch him because the moat between the rail and the stage was beyond arm's length, but I tried and retreated. And so did the band, into their back catalog of *I Will Follow*, the tune Chad Kaperak introduced me at the beginning of my U2 venture. The rawness came through as Bono played the guitar and ripped the chords while Edge played the arpeggio. Intermixed into the song was an ode to the Park West where the band first played in Chicago. We were being given a U2 history lesson that swung through *Sunday Bloody Sunday*. An Irish tricolor landed onstage. Bono grabbed it in solidarity and the band marched on with us singing the chorus. It was electric.

Missing tonight was the beautifully lit *Bad*. Instead, we were treated with *All I Want Is You*, followed by my favorite warhorse song in their collection, *Where the Streets Have No Name*. Tonight, the lead singer stood there like a Christ figure behind the microphone, belting out the tune and knowing this was the song that pushed U2 over the top in success, and I was there marching in step right behind them when it happened. When the tune faded, the band moved through *Mysterious Ways* to *The Fly*, which two tours later, was more dangerous and raw. The tune was turned into a post-apocalyptic punk song with Edge driving his guitar with relentless abandon. Larry and Adam kept the rhythm section tight, while Bono belted out the lyrics in anger as he stalked the stage, stopping every so often to make his point. When he reached the tip of the heart, he jumped into the crowd with careless abandon. Within seconds, he was propelled back up onstage by his security. Flushed red with fury, Bono ran in front of us on his way to the back of the stage, where he splattered himself, like a fly, against the video wall as it pulsated tropical colors. An echo of his voice pushed through the venue as the show came to an end.

Since we were behind the stage the previous night, Clint never saw the opening video to the encore we were about to witness. The short film featured Charlton Heston discussing responsible gun ownership. Heston's comments were haunting, as the video following the interview was of a little black girl, about the age of three, pulling a firearm out of a bag with no parental authority in sight. Suddenly, the stage became drenched in blood red light and Edge ripped into the intro of *Bullet the Blue Sky*. In the meantime, Bono returned to the stage belting out the lyrics, adding to the tension already created by the band's tempo. When the song moved to Edge's Jimi Hendrix-like solo, Bono roamed the stage with his arm bent across his face like Dracula, covering his eyes so as not to be witness to what was just projected to the audience on the screen. In his right hand, he held a spotlight. Suddenly, he dropped the arm concealing his eyes and panned the crowd with the light, telling us that we are all in on the crime of ill-fated gun control. Bono intermixed the last lyrics of the song with references to WalMart and the ease which guns can be purchased in America. A chill rolled down my spine when he commenced his rant within earshot of us while shining the spotlight on the crowd over our left shoulders. The band stopped, the stage went dark, as did his light. The crowd was stunned by the theatrics. Slowly, we heard the intro to *With or Without You* and the tension in the arena was tempered. Bono was now at the tip of the heart, and dragged a fan to lie next to him as he sang the lullaby-like tune. The girl next to me began to tear up. The emotional connection had been made.

As we filed out of the United Center with the masses, more

exhausted than the previous night, I was at a loss for words. We were so close. Every intimate moment we had would be inscribed in our memory. Two nights of U2, the opportunity to have an intimate meeting with them and finally being so close to the stage was fulfilling. Yet, I had a ticket for a third night, but I needed a break, thinking of Jessica sat in the back of my mind. What I had done to her the night before was uncalled for and I was about to blow an opportunity. Deep down inside me, I wanted to know things were okay with her. I made a phone call to her prophetically apologizing for my actions, explaining how my U2 excitement got in the way. I admitted to her that I made a huge mistake, impeding on her evening. Jessica graciously accepted my apology.

Two nights later, U2 carried me further into the their galaxy of great shows. It was the third show in four nights and the band was making the United Center their home. Overall, they were loose as they laughed and bantered among themselves between tunes. Songs weren't rushed and the vocals were better. I sat behind Adam Clayton, at an angle, about fifteen rows off the stage. I was solo and had very little disruption other than the three eleven-year-old girls sitting next to me. When old tunes were exhumed from the vault, the girls became chatty, interrupting my first account of *The Electric Co.* being played live. I gently tapped one on the shoulder and put my finger to my mouth. They understood. I chuckled with the thought of these kids being conceived about the time the *Rattle and Hum* track, *Desire*, hit the radio waves thirteen years prior. As the show closed, I knew I made the most of U2's visit to Chicago.

The next day, I took the afternoon off from work and ventured to the hotel one last time, knowing they may be checking out before their last Chicago show. When I arrived, I was too late to get a good viewing spot as a crowd of about sixty fans had already planted themselves outside the entrance. Anyone walking down the street, or driving by, knew something was going on and only time would tell before it got out of hand. And, it did when a car passed slowly in front of us. A woman stuck her head out of the window and asked, "What are ya'll waiting for?"

"Bono and U2!" we replied in unison.

"Bono's here! Stop the car!" she shouted to her companion, driving the car.

Suddenly, the vehicle stopped in the middle of traffic. The woman flew open the passenger door and jumped out wearing high heels, a mini skirt and something that resembled a top covering her upper body. She proceeded to strut her way to the front of the line. Her boyfriend, the driver, got out of the driver's side door, in traffic, and followed suit. As he wooed her back into the car, the woman turned around to her beau and said, "Park the car dammit and come back. I'm goin' to meet Bono."

The crowd's focus turned away from the hotel's entrance and onto the commotion that lay at our feet.

"When's he coming out?" she asked us.

"Honey, come on. Just get back in the car," her boyfriend said, who was five paces behind her. Their parked car was causing traffic to jam in front of the hotel. The blaring of horns began.

She turned and shouted back to him, "No, I'm here to meet Bono!" She was now making every indication of what her intentions were going to be.

"Come on. Don't make a scene. We're holding up traffic. Let's go," her boyfriend said, as he caught up to her and grabbed her arm. She pulled away.

"Fuck you. You get back in the car and park it. I'm staying here to meet Bono."

A hush now covered the crowd.

"You're an asshole anyway," she added.

"We can work it out," her boyfriend said, as he turned and tried again to pull her back to the car.

"Stay away from me! I wanna to meet Bono," she countered, as she threw up her arm to release herself from her boyfriend's grasp.

"Miss, you cannot come in front here. You're going to have to stand back there," a hotel security staffer said to her as he approached the disturbance. He gently tried to move her back to where she came from. Meanwhile, her boyfriend returned to the car and backed it up as to fit into the hotel's valet area.

"I wanna meet Bono!"

"Sorry M'am. Everyone else here has been waiting patiently," the security guard said with a soft approach.

"When's he coming out? Have you met him?" she asked while standing with her hands on her hips.

"I don't know," he said, as he gently nudged her to the sidewalk.

"I'm not going anywhere until he comes out."

"Honey, you are embarrassing yourself in front of all of these fans," her boyfriend cooed.

The woman turned, pointed to her boyfriend and said, "We're over. No more. Finito!"

The boyfriend then leaned into the backseat of the car, on the driver's side, and retrieved the woman's purse, some clothing items and a computer printer. He brought them around the back of the car and neatly stacked them on the curb. He looked back at her and said, "Go meet Bono. We'll chat later."

"Hey! What's my shit doing on the curb?" she asked.

"I am leaving it with you and Bono."

She passed me to collect her stuff and on close inspection, she wasn't completely sober. She bent over, as best she could, and started to pick up her life up off the curb. She struggled to open the back door of the car, piling her belongings into the vehicle. Her boyfriend, chivalrous as he could be, came around and helped her. We all clapped. He nudged her into the front seat and shut the door. Within a minute, the circus took off down Chicago Avenue and our focus returned to the hotel entrance.

Security began to enforce the rules about keeping the sidewalk free and clear for people to walk by as white vans had now pulled up in front of the hotel. The U2 entourage slowly exited. *Pop* producer, Howie B, U2's soundman, Joe O'Herlihy, and others were making their way into the waiting vehicles. What I was observing was nothing like the calmness of the previous Saturday afternoon. Fans became restless and rowdy. I became turned off and decided to leave the spectacle behind. This wasn't what I wanted to see, especially after the intimate afternoon we fans had just a few days before.

24: "i'm the monkey dancer"

During the late summer of 2001, Jessica and I were in a comfortable groove. I no longer had to call her on Tuesday for a Saturday night date. We spent Labor Day together, in the city, enjoying the warm weekend. In the coming days, the world would be in shock as New York yielded to a terrorist attack, opening a floodgate of emotion. The weeks following the events of that tragic day were rough on everyone plus, I was laid off. Thankfully, Jessica, on the other hand, landed a great job around the same time. She looked out for me by helping me find freelance graphic design work. We were a team, facing the autumnal color change, which blanketed our city with optimism.

While the world had been turned upside down in one day, on September 11, I headed to seek calmness and U2. I yearned for them. However, I had no impetuous to get tickets for their fall return to Chicago. I wasn't sure if I should see them again because I didn't want my memories of the magic during their last visit to be tarnished. Nick, however, convinced me otherwise and bought tickets for himself, Jessica and me. We were ready to do it all over again and why not, it was U2.

When Nick arrived for that fall U2 show in Chicago, the three of us, Nick, Jessica and me, decided to dine the night before the show. Nick met Jessica briefly over the phone one night and they hit it off. He had no trepidation about her. In fact, he wanted to have some fun with her. So, at dinner, we devised a plan to determine her worthiness by having Aunt Bev interrogate her over the phone while we watched in anticipation. I snagged the idea from the movie *Diner*. Nick and I came up with twenty questions, covering the gamut from sports, to Chicago and yes, U2. Jessica had to answer ninety percent of them to be a member of our fan club and get her official "club" badge.

At dinner, Nick pulled out his cell phone and called his mom back in Vinton, in order to begin the game. Jessica, although nervous, was a good sport. The first round of ten questions went quite well. We weren't sure about the following ten, which were a little harder. Jessica finished the second round only missing two, but still able to join the club. We gave her an official letter of entry to the club, along with a badge and T-shirt, which she would have to wear in our presence during the following night's show and every subsequent concert we attended together for the coming year. On the following evening, she wore them proudly.

Nicholas' tickets, located in the Mezzanine level just behind Edge's side of the stage, put us in a great vantage point. We observed the excitement of the crowd in the front row of the heart area, feeding off the energy of the band. U2 were loose and never wavered during any part of the show. Six weeks had passed since the destruction of peace in New York City. Bono and the boys were here to help heal the wounds of the country. They were very aware of terrorism, growing up with the Irish Republican Army acting out in Ireland, and honored the victims of the New York tragedy by listing all who passed away on their video monitors near the end of the show. It was a fitting tribute as Bono, once again, had the audience in the palm of his hand. He told us from the U2 pulpit to go out and make peace. Whatever he said, we would do. There was no doubt.

As soon as the last song began, Nick, Jessica and myself bailed for the venue's exit in order to grab one of the last standing cabs outside the United Center. Within minutes, we arrived at the fabled intersection of Chicago and Michigan Avenue. Once more, we tried to coax Jessica to join us in going to U2's hotel bar for a drink. She graciously said, "No thank you." We gave her cab fare and headed out into the crisp night. Nick and I looked like Frick and Frack, wearing matching khaki slacks, sweaters and jackets.

When the bellhops opened the door for us, we knew the rules and took the elevator up to the bar. I said to Nick that I needed to hit the bathroom before venturing into the bar. He agreed and during our bathroom discussion, Nick said he wanted to meet U2 on the street. I was hesitant to go back downstairs. The fatal flaw was leaving and not being able to return. I caved into Nicholas' idea. We exited the loo. I looked into the foyer leading to the bar. My stomach tightened as we may have passed up one of our greatest U2 moments. We stood by the elevator to make our way downstairs per Nick's request. The doors opened. We entered and made small chat with the operator, who rode down with us to the lobby. When the elevator doors opened, there stood the members of Garbage, U2's opening act. My heart sank. We nonchalantly exited the building and walked around it. Upon our reentry, we were stopped in our tracks by hotel security. She told us there was a private party in the bar. No one was allowed upstairs.

"My cousin here just graduated from Harvard Law School

and just had a celebration dinner. I want to treat him to a night cap upstairs while looking out on the city," I said, ramping up the charm.

"I'm sorry. The bar is closed for a private party."

"I see. Would you be so kind to recommend one of the same stature within walking distance?"

"The St. Regis Hotel has a bar around the corner," she said, as she pointed to the building across the street.

"Much appreciated. Have a great night," I said with a smile.

Within a few steps, we entered a dark, wood-paneled room, which was styled like Ralph Lauren. We sank into the leather chairs and ordered drinks. We shot the shit over the next forty-five minutes about our blunder of bypassing such a great opportunity at U2's hotel bar and hitting the street instead. In my opinion, we made a rookie mistake and ordered another round of Manhattans, which went down, just as smooth as the first. We ended up discussing Nick's life in Minnesota and what happened to the girl he dated before leaving law school. When our second round of cocktails ended, the house lights came up and we paid the king's ransom of a bill. Nick's eyes told me what the coming mission would be, go back to U2's hotel and wait outside.

When we arrived at the palace doors of U2's hotel, Nick was a step ahead of me and had no intention of stopping. Instead, he proceeded into the hotel's vestibule as a pale white man came towards him. I kept walking, but Nick stopped and paused.

"Edge, what a great show tonight! Man, you were awesome," Nick drunkenly shouted.

"Oh shit!" I screamed inside my head. "Here comes the Chicago paddy wagon for us. I better go save my cousin." Instead of turning around, I headed to the elevator hoping Nick would follow suit. He didn't. Bono passed me and headed in Nick's direction. I made an immediate U-turn in order to beat the singer to the exit. Luckily, Bono paused, with his companion, as I went out the front door of the hotel.

Upon my exit, there was a car waiting with Edge by its side. Nick was about six feet behind the vehicle's trunk taking pictures with his disposable camera, getting every angle he could have of Edge. Within seconds of me joining Nick, Bono came out the door of the hotel. Nick shouted, "Bono! How are you?" The lead singer waved and proceeded to dance his way into the awaiting car, proclaiming at high volume while skipping on one foot, "I'm the monkey dancer!" Edge nudged Bono into the car and shut his door. The guitarist hurriedly came around the rear of the car and hopped in the back seat behind the driver. The street was an empty witness as the vehicle drove off into the night. The rocker's bodyguard, Mike, came running out of the hotel in hot pursuit, yet to no avail.

Nick headed back to Minneapolis the next day as I was coming down from the high of the incident the night before. A fellow fan told me U2 would camp out in Chicago for a few days beyond the second night's show. I acted upon the insider information and decided to go to the hotel. Lo and behold, she was right. When I got there, I saw bags with their hang tags on a cart as Larry made a swift exit into a waiting car. Adam walked out of the hotel soon after and lingered for a minute to give us autographs. He too entered the back seat of the car. Edge wanted nothing to do with us. He was on the phone. Bono followed a couple minutes later. The rush was on. Several people ahead of me got their photos taken with him as he graciously signed memorabilia. I approached him with the CD insert of *The Joshua Tree*. He took the booklet and began to sign it. I interrupted him.

"Bono, please sign the insert, 'Nick, I'm the monkey dancer. Bono.'"

The lead singer honored my request and then looked at me

over the top rim of his blue-tinted shades. He asked, "How do you know about the monkey dancer?" His eyes were glowing like crystals behind his shades.

"We witnessed you Tuesday night dancing your way, on one foot, into a waiting car and exclaiming it at high volume," I said.

He laughed. "No one should know about me and the monkey dancer. Your lucky to have witnessed it," he said, as he gave me back the booklet and shook my hand. He then turned and nodded to Edge. They climbed into the second limousine and drove off. It was the perfect end to their fall visit to Chicago. It elevated my spirit, as I was jobless and in an emotional haze trying to understand what happened six weeks earlier in New York City.

25: the invited guest

"Would you like to hear Bono speak on Sunday night, Jess?" I asked as the "L" train we were riding rattled towards Midway Airport.

"I'm not sure. Did you get the tickets for Bono's lecture?" Jessica inquired.

"Dominic said he got them for me. He's going to put them at Will-Call on Saturday at Memorial Stadium before the Husker game."

"You and U2? Seriously, how could I say no to you, Eric?"

"Then we're extending our Thanksgiving holiday in Omaha?" I asked.

"I need to give it some thought. We're flying Southwest which is cool. We can change our tickets without penalty."

Jessica paused as the "L" came to a stop. The doors opened. A rush of late fall air entered the train car.

"I know. Bono's speaking on Sunday night after the holiday and you need to get back to the office. I don't want to impose."

"It's all about you and U2, Eric. Isn't it? Seriously, if we get married, will they sleep in our bed? Hmmmm?" she asked with a smile that leaned towards sarcasm.

"Hey, when I heard Bono was speaking in Lincoln, I pulled the trigger on my connection at UNL. It goes back to my philosophy of 'make shit happen.' It isn't like I'm flying halfway across the country with no ticket and no chance to see the band. We'll already going to be in Nebraska anyway. What's the harm?"

"I know. I need to see what's on my plate at the office. I'm sure I can go. I just hope we can get out of Omaha on Monday," Jessica said caving into my Bono lust.

A professional through and through, Jessica could get me to eat dirt more easily than I could get her to take a chance. Besides persuading Jessica to see Bono, I had one other hurdle on this journey to Omaha, request Jessica's parents for her hand in marriage. Of the two issues, seeing Bono and getting my future wife's blessing in marriage, the nuptial request was the easiest. Jessica was unaware of my second feat. Since we moved in together earlier in the year, she had been pushing the marriage topic ever so slightly. We had been through so much together and had the glue to make it work. Our friendship, above all, was the key and we had the fortitude to move forward. She needed to retain a certain level of control always wanting to know what the plan entailed. In this case, it was marriage. I too wanted to tie the knot, but was comfortable flowing with the wind and not rushing into nuptials.

When our plane landed in Omaha, Jessica's brother, Alex, greeted us. I met Alex the previous Thanksgiving, after Jessica and I had been dating for six months. Most of Jessica's relationships were fated in the number three. She seemed to have a string of them, which took a turning point, good or bad, at three months, three years and even three weeks. I, on the other hand, had lasted well over three months and considered myself fortunate. Now, going on our second year as a couple, Alex was supportive of our relationship.

When I pulled him aside a day after our arrival, I told him of my intentions. He gave approval.

"Does Jessica know you're asking mom and dad this weekend?" he asked.

"Alex, she has absolutely no clue."

"You know, she's not the best driver," he said, as we were headed to the grocery store to pick-up some last minute items for Thanksgiving dinner.

"What do you mean?"

"She had to go to driving school," he laughed.

"Huh? Why are you telling me this now?"

"Oh. You didn't know. Mom and dad had to hire a private instructor so she could pass the driving part of the test when she was in high school."

We came to a stop sign. Alex looked left and then right. We proceeded.

"I love her to death, but she has her moments," he said, as we made the turn.

"She seems to drive okay whenever we are here in the Big O," I replied.

"Oh yeah, that's cause she knows it like the back of her hand. Wait 'til you get a car in Chicago. I'd advise you to become the household driver. Look, you're going to be all right. Mom and dad like you, which is most important. I hear you may see Bono speak on Sunday?"

"Yeah, I've a connection at Nebraska. He got me two tickets to the event. I'm trying to get Jessica onboard."

"Sunday night? She'll go."

Alex put the car in park. We opened the doors and continued

the conversation into the grocery store.

"When are you asking mom and dad about marriage?" Alex always made conversation comfortable.

"Tomorrow night, when Jessica goes to bed. I'm sure the folks will still be up." I looked over to Alex for confirmation.

"You'll be fine," he replied, as he picked up a shopping basket.

Alex was right. Asking for Jessica's hand in marriage was a cakewalk compared to my anxiety of seeing the Irish boy wonder. I don't know why I have these anxieties. It started fourteen years ago and I should have been over them by now. There is something mysterious about the man, maybe it's his aura. I don't know, but I have always asked myself what would I say if he walked into our house and made himself at home. I'd probably say, "I'm a fan of you and your band" and treat my meeting by having a comfortable conversation about life and not indulge in hero worship.

The following evening arrived and like clock work, my girlfriend was headed to bed at ten o'clock, one hour later than usual. Jessica's parents were in the kitchen preparing for another feast for friends. Elizabeth, Jessica's mother, was peeling shrimp over the kitchen sink as I stood with my back to the cabinet along side her.

"Elizabeth and Steve, I have a question," I said forthright. "I think it's appropriate to ask you this even though Jessica and I are older." There was a natural pause. I continued, "I would like to ask for Jessica's hand in marriage."

Elizabeth looked up from tending to the shrimp.

"Do you really think you need to ask?" she asked me with a smile. She then asked Steve over her shoulder. "Steve, what do you think? Should we grant him permission?"

"If you want her, she's all yours," he turned and smiled after his response.

The weight of the world was off my shoulders. I knew her parents would respond well. I'm old fashioned in some ways and I did what every man should do. Over the coming months, Elizabeth and Steve would be waiting by the phone for Jessica to announce our engagement. It would not be until the following 4th of July, but for now, everything was on pace. I felt warmth inside me as I stood in the Kahn's kitchen. Jessica would be my bride and we would make a life together. After having lived together for nearly a year and getting a dog, you could say we were already married. The anticipation of a wedding floated through the house. Everyone, but the bride-to-be, was in on the conversation. Added to it, we made the decision to stay on and attend Bono's lecture.

Jessica's mother knew of my interest in U2. Throughout our conversations in the days before the event, she continually asked the rhetorical question about my fascination with U2 and Bono. She was having a hard time wrapping her head around the phenomena.

"Remind me, why do you stand outside U2's hotel all the time?" she'd ask.

"Ah, to meet the band and get autographs."

"No, seriously, what do you see in him?"

"Besides rocker? He's a humanitarian, philanthropist, artist and I think he's a cool dude who stands behind his convictions whether popular or unpopular. He uses the concert stage as a pulpit."

"He sounds very interesting. I told Jessica that you kids can take the Volkswagen to Lincoln for the lecture."

"Thank you. We're going to have a great time."

The evening in Lincoln was one of enlightenment as it pertained to Africa's struggle with the AIDS epidemic. Jessica and I were able to get seats in about the 20th row. Not bad, I thought, as we sank into an evening of lectures, statistics and singing. While learning about the horror of what was happening in Africa, we were overwhelmed as Bono brought it home. AIDS would leave 40 million children orphaned by the end of the decade. It was troubling, but now I understood why this event was taking place in the heartland. Bono was attempting to connect with two factions in America, those who were well educated and those hard-working Midwesterners, willing to take up a cause as long as they knew the whole story.

Tonight, we were a witness to Bono, the humanitarian. The compassionate side was no different from the rock star. He knew how to capture audiences and hold them in his hand. He had the facts and visited the regions affected by AIDS in Africa several times over the years, which validated his insight. He was now a spokesman to the world about this devastation. Jessica and I held hands as we continued to learn that more people die of AIDS in one day in Africa than were killed on September 11. One woman spoke of losing her husband to the deadly disease, which left a devastated family behind. Miscommunication and poor education about the spread of the disease seemed to be the cornerstone of the epidemic. Infected men were under the belief that having sex with virgins would cure them of AIDS. Instead, the disease spread. Bono wanted to make antiretroviral drugs available to everyone in Africa no matter what the cost. At the end of the evening, several children, from the same tribe, joined the lead singer on stage to sing a song about Africa. The song wasn't U2's, but something Bono wrote for this mission. The performance capped an emotional and thought provoking evening.

Jessica and I felt lucky to witness the lecture as the emotion felt in the lecture hall was somber. We slowly exited the room, but I had no intent of going back to the car. Instead, I had the itch to catch Bono outside the venue. As Jessica finished putting on her overcoat, I grabbed her arm and headed out into the night. She knew exactly where we were going, to the back door in hopes of some face time.

When we came within earshot of the rear exit, we ran into Bobby Shriver. I asked about Lance Armstrong, who had also spoken during the evening. Bobby said he had left the premises. A moment later, we heard commotion from behind us. It was Bono, with a swarm of students around him, leading them like a Holy figure to the curb. Traffic stopped. Photographs were snapped. Autographs were attempted. Jessica and I filed in with the mass of fans. I circled the group, looking for a way in. Jessica tagged along in the back as the human school of fish shuffled its way across the street. Obviously, this was no time for a personal conversation. The lead singer's bodyguard protected his client and kept the procession moving. Bono was answering questions as best he could. Those few who got an autograph were lucky. The mass hung on as the lead singer walked up the stone steps to the doorway of the Union Hotel. His bodyguard cut off the gathering and told us that the lead singer was retiring for the evening.

Jessica and I awoke the following morning to the news that a snowstorm blanketed Chicago. We were on the first flight out of Omaha, hoping to get out, but no such luck. Jessica worked the phone and got in touch with her office while I was knee-deep into the *Omaha World Herald*, reading about the previous night's event. Bono definitely made an impact. While in Nebraska, he met with Warren Buffet whose estranged ex-wife was interested in raising money and awareness for the AIDS in Africa cause. The Buffett's had become champions of the U2 front man's work. Meanwhile, Jessica and I arrived back in Chicago seven hours later.

Eight months would pass before Jessica and I were engaged and another ten months before we married. In that span of time, my mom and dad came together too. Due to engagement parties and wedding events, we saw them often and together. The boxing gloves of their relationship had long been put away. Jessica was the bridge I needed to get them to reconnect. Dad's laugh and mom's reminiscing about old friends helped the renewal of their friendship. Around this time, we noticed a change in my mom. Something about her reaction to things, and sudden spurts of disillusionment, told me her wiring was going bad. I didn't know what was going on, but would soon learn it was the beginning of the end of the woman I came to know as mom. Soon, she would succumb to dementia.

As the joy of our wedding season came upon us, I was yearning for my stepfather, Stefano, to join the festivities. The pain of him not being at my wedding wasn't easy to deal with, as I wanted him to meet Jessica and her family. His love for cooking would have granted him inroads into my future mother-in-law's kitchen, as she loved to entertain. Even better, he would have fallen for Jessica as I did. I knew I wanted to invite someone with the same zest for life and, of course, this meant sending a wedding invitation to Bono.

"Why would he come, Eric? Seriously?" Elizabeth asked over the phone.

"I don't know, but I feel as though inviting him may help close a gaping hole in my life," I replied, as I sat at my desk resizing images in Photoshop.

"Well, I did order extra invitations. I'll send one to you," she replied. Elizabeth was more than willing to engage in my U2 behavior.

"I'd appreciate you not telling Jessica. I want to invite him on my terms," I said, as I stared out the window on the February day.

"Do you really think he'll come?" Elizabeth asked.

"Oh, you never know until you ask. I'm planning on including a note with the invitation, clarifying why I am asking him to attend."

"Well, if he comes, I'll eat my panty hose that night," Elizabeth said with a laugh. She was hoping the event was not all about Bono.

"I wouldn't worry about him coming," I said. "More importantly is the event itself. I just want to add a little of my personality to it."

"Okay. I will get them in about two weeks. I should send the invite to your office, right?" She ended the sentence on a high note.

"Yeah, to the office."

"You really think he's coming?"

"Probably not, but wouldn't it be cool to get an RSVP from him, or his office, telling us he couldn't make it?"

"Yes, it would. Have a great rest of the afternoon!"

Elizabeth hung up the phone. I followed the cursor on screen. Bono_letter.doc file was aliased on my desktop and I opened it for another review.

Dear Bono,

Ten years ago this coming summer, my stepfather, suddenly passed away. He was a man who showed me the world of art, how to have a sense of humor, his love for the kitchen, and more importantly, introduced me to your country – Ireland.

Stefano, as I called him, went beyond being a father figure. He took me under his wing as a son of his own. To me, he was a stepfather, but to the academic world, he was one of America's foremost scholars on James Joyce. His passion for Irish literature, culture and music attracted my mother, a Joyce scholar herself, to him.

During my youth, my stepfather made it possible for us to spend two wonderful years abroad in England and the South of France. They are memories that I cherish to this day. When I left home and went off to college, he became one of my biggest fans and ardent supporters. My endeavors, however big or small, were triumphed through his conversations with his colleagues and friends.

On May 8, I will walk down the aisle with my friend whom I will call life partner. My fiancée, and I have been together for three years. During which, she has only heard of my stepfather through the tales of my mom and her friends. I know that if he were around, he would praise her as well. Jessica's interests remind me so much of my stepfather's passions in life: cooking, reading, theater, and travel. These are just a few of the reasons why we have fallen in love and chosen to marry.

I know that your time is precious and limited being a humanitarian on the frontline of the AIDS crisis, the front man of a cutting edge band and being a father yourself. Having said that, I extend to you an invitation to our wedding. Not because you are a rock star and it would be 'cool' to have you at our wedding (Although, it certainly would be 'cool.') More importantly, you represent the Ireland that my stepfather fell deeply in love with, and for you to take his place in our wedding would mean the world to my mother and me.

Please accept this invitation in confidence between us.

Best,
Eric Shivvers

Within nine weeks, Jessica and I were married. We celebrated in style, heading to Hawaii for ten days of paradise while learning, shortly after our return, that Susan Buffett, wife of Warren Buffett, had passed away. Bono flew into Omaha to attend the memorial service where he performed *Forever Young* and *All I Want Is You*. Pandemonium swelled around the Buffett neighborhood as fans caught word of the Irish rocker's attendance. Omaha was becoming Bono's second residence. I thought how coincidental it was for him to be in Omaha months after our wedding. "If he only knew I had invited him to our wedding two months prior," I said to myself. The thought vanished until one afternoon, when the phone rang at home.

"No seriously Jessica, get Eric on the phone," Elizabeth said. I could hear her yell for my father-in-law, "Steve! The kids are on the phone. Pick the phone up in the den and get on the line."

"Hello," Steve greeted us kids.

"Hi dad! I heard you have a story for Eric," Jessica said, as I listened in.

"Oh yeah, I went over to pick-up your mother's linens from the Delaney's house and just happen to catch the caterer of your wedding leaving. I asked him how life was since your big event. He said incredibly busy, especially catering the Buffett Memorial luncheon. Johan went on to tell me how difficult it was to get his truck and servers down Warren's street. He said it was wall-to-wall cars driving through the neighborhood at a snail's pace. Once he got to the Buffett's house, he unloaded his wares for the event and proceeded to the kitchen. His staff helped in getting the food prepped and while doing so, there was a man who wouldn't leave the kitchen. He tasted everything being plated. It turned out to be Bono."

"And then what dad?" Jessica asked with curiosity.

"No way! The Bee-oh-en-oh. Bono?" I interrupted.

"Yeah, it was Bono, Eric," Steve said with a laugh.

"No shit," I said.

"Yeah, no shit's right. I said to Johan you were a big fan of his," Steve replied.

"If Johan only knew Bono was invited to our wedding, he could have leaned over and said, 'Dude, you could've eaten all of this at the Shivvers' wedding too!'" I said, as I laughed.

"Yeah, we should have told him in the invite that we started with chocolate cake and ended with wedding cake. I guess the rocker doesn't have a sweet tooth!" Jessica chimed in with a laugh.

As we said our good-byes and hung up the phone, Jessica and I looked at one another in bewilderment. I guess my invitation to Omaha came full circle.

26: the anxiety of vertigo

In the fall of 2004, Jessica and I descended on San Francisco for her cousin's wedding. On the first evening in the California wine country, Jessica's cousin Ethan, a fan of Bob Dylan, leaned over the dinner table in order to start a conversation about U2.

"Rumor has it there's a new U2 album on the horizon," Ethan said, as he poured me a glass of wine.

"Yeah, have you heard the new track?" I asked.

"'Vertigo?' Isn't that the title? I think I heard it on a television spot for Apple's iPod."

"Yeah, that's the one," I said, as I leaned forward and grabbed the breadbasket.

"Very punk. I like it. Not sure about the Apple tie in though," Ethan said.

"Yeah, me neither. I feel they're selling out," I replied, as I swiped butter onto a piece of bread and popped it into my mouth.

"What do you mean?"

"Well, there's a history with U2 and advertising."

"Really? Explain."

"They were approached in the 80s about using one of their songs for a car commercial and the band turned it down. Now, however, they have changed their tune, excuse the pun, and are promoting themselves on television with Apple."

"Wouldn't you call this self-promotion? Are they not trying to reach a broader audience?"

"Yes, but it still has a corporate undertone. We all know the record industry is in the shitter and this is a move for them to get to a broader, more youthful and wired group. My fear is that they will go the way The Rolling Stones did in the late 80s."

"You mean like Budweiser's underwriting of The Stones' Steel Wheels Tour."

"Exactly. U2's musical influence came from punk and I feel it's not very punk rock when you invite a corporation into your bed. I'm scared of what might happen when U2 does turn to a corporate underwriter. The backlash from fans may be great. Fortunately, they've never had a tour sponsor because the band has always figured out a way to fund them personally, which means sticking their necks out. I have always found their self-funding quite commendable."

"I understand and agree with you. However, I feel the musical landscape is changing and bands have to adapt no matter how long they have been around. U2's iPod and iTunes exposure are a way for them to widen their audience base and I'm sure they felt it was the way to go."

"True, but I just don't want to see their commercial all the time on television ad nauseam."

"Sounds as though you are falling off the U2 bandwagon."

"No, never. Just dismayed. I want this new album to be on the level of "War," "The Joshua Tree" or "Achtung Baby." Not as a copycat album, but in the sense of pushing the creative envelope again as they did before," I replied, as I took a drink of my wine.

"Didn't they scrap a part of the new record?"

"Yeah, producer Chris Thomas, who worked with INXS, Midnight Oil and I think the Sex Pistols, was at the helm for the first round, but the band just wasn't feeling it. I think the history with Howie B, and how the "Pop" record came out, forced them to go back to the familiarity of working with Lillywhite, Lanois and Eno."

"I hope you feel that scrapping a record is no indication of the creative process or lack there of," Ethan said, while he put his wine glass near the edge of the table and leaned back in his chair.

"No, I call it knob fiddling. It has been happening ever since the recording of "The Unforgettable Fire" album."

"Dylan wouldn't do that."

"What? Scrap an album or knob fiddle?" I asked.

"Overwork the production."

"Oh, I agree completely. Dylan's a control freak. Once it's done, it's done. That's my observation of his work and I say that with all good intentions. Plus, he has been at it quite a bit longer than the boys of Ireland and could give a shit less about what people think of his work," I said, picking up the menu in front of me and moving on with my diatribe. "U2, on the other hand, ebbs and flows both sonically and lyrically. If they don't feel it in the studio, they move on. The other issue is getting all of them in the same workspace at one time, which has become a burden with the four hundred pound gorilla in the room, if you know what I mean." I paused and collected my thoughts. "Not that I'm knocking Bono and all of his great deeds, but their albums are now taking longer to execute because of all of his good-hearted endeavors."

The intellectual music discussion with Ethan fueled my hunger for a fresh U2 album. With reports of the impending release of *How to Dismantle an Atomic Bomb* on the horizon, fans were getting excited and glad that an ending was near to their start and stop recording process of the last four years. Bono preached to us, in the press, about how Edge was finding his groove and the album was their best work to date. What he was really trying to do was get in front of a potential album leak since a copy of their upcoming album had been stolen a few months earlier from their compound in the South of France. A potential leak to the Internet, within days before the album's release date, could have been devastating for the band.

On the eve of *How to Dismantle an Atomic Bomb*'s release, U2's long-time fan club, Propaganda, was being dismantled. For over twenty years, band management had overseen the fan club. With *How To Dismantle an Atomic Bomb*, however, U2 decided to move the club to the Internet to gain a wider fan base and make a connection to fans in real time. Gone was the quarterly printed fan magazine, *Propaganda*, with it's in depth interviews, band commentary, observations on politics and merchandising specials. Now, with them moving to the web, access to band information was easier, but the intimacy was gone. Long-time fans felt misplaced and taken advantage of due to increased membership fees and inadequate customer service from the site. Regardless, Nick and I, true-blooded U2 fans, joined up as we were told we would have priority in tickets sales, as long time Propaganda members. Added to the enticement, were web exclusives and an annual membership gift of a limited edition CD not available anywhere else.

Days before the album's release, I heard thirty-second snippets of songs on the band's Web site. I started to feel uneasy about their next creative venture. All of this came to a head when *How to Dismantle an Atomic Bomb* hit my CD player. My auditory sensation was confused because *Vertigo*, the album's lead single, was such a heavy guitar driven song that the rest of the album paled in comparison. I felt the tune *Love and Peace or Else* was a stretch to capture the fire of *Bullet the Blue Sky*. For that matter, the second track, *Miracle Drug*, was searching for the emotional connection found in the song *One* from *Achtung Baby*. My conclusion was leading me to believe the album was a little too paint by numbers until I found the real gems, and saving graces, which were *Crumbs From Your Table* and *One Step Closer.* *Crumbs From Your Table* is quintessentially U2. It is a stripped down track with Larry's rhythmic drumming, Edge's full on use of his beautiful arpeggio style and Bono singing from the heart. *One Step Closer* follows *Crumbs From Your Table* with a haunting simplicity, much like *Wake Up Dead Man* from *Pop*. It is a soft, steady track with Bono telling the story of how his father, nearing death, was getting one footstep nearer to figuring out what was waiting for him on the other side. The memorable triptych of songs from this album closes with *Origin of the Species*, which was an anthem to youth about loving yourself, no matter what you looked like or what your sexual orientation was. It was a reflection of U2 raising their children giving them the direction. The brilliance in the three songs was how they worked together in harmonious fashion and how the band had always been able to work in one of these trios of beauty into every album since *The Unforgettable Fire*.

Three months later, we received confirmation about the Vertigo Tour, the title of the tour supporting the new album. Nick and I awaited a first shot at seats via the online club pre-sale. Our subscription granted us passwords and a time slot to buy tickets for the May shows. When our time arrived, we jumped online and punched in all of the information we were given as fast as we could. Nick, who was now working in downtown Chicago, was on a high-speed LAN line. I, on the other hand, was on a chopped-up and untrustworthy DSL connection, hoping to land those much-coveted general admission floor seats. Within seconds, they were gone. Never had a chance. The best tickets I could get were in the third level at fifty-five bucks a piece for the second night. I felt snubbed as I was a twelve-year fan club member and wasn't happy. Neither was Nick.

"Nick, we've got to keep the faith," I said on the telephone.

"This sucks! What a load of horse shit!"

"Did you buy anything?" I asked.

"Fuck no! I wanted General Admission tickets. All that came up were the one hundred fifty-dollar seats. We've been long-time fan club members for Christ's sake!"

I could only imagine what Nick's inflamed face looked like by now.

"I bought fifty-five-dollar seats in the nose bleed section," I replied.

"Why?" he responded.

"I had to, Nicholas. Something is better than nothing. I may have a better shot when we go to the venue this weekend along with the masses."

"I agree. You're right. This is such bullshit, Eric."

"I'll pick you up Saturday morning at about seven. Can you get your ass out of bed for the sale?" I asked, knowing he'd probably still be up from his Friday night soiree.

"Yeah, I'll set two alarm clocks. I gotta go. Drop me an e-mail before Friday. Love ya."

Saturday morning came early as my alarm rang. I looked at the clock. Six in the morning was staring me in the face. I hit the snooze button. Jessica rolled over. She wanted me out of bed before the buzzer went off again as it was her day to sleep in. I could feel her palm in my lower back; reminding me I had to get my feet on the ground and ass out of the bed. I slid the alarm button to the right and put one leg on the floor. The dog arose and we slowly walked down the darkened hallway to the second bedroom. In my daze, I dressed myself and headed to the kitchen to make coffee. I needed a jolt before sitting in a car all morning, freezing my ass off.

When I rolled up in front of my cousin's apartment building, the clock in the dash showed seven. Nick slid into the car and I drove us to the United Center while still being half-awake. Debauchery greeted us as we pulled into the parking lot. Several drunken U2 fans arrived well before us, wearing next to nothing while doing a few Irish jigs in the back of a pick-up truck. None of them seemed to care that the outside air temperature was hovering just above freezing while they were topless and wearing tricolor clothing of national, Irish unity. We needed the entertainment to kill time, leading up to the sale. Nick, as usual, had to devise a plan. Ironically, his friends pulled up next to us. He hopped cars to strategize. I could have cared less. I preferred to stay in my warm vehicle rather than get involved in an early morning meeting of U2'dom because all I wanted was a shot at purchasing floor seats or at least, obtaining better tickets than what I had via the fan club pre-sale. Eventually, we all trekked to the lone security guard, sitting in a pick-up truck, handing out line numbers. Our bare naked Irish brethren, who were still whooping it up, preceded us.

For the next two hours, I remained cloistered in my car while Nick was with his friends in a car next to us. I kept turning the car on and off to stay warm. The parking lot slowly filled with other fans filing towards the same pick-up truck we did an hour earlier. Nick eventually came back to our car. He complained of being famished. Actually, he had to go to the bathroom. I looked at the clock. We had half an hour before we were to line up and had limited options.

"There's a Mickie-D's over on Western we could go to," I said.

"Cool. Let me tell the others," he said. Nick then rolled down the passenger window and shouted at the car next to us.

"Hey, Leo. Roll down your window," Nick said. He waited for a moment and continued, "Follow us. We're going to McDonald's. I gotta piss. I also want to get some hot chocolate in order to warm up."

It was typical of my cousin to make the wrong call during something important with U2. I would've walked a few blocks away and found an alley. Instead, we had to drive somewhere, taking God knows what chance, while Nick bantered on about the "what ifs" when it came to buying tickets. He was driving me crazy. By the time we entered McDonald's, I was fed up with my cousin's anxieties because the closer we got to the witching hour of the sale, the worse Nick panicked. To me, I could have given a shit less what the ticket strategy was for the day. I was worried that our short jaunt to McDonald's was going to put our whole ticket purchase in jeopardy.

Upon our return to the United Center, security was preaching the rules about the purchase. It was the same spiel for every other show we bought tickets for, followed by randomly drawing the starting number. Seconds later, shouts of glee and spirited disappointment came from the amassed crowd as we learned our numeric fate. The drunken, Irish contingent found out that none of them had a number anywhere near the first twenty spots for the sale in order to acquire general admission seats. They were visibly upset. However, their numbers were better than ours, but not by much. To me it didn't matter, I just wanted to get the process going. Within minutes, the line started to move and when I got to the ticket window, both shows had sold out. In anticipation of more concerts being added to the existing two night run, I ran as quickly as I could around the huge arena, just to get back in line. I waited to hear those magical words.

"Two more shows are up for sale," said the United Center employee, running the show.

Nick and I were excited. I headed back to the window in anticipation of buying a golden floor ticket. I asked and scored two of those coveted seats in the general admission section. Again, I circumvented the venue in order to get back in line and buy more tickets. Within minutes, I had bought seats for the fourth and final show in the second balcony, looking straight onto the stage. I was euphoric. Nick wanted to stick around the venue to discuss his victory with his friends. I encouraged him not to.

"Nick, we got'em. Let's go," I said, as we headed back to the car. Lack of sleep was taking over me as my bed was screaming for my slumbered return and dreams of the coming May U2 shows.

27: the birthday gift

Jessica and I left Austin exhausted after celebrating our one-year wedding anniversary in the Lone Star State. Our traveling weariness almost gave way to us missing the last leg of the trip from Houston to Chicago. Thank God we didn't. The next direct flight back to the Windy City wasn't leaving until the following morning. Luckily, when we got on our plane, we found an empty row consisting of three seats on our Southwest flight and as chance would have it, a woman hastily took the last seat next to me, obviously out of breath.

"Is this seat taken?" she asked in a familiar Texas twang.

"No, it's open," I replied, as I looked up and over my newspaper.

The woman was wearing a black T-shirt with recognizable red concentric circles on the sleeves. She heaved her bag into the bin above us and twisted herself into the seat with a semi-thud. I leaned over.

"Did you see the band in Houston?" I asked.

"No. What band?" she replied with a smile.

"Aren't you wearing a U2 shirt? I recognize the red circles."

"No, darlin', I bought this through the fan club," she said, as she was rummaging through the seat pocket in front of her.

"Are you a fan of U2?" she asked me in return.

Jessica heard the question and leaned forward.

"Are you kidding, if it weren't for me, he would've married the band," Jessica giggled.

"Stacey," the woman said, as she extended her hand forward, across me, towards Jessica.

"I'm Jessica. This is my husband, Eric. Very nice to meet you."

"Ya'l from Chicago?" she asked.

"Yes," Jessica replied. "And you? Houston, Stacey?"

"Born and raised..."

"You're going to Chicago for what reason?" I questioned.

"Hello! Can't you tell? I'm going to see U2 and their live DVD taping," she said, as the jet engines started to growl.

"How long have you been a fan club member?" I kept up the conversation over the background noise.

"Since 'Pop' and I've seen them a few times since then too," she said, leaning back in her seat as we felt the plane abruptly turn towards the runway.

I could hear Jessica's thoughts, "Only you could find a complete stranger who is as big a U2 fan as you, if not bigger."

We accelerated down the runway. The lift, underneath us, began to bounce the plane as we became airborne.

"I hate flying," Stacey confessed as she raised both hands and covered her eyes.

"I hear ya," I replied softly.

Keeping the conversation light, I had to continue on with my U2 interrogation.

"How many times have you seen them?" I asked.

"Four times. First in Dallas on PopMart and then Dallas and Houston for the Elevation Tour. I also went to the second Slane Castle show in Ireland as well," she said, as she looked towards the ceiling of the plane with her eyes still closed.

"And you?" she asked.

"Mine goes back a bit further. The band made an impromptu stop on my college campus on the Joshua Tree Tour and I got hooked. Since then, four times on Zoo TV, both indoors and out, PopMart at Soldier Field twice and five times on Elevation," I said. "But, I've never seen them on their home turf."

"It was cool. Very cool. But I hate flying."

"How did you make the trip to Dublin?"

"Many cocktails," she laughed and opened her eyes. "I left Rudy, my husband, at home and went by myself. I met several fans on the plane over to Ireland. It made me feel comfortable. As I said, add a couple cocktails and the flight was just fine."

"Wow! Slane Castle. Seeing U2 in Ireland. That's amazing," I said wide-eyed with excitement.

Jessica leaned into my left ear and said, "Sounds like she's one up on you. You've never seen the band in Ireland. I should keep a tight hold on you. She may invite you the next time she goes."

As we bounced through the spring storms hovering the Midwest, Stacey was settled, not only by our conversation, but by the gin and tonic she ordered mid-flight. We discussed our professional lives. She was a nurse and the conversation moved to health care. I discussed the diagnosis of mom's Alzheimer's, which happened the previous fall. Stacey and I began to create a bond as her career was in cancer patient care. While we discussed life, Jessica remained nose down in a book. She lifted her head every now and then to take in my conversation with Stacey.

When our plane landed at Midway Airport, we taxied for what seemed an indefinite amount of time, covering the whole airfield of the airport. In doing so, and trying to figure out where we were, I leaned across Stacey to look out the far window across the aisle from us. What caught my eye made my mouth drop.

"There it is!" I pointed to the window.

"There what is?" Stacey asked.

"U2's plane," I replied.

"Where! Where's U2's plane?" she exclaimed almost jumping out of her seat.

"We just passed it. It had concentric circles on the tail just like the ones on your shirt," I said.

Now everyone was looking out the window.

"Na-na-na. You're saying shit again," Stacey said, as she pulled out her business card and handed it to me.

"My cell's at the bottom. Call me tomorrow and we'll hook up at the show."

Jessica nudged me, implying that I wasn't to runaway with Stacey. I laughed and looked back at my wife, knowing exactly what she was thinking.

For the first night of U2's Vertigo concert in Chicago, I invited Mick, my old neighbor and dear friend, to join me. Our seats were in the third balcony, looking across the stadium at a slight angle. Not a bad perspective, but we were quite a ways away from the stage and were going to have to rely on the video monitors above the band to see any facial expressions. Mick could've cared less, as he was just eager to see a live U2 show. I, on the other hand, should have been excited because the band was taping tonight's show for a future DVD release, yet I still didn't feel the same U2 buzz I usually have for their concerts. I knew why.

It started seven months prior with the launch and promotion of their Special Edition U2 iPod followed, shortly thereafter, by an album, which just wasn't doing it for me. And finally, a tour, which used the same stage layout and video monitors above the band as found on the previous outing. All that had really changed in stage set-up was the catwalk, which was now in the shape of an ellipse instead of a heart. I was a little disgruntled because I knew U2 had more creative firepower, but weren't showing it. The only added effect would show up later in the show when a curtain of glowing balls, each about the size of a 16-inch softball, would be lowered from above the stage and acted as a backdrop. Willie used them as a crude screen, or canvas, projecting text and graphics through them. The concept was cool as it allowed fans, seated behind the stage, to have a decent view of the band for most songs. This appeared to be an extension of the Zoo TV Tour, pushing video media as far as it could. It was a nice addition, but nothing groundbreaking as I felt we were witnessing something old in new packaging.

When the house lights finally dropped. U2's stage manager came out to excite the crowd for the taping. I was melancholy at a point when excitement should have been running through my veins. After all my years of fandom, I couldn't believe my mood. Bono acerbated the situation when he began to sing. It was harsh and rough. He was over excited. Then he coughed, with a frog in his throat, and had to restart a tune. I crumbled and was mortified, but after the initial hiccup, and a few songs into the show, the pressure lessened.

When the band ventured into the *Boy* album classics, *An Cat Dubh* and *Into the Heart*, the show, I thought, was starting to take off. The songs were a throwback to the good old days of punk rock which was exciting given that *How to Dismantle an Atomic Bomb* was trying to emulate the genre in certain songs. However, the band made a mid-concert U-turn and went into a trio of tunes, pulled from the new album, which didn't jive with the punk vibe they created moments earlier in the show. The rest of the concert tromped along as the band dug deep into the war-horse vault and extracted *Bullet the Blue Sky, Pride (In the Name of Love)* and *Where the Streets Have No Name*. The saving grace came at the beginning of the encore when they ripped through thunderous versions of *Zoo Station* and *The Fly*.

While the band closed out the evening with the song, *One*, Mick and I hopped a cab back to U2's hotel to grab a bite at the bar, hoping we would catch a glimpse of their grand entrance. It never happened. Instead, we made the best of it and conversed about our bachelor lifestyle before we met our respective spouses. During those unattached days, Mick made my crummy, single life more enjoyable as I would invade his apartment, next door to mine, in my boxer shorts, carrying a plate of pasta and zoning out on ESPN.

After downing the last of our drinks, we headed out into the evening, witnessing several stragglers attempting to get into the hotel we just exited. Some were singing to the radio station blaring out of their cab as they stumbled onto the sidewalk. Mick and I watched with humor while we said our good-byes. He headed west on Chicago Avenue to his condo on the river. I hopped a cab in search of some much-needed rest because two days later, I would be right back to the very spot I was leaving to hang out and get an autograph from Bono on his birthday.

When the late spring sun poured into our bedroom on the morning of Bono's birthday, I slowly awoke with the tune *Vertigo* pounding in my head. It was just after eight. Jessica had long since left for the city. I went along with my normal routine, walking the dog and making some coffee, followed by prepping my bag for the day's activity. Packed into my messenger bag was a bottle of water, two PowerBars, the camera, some U2 paraphernalia and a Sharpie pen plus a custom-made birthday hat for Bono. The pointed cone was covered in images of the lead singer, throughout the years, and emblazoned with yellow and orange type screaming, "Happy Birthday, Bono." My goal was to hit the hotel by ten o'clock and not much later. The one potential issue was drinking too much liquid. I could ill afford losing my place in line especially on Bono's birthday, just to go to the bathroom.

Upon my arrival, I was near the back of the pack of groupies hanging out. In front of me, were obnoxious youngsters half my age. I knew nothing happened until three in the afternoon, but what time this lot showed up, boggled my mind. My watch said nine-fifty. Within two hours, a spot opened up under the canopy next to the door entering the hotel. I slipped in unnoticed. It was fate. I took up the new post and put on my party hat. I then called my wife with the exciting news. Within an hour, Jessica was on the scene.

"Oh my God. Look at you!" she laughed.

"What?" I asked.

"The hat. It's so cute. Where did you get the idea?"

"Linda, at the office, told me to be creative and make a custom one."

Rumblings, from the fans next to me about Jessica coming to the front of the line, were bothersome. "She's my wife and here for a visit," I said, as I turned to the three catty women standing next to me.

"Will I chat with you later?" Jessica asked me.

"Without a doubt. Here, hold my spot. I need to use the bathroom at the bar around the corner."

Upon my return, we continued the conversation as I put my birthday hat back on. She laughed again.

"Call me this afternoon when you're done chasing Bono."

"Of course," I said, as I leaned forward to kiss her.

Jessica turned away and slipped into the masses walking the

Mag Mile. Within minutes of her vanishing, Stacey exited the hotel with a lot of under-the-breath gossip about seeing Bono at lunch and discussion about that evening's meet-up spot on the floor of the United Center. She was amused at how far I had taken Bono's birthday. Like Jessica, Stacey and her friends disappeared into the crowded street. I was hungry. I looked at my watch and knew we had about another three hours to wait for the lead singer's exit. To kill time, I hunted for my CD player in my bag and a PowerBar then lulled myself into some vintage U2.

Two hours later, my boredom was broken when a roving camera crew arrived in a cargo van. I couldn't tell whom they were with, but the cameraman randomly filmed the gathered crowd around me. My hat seemed to capture the attention of the woman holding a microphone and calling the shots. She approached me and asked about my fandom. I was flattered. Anticipation was now in full swing. Fans were also lining up across the street as my cousin, Nick, arrived a few minutes after my interview. We chatted while I retrieved a birthday hat for him from my bag. He pushed his way back into the crowd. Mike, Bono's bodyguard, came out and told us the rules.

"Hello. I have some rules we will follow this afternoon," Mike said. "One, there's to be no crowding around Bono. Two, if we feel that someone is getting out of line and out of hand, we'll put him into the car and that's it. Three, we're on a tight timetable. I'll bring him over to my left first and then to my right. Four, we don't have enough time for everyone. Get whatever photos you can get. This means that he'll not take requests for photos with you. Understood? Great."

While my camera dangled from my wrist, I was all set. I felt good about my spot until a woman cut behind me and forced her way to a better vantage point. I gently nudged her out of the way. Within minutes of the announcement, Bono emerged from the hotel to great fanfare. Mike wrangled the Irishman and moved him to the far side as the crowd serenaded him with *Happy Birthday*. When the singer finished his autographs stage left, Mike brought him to my side. I put my hand out to greet him while handing him an envelope, which he proceeded to autograph.

"Bono, wait, don't sign it. It contains a birthday gift for you," I said over the chaos of fans trying to garner his attention.

"Wow! Thank you," he replied.

"Inside is a photograph of your friend Michael Hutchence during his last stop here in Chicago. I took it backstage in the fall of ninety-seven."

He looked at me. He was stunned as I hit an emotional chord.

"I also have a birthday hat for you as well," I said to him.

He took the hat and began to draw on it. He doodled glasses on one of the images and proceeded to sign it. I kept our conversation going.

"My mom is a James Joyce scholar and I would like you to have her copy of "Finnegans Wake" she used for her dissertation," I said, as he wrote 'Happy Birthday to me' on the hat.

"Send it to me."

"To Principle?"

"Yes, please."

Bono moved away from me into the throng of people. Nick extended his party hat to him, which he gladly signed. Within five minutes, Bono was ushered into a waiting limousine. Nick and I hugged. Adrenaline was flowing through me. I called Jessica from the bus on my way home. I must have sounded erratic. I couldn't put a sentence together.

Upon my arrival home, I had very little time to collect our tickets, walk the dog and prep for the show. I quickly grabbed the extra birthday party hats, threw on my custom-painted U2 jeans and headed back to the bus stop. Tonight, Jessica and I had general admission tickets and could quite possibly get into the interior of U2's stage called the ellipse. Admittance into the elliptical opening was now a random chance by scanning your ticket upon entry into the venue and not by first-come, first-served to those who stood in line like the previous tour for the heart. I was hoping one of our tickets was the lottery winner, but when Jessica and I arrived at the venue, all hope faded. The scanners for the entrance into the ellipse were being hauled away. I moved to plan B, which was meeting Stacey next to the mixing board.

As Jessica and I waited for Stacey's arrival, we stood at the back of the arena floor, taking it all in. Way up above us, in the rafters, were fans dangling Irish flags off the balcony. To our right was a video camera, readying for the evening's taping of the concert. Behind us was the *Good Morning America* crew shooting a promo tying U2's concert into an upcoming episode. Stacey arrived momentarily and we went into our hyper state of U2 conversation. She told us to keep an eye out for workers handing out wristbands as to appease us in the back for not getting into the ellipse upon entry into the venue. Jessica and I saw someone dispensing the bands and we joined the surge with Stacey, but were unable to get one as the lights came down. The venue became awash in red. It was time for the intro to the show opener, *City of Blinding Lights*. We braced ourselves. Jessica was eager to see the show, which lessened the anxieties I had two nights prior. From our spot on the floor, we gazed over a sea of fans with arms raised, singing to the chorus and pogoing to the beat. The vibe was intoxicating, the energy was electric and I was dancing in the back of the venue with the gal who understood my U2 fandom.

28: an old friend

In the fall of 2005, and a few days after the band played the United Center, I stood outside their hotel with two others in anticipation of seeing the Irishmen on an off day. Hotel staff allowed Victoria, Rebecca and I take cover under the canopy from the soft rain as long as our gang of three didn't grow. We all had a hunch that the band was still in town as we discretely clutched our collectables. Rebecca brought a copy of *The New York Times Magazine* in which Bono was interviewed for the feature article. Victoria had a copy of the *Boy* album and I had a program, purchased off eBay, from the Zoomerang leg of the Zoo TV Tour. You could tell by the grins on our faces that the three of us had the biggest secret in town.

As the passersby looked at the entrance and ducked under the canopy for protection from the rain, Bono's bodyguard exited the hotel carrying a duffle bag. He noticed the three of us huddled in the corner. We waved him over and asked casually if the band members were coming out and would they sign. He informed us they were running behind schedule due to the weather and would be departing soon. Moments later, Edge exited and headed towards one of the white vans parked just over my right shoulder. With a newspaper tucked underneath his arm, he was unwilling to stop for an autograph. Instead, we got a brief wave.

"Edge, may we please have an autograph?" I inquired, as he directed his roadie where to put his Gibson guitar case in the back of the van. He turned around, still clutching his *New York Times* and Blackberry, and saw me holding out a pen as enticement to sign autographs. He came towards us. My olive branch worked as he took my pen and graciously signed our soon-to-be collectables. Rebecca asked for a photo.

"On one condition," he said. "It has to be a group shot."

Without hesitation, we asked a hotel staffer to be the photographer as we flanked the guitarist. On the count of three, the flash exploded. We were overcome with excitement as the guitarist slipped away and gave us a good-bye salute as he entered the white van.

Again, the front of the hotel was quiet. No other fans had arrived for the impromptu meet-n-greet until a woman, with a young child in tow, cut between the door to the hotel and us. Her timing was impeccable. We not only looked dumbfounded, but also visibly upset. We mutually agreed we would cut her off from Bono if she took too long. Minutes later, we saw a reflection of Bono's bodyguard, Mike, in the revolving door. We knew the singer wouldn't be that far behind. Actually, he wasn't. He was right in line with Mike, wearing loose fitting clothing and sandals. Immediately, he was hounded by the woman and child. I have seen it countless times, Bono cannot resist a child. Rebecca was smart. She let the woman introduce herself and her kid to the lead singer and then gently infringed upon their conversation, launching into her sales pitch about being an advocate for

AIDS research in America while studying social policy in college. It was brilliant.

My game plan was to be the last one to talk to the lead singer. I waited patiently. When I knew it was my turn to talk, I pounced.

"Bono, I'm not sure you remember me. I gave you a picture of Michael Hutchence for your birthday this past May."

He looked at me and began to sign my tour program.

Without skipping a beat, I said, "I also sent you my mother's copy of "Finnegans Wake." The one she used for her dissertation."

"Here, to the hotel?" he asked, looking at me with his steel-blue eyes through his wrap-around shades.

"No, to Principle in Dublin."

"Hmmm. Not sure I got it. I'll need to look for it when I get back."

"One thing to add. I married an Omaha girl. Her mom plays bridge with a friend of yours, Warren Buffett."

He looked up from the program. His ears perked up.

I kept the conversation moving. "Anyway, I have run out of my allotment of tickets through the fan club and she's interested in seeing the show in Omaha."

"What's her name?" he asked.

"Elizabeth Kahn."

"Done! Give me her information and I'll take care of it."

Blown away, I pulled out my cell phone. Elizabeth's phone number was three clicks away. I took the massive envelope holding my tour program and ripped off a piece. Shaking, I jotted the information down at a feverish rate. While doing so, I looked over the edge of the paper. There they were. The most immaculate toenails I had ever seen in my life. Bono's toes were peeking out of his sandals to soak in the humid air. The observation caused me to pause on my much-needed concentration. I wasn't worried. No one else was hounding him as I scribbled Elizabeth's information down. Once finished, I leaned into his SUV and gave him the torn piece of paper, just as the bellhops were closing the doors of the vehicle. We waved and shouted our good-byes as the black SUV crept out of it's parking spot in the hotel's valet area. I stood there watching it vanish into the Saturday afternoon traffic.

As I said my good-byes to Rebecca and Victoria, the soft rain turned into a downpour. I flipped open my umbrella and made my way to the bus stop half a block away. I couldn't contain my smile. I had just scored a huge coup. Yes, I had another autograph but even better, I scored a connection for my mother-in-law. I flipped open my phone and called home. I told Jessica that my trip to the city was a success and about the intrusive woman outside the hotel. However, I held back on the last part of the story until I got home.

"Oh, you have to call my mom," Jessica said, as she was stretched out on our couch upon my return home. "I cannot believe you asked him to put my mother on the guest list. Eric, you are too much."

I picked up my cell phone and began to ring Jessica's parent's house.

"Hello?" Elizabeth answered.

"Elizabeth? It's Eric, your son-in-law," I said with excitement.

"Oh, hi. How are you?"

"I'm good, thanks. Do you have a minute?" I said, moving onto my story without confirmation.

"I was just in the city outside U2's hotel and had a moment to chat with Bono. I told him that my in-laws were from Omaha and that they played bridge on-line with Warren Buffett." I paused and continued, "Bono's ears perked up. I asked him if there was a way I could get you and Steve into the show. He replied and asked for your name and number." I was out of breath.

"You're kidding me," Elizabeth said. "Are you serious? You said this to Bono?"

"Yes, can you believe it?"

"Were there others on the street with you?"

"Two other fans."

"Seriously? You gave him our number?" Elizabeth couldn't believe her ears.

"Yeah, they'll probably call and confirm," I said.

"Bono's calling me?" She asked and then laughed.

"No, probably someone from his staff'll ring you."

"Oh, I'll be waiting for this. I'm going to run a hot bath right now and get ready for Bono's phone call," she laughed. "When's the show? I need to clear my calendar!"

"December fifteenth."

"Oh, that's near my birthday. I cannot wait. Is Jessica there?"

I turned to Jessica with the phone in my outreached arm and said, "Your mom wants to talk to you."

"Hi mom...Yes, he was out there yesterday too...Can you believe it?...Yes, he gave him your number...Yes, he has pictures..." Jessica's voice faded away as I walked to the back of the condo.

After the high of meeting Bono, my life took a downward spiral. I was working at a non-profit where budgets were very tight and I had to be resourceful in getting the best bang for our buck developing ad campaigns, direct mail and printed collateral. It was bleeding me dry creatively. The tough economy added pressure to raising money, as well. It was a burden that employees carried around the office. Added to the emotional pot of soup was my mom. Her Alzheimer's was progressing. Facing the reality of the disease, I collapsed inside. Mom and I had spent the past two years talking on the phone, at least twice a week, in order to stay close and deal with the situation. She was now unable to pick up the phone with any regularity. I knew what was coming and so did she.

To have mom's life stolen away from her by this disease was

taking an emotional toll on me. I knew mom would never be the same woman captured in the photo, gracing my desk. In it, she was impeccably dressed and wearing a broad smile on my wedding day. It was the reality of her succumbing to the disease, as well as keeping all of life's other plates spinning, which was pushing me to the brink of collapse. I was emotionally over-whelmed. I huddled in my cubicle daily watching the clock move ever so slowly towards five o'clock, the magical hour when I could escape from my office woes and return to the sanctuary of our condo. I knew I was an "L" ride away from the safe haven of home, but even walking those four blocks to the train was ardu-ous. I was desperate to keep the onset of my depression from Jessica. She knew something was up, but waited for me to reveal what I was going through.

By July of 2006, I was near the end of my rope. I was so debil-itated by the claustrophobia depression produced that I couldn't walk to the train, either going to or returning from work, with-out having a severe anxiety attack. One night, it was so bad at the office that I had to call a cab to take me home. I collapsed into the backseat and never looked out the window until I arrived in our neighborhood. I was traumatized. Jessica heated up leftovers that evening as I sat at the breakfast bar in our kitchen. She knew something was up while she was plating dinner. I said nothing. I was a shell of myself as I moved my fork through the food, which was now in front of me. Jessica came around to my side of the counter, seated herself next to me, and proceeded to rub my back. I then spilled everything to her.

"Eric, I want you to leave your job," she said, as she put her arm around my shoulder.

"We have bills and responsibilities. I can't quit tomorrow. We also have a benefit for the center in five weeks. Its all hands on deck," I replied, staring at my plate. I wanted to eat dinner, but couldn't muster the manpower to lift the fork.

"Okay. When the event is over, I think you should hand in your resignation. The fall is a great time to look for work. Plus, you can ride your bike. I also think you should look into seeing a therapist. When you walk around this house, I can tell something's brewing inside you. I can only help you so much. The issues you are dealing with are very difficult."

I looked at her for confirmation. Water was beginning to fill the lower lids of her eyes. She was holding back tears.

"I agree. I'll look into seeing someone," I replied and leaned into her arms.

"I can help you find a therapist. Why don't you call our insurance tomorrow and see what the co-pay will be," she said.

We embraced in a hug of comfort and held one another. It was the emotional nourishment I needed. As Jessica slowly pried herself from me, she stood up and took away my plate. I moved to our couch, where I could stretch out. I fell into a dream-like trance where I told mom what I was going through. She was coherent in my daydream as Alzheimer's had yet to completely debilitate her. Mom confirmed what Jessica said to me at dinner and was sympathetic. She too had waged her own battle with anxiety. I recalled a time long ago when she suddenly stopped our big, brown Buick on the side of I-74. We were on our way home from a Wisconsin ski vacation in the dead of winter. She succumbed to a panic attack and I had to console her as she breathed into a paper bag, which kept her from hyperventilating. Stefano, a Brooklynite, couldn't drive. Instead, he stood on the side of the road in the last rays of winter's afternoon light, flagging down truckers in order to get mom help. Within half an hour, we were in the back of an ambulance as mom was rushed to a hospital. It was a traumatic experience for me to see my mother in such a helpless situation.

I had been to therapy multiple times before in my life and now starting the process again, along with medication, which ended my sleepless nights. Gone were the traumatic middle of the night horrors waking me up in a cold sweat. Here to stay was the safety net of Jessica, who stood nearby and lulled away some of the pain. I needed Jessica's support, but also had to face my mother's diagnosis of Alzheimer's head on and the eventual result. For now, I had to stay positive. However, I was scared. I knew what it was like to lose a parent suddenly, yet to watch my mother suffer with a prolonged sickness wasn't painless. Luckily, she was still cognizant of her surroundings. Mom knew I was struggling with some lifelong issues, above and beyond her illness, and blessed my seeking therapy. Now, the challenge was to be the emotional, steadfast adult. Since Mom championed me during my toughest times, I had to let her know things were going to be all right for the both of us and I did, but there was something missing, the comfort of her touch. I remembered how she always put her arm around me when I was growing up, letting me know she was there for me. It was that mother and child connection we always had together, which would soon vanish completely. I was now fighting for my emotional life trying to keep it together.

29: i sat on her couch

As I worked from home in the fall of 2006, my interest in U2 gradually came back. I checked in with atu2.com, one of many fan-run Web sites for the band, and found information about Bono being Oprah's guest for the second time in his musical career. Of course when I went to Oprah's site, the competition to get tickets, an essay contest about how Bono inspired you, was closed. However, I had a trump card. Our old neighbor Denise, who used to live above us, was a producer on the show. I'm sure she knew of my U2 fandom by the painted jacket I would wear in and out of the building every so often. I never thought about requesting a ticket to *The Oprah Show* because it wasn't my style, but this was Bono.

As I started to craft the note, I mentioned we were both alums of the University of Iowa and it was at our Alma mater where I really got the U2 bug. The words floated out with ease and before I knew it, my e-mail was composed and I sent it off. A day and a half later, I received a response from her assistant stating there was one last seat for the event and asked whether I wanted it. I immediately replied with a confirmation e-mail and in return, obtained a voucher imprinted with the date of the event. I was ecstatic.

"Jessica! I just got a note back from Denise's assistant with a pdf ticket for the show," I said into the speakerphone to my wife.

"You're kidding me! I would have never thought in a million years she would've responded. Good for you. What's the date?"

"October twelfth."

"That's next week. Are you excited?"

"Jess, what do ya think, silly?"

"Let me guess. You're going to wear your custom-painted jeans."

"Hell yeah! I hear the show is going to tie into the Red Campaign that's raising money for AIDS in Africa. I'm going to wear the red CBGB's shirt you bought me in New York."

"Very cute. Gotta run. Love you," Jessica said. Then the phone clicked dead.

On the day of Bono's interview, I arose at six o'clock in the morning and made a pot of coffee. The excitement of the day was already mentally exhausting. I kept pacing around the house with my mug of joe so not to fall asleep. When it got time to dress, I looked at my custom-painted jeans, which lay lifeless on the bed in the second bedroom. For a brief moment, I thought how far I had come from painting those jeans to attending *The Oprah Show* featuring Bono. I stopped my thoughts and slid on the jeans. The stiffness from the paint made a swishing noise as I walked around the apartment gathering my things. I hadn't worn them in a while and they were tight. I threw a belt on just to cover up the unbuttoned waist. Roo, our dog, sat in the hallway and took it all in. Seldom had he seen me in full U2 regalia. I'm sure he was questioning my sanity as well.

As I put my house keys in my pocket, I contemplated taking my copy of *Vertigo 2005: Live From Chicago DVD*. I had been to *The Oprah Show* before and had a good idea that taking the DVD into the studio wasn't allowed. It was contraband and I would be asked to leave it with security until the end of the show. I wasn't willing to take that chance. Again, I was thinking about making shit happen. If Bono signed autographs, the possibility of not bringing anything would have bothered me for quite some time. However, I already had his autograph, in the crotch of the painted jeans I was wearing, which satisfied me.

Once I was ready, I headed out into the dark morning. I hopped a bus and realized I was never going to make it to the studio on time. Before the bus moved onto Lake Shore Drive, I bailed and jumped a cab. I was anxious as we cruised through the caverns of the city at daybreak. Since I had been to *The Oprah Show* years before, I knew how they called groups from the waiting room. Today, I had a ticket for myself, but was worried I would be thrown in with the general audience cattle call to the studio and wouldn't get a good seat. Yes, I was thinking selfishly, but had to stay focused on the positive, I had a ticket to see Bono at Oprah's studio.

Upon my arrival to Harpo Studios, I paid the cabbie and entered into the warm studio. I was familiar with the drill. However, on this morning, I had to stop by the coat check girl first in order to drop off my jacket and obtain a Red T-shirt, donated by The Gap and inscribed with the word INSPI(RED), which was to be worn during the taping. I was then pointed to the check-in desk where I showed my driver's license. With ticket in hand, I headed to the metal detector where I dropped my keys into a plastic bowl and calmly walked through. I then walked to the base of the stairs going up to the waiting room where I heard quite a few voices from above. My heart started to pound while I climb the stairs, slowly. When I got to the top landing, I noticed I was the only man in a sea of about two hundred women. I felt out of place as my jeans began to cause a stir. In order to stave off more attention, I took the first available seat

Once seated, I made small talk with my neighbor, a suburban housewife from Indianapolis. We engaged in conversation about my custom-painted clothing and my interest in the band. She had knowledge of U2 visa vie her daughter, who sat next to her. As conversation rambled, an elderly usher from afar was watching me. She came over and asked me to stand up so she could get a better look at what I was wearing.

"Where did you get these?" she asked, as she pointed to my painted jeans.

An announcement came over the intercom, "Barbara Howe, please bring your party to the studio entrance."

"I painted them," I said after the announcement had passed.

"Oh, they're smart. What does it say there?"

"U2. It's Bono's band back in Ireland."

"Turnaround. I want to see the back of them."

"What does it say on the back?" she asked.

"'Achtung Baby,'" I replied with a smile.

"What's that?"

"Oh, it's one of U2's finest albums."

"Can you make me a pair?"

"Sure. Give me your size. I will paint a pair and drop them off here next week," I said, laughingly.

As I said that, I noticed the slow drift of audience members, making their way across the waiting room and heading downstairs. More names were being called. I knew I had to wait.

"Eric Shivvers' party, please come to the studio entrance."

"Shit. That's me!" I screamed in my head.

I got up out of my seat and quickly made my way down the stairs to the entrance of the studio. As I crossed the threshold into the stage area, I immediately spotted someone with a headset. I pointed to my jeans and asked them point blank, "What does a pair of funked-up jeans like these do for me?" Without hesitation, she pointed me to the front row of the balcony. Not a bad spot, but a group wanted the whole row and I was moved out. Immediately, I found another stagehand with a clipboard. Again, I asked the same question and was pointed to the last remaining seat, in the middle of the back row, on the main floor. I was in heaven, four rows off the front of the stage and dead center. I sauntered down the wide aisle behind the last row of seats, climbed over the back of them and sat down. My painted jeans opened conversation with my neighbor to my right. We fell into a discussion about U2. Within a few sentences, I found out that we were University of Iowa brethren. He too attended the same show I did at Carver, but his love for the band went back even further than I. He just happened to see their first Chicago show at the Park West.

Once the studio audience was seated, U2 tunes began to permeate the studio PA. A sense of excitement settled over us as the stagehands brought out the famed, tan-colored couch and dropped a backdrop. My conversation with my neighbor came to a close when the staffer, who pointed me to my seat, grabbed a microphone and crisscrossed the stage, discussing the interview process. She stopped momentarily and asked the audience questions, mostly about Bono and U2. A show of hands rose and fell. When she asked about our knowledge of Red products, I put up my hand immediately.

"Sir, you in the middle. What's your question?" she asked, as she was pointing to me.

"I know that the Red Motorola phones are available," I began.

The gal interrupted me and said, "Please, stand up and ask your question."

"I know that the Red Motorola phones have been available in Europe for a year now. When can we get them here?" I asked.

"Great question. We have the Motorola people here, but before I turn the question over to them, I want to ask, where did you get those jeans?"

"I painted them."

"Really?"

"Yeah, I sent the band a pair about twelve years ago or so."

"I want to hear more about them. Would you like to come up onstage?"

"Yeah! That'd be cool."

As I climbed out of my seat, the Motorola representative answered my question. I swiftly walked across the studio, up some stairs and onto the stage. The lights were blinding. I put my hand over my eyes as I approached the MC.

"Those jeans are something else. Turnaround, I want to see the back of them too," she said.

"No problem," I replied, as I spun around onstage.

The MC and the rest of the audience looked on in bewilderment at my creation. I could tell she wanted to know more about me as she pointed to the tan-colored couch and said, "Here, have a seat."

Without hesitation, I parked my ass on the leather couch, which had seated so many famous guests before me. I turned around looking for scuff marks left by Tom Cruise after his own monkey dance. No, seriously, I had to look. Sadly, none were found.

"Tell me about your jeans," she inquired, as a microphone was now in my face.

"Well in 1994, I sent Edge, U2's guitarist, a pair jeans, just like these, in a FedEx bag to the band's management office in Dublin. I went through the chain of command. Initially, they were interested, but as you know, there are many decision makers and I didn't make the cut."

"You're still a fan even though the venture didn't work out, yes?" she asked.

"Oh, yeah. That didn't heed my fondness for U2."

"Really?"

"Yeah, my zeal for the band isn't based upon them hiring me for my merchandising idea."

"Interesting," she said and paused to collect her thoughts. She then continued the conversation and asked, "You know you're sitting in Bono's seat? What's it like to be sitting where he will be in a few short moments?"

"It's a couch," I replied. The audience laughed.

"I know, but what's it like sitting where he's going to sit?"

"I'm not sure. I'm a little overwhelmed. We all know he's special and where he sits has no bearing on me. Like me, he puts his pants on one leg at a time."

"What is it that attracts you to him and the band?"

"U2 has always stood behind their convictions and have championed great causes, such as Greenpeace, Amnesty International and the like. Bono, more specifically, is one of my heroes because he's passionate about his causes. He believes what he's doing socially is for the betterment of all of us. The kids of today need more heroes like him. Sadly, too many of our kids are hung up on sport's figures, or celebrities for that matter, who end up falling from grace and become a disappointment."

I paused. The MC looked at me and tried to get a word in edgewise. I interrupted her with my follow-up thought.

"As I sit here, I see moms, dads, cousins, and possibly grandparents in front of me. All of whom could be a mentor or hero to someone. If we took Bono's philosophy of reaching out to others and made an impact on one person who crosses our path, we could change the world. It's that easy. We've the power to do that. We just need to make it happen."

At the end of my manifest, I arose from the couch and shook the MC's hand. I thanked her for the invitation and went back to my seat. Like Andy Warhol said, "In the future, everyone will be world-famous for 15 minutes." On this day, I cashed in a few of those minutes. It was my jeans, which granted me that opportunity. Who cares if the band didn't run with the merchandising idea I presented to them twelve years earlier? So what! Instead, my custom-painted U2 jeans opened some doors, which just happened to be a tan-colored couch, on a famous stage, allowing me to reveal to a room full of strangers why I have been a fan of Bono and U2 for more than 20 plus years.

Epilogue

In October of 2006, I headed to Iowa by train to see my folks. My wife had just bought a laptop and I asked if I could take it with me. Within three days, I had written forty-five pages of stream of consciousness. I knew I had a story to tell about my U2 fandom, but I didn't know how to craft it until I lent an early chapter to a friend. After struggling through the rough copy, she pricked my wife's ears and said I should attend the Iowa Summer Writing Festival at the University of Iowa, my Alma mater.

Two years later, for my fortieth birthday, my wife Amy sent me packing to Iowa City for a week's residency where I began working earnestly on my book. The class was very instructional and in the end, I was grateful that my wife didn't deliver on the Gibson Acoustic Songwriter Deluxe guitar I had asked her for. During the workshop, we each read aloud part of our book. Mine was the last work read in class. I had admirers who liked what I presented, but said a massive rewrite was needed. I took their advice and for the next nine months, I rewrote every chapter. In time, I learned how much discipline it took to be a writer and discovered how tough it is to self-edit.

The four years I have spent writing this book has been therapeutic as I observed my scholarly mother slip into the night with the debilitating disease of Alzheimer's disease. She's the one who played the guitar late at night in order to lull me to sleep as a young boy. I would like to think this book is a testament to her enthusiasm for writing. As for my father, his zeal for music is the other part of the story. His record collection and witness to the beginning of rock 'n' roll in the 50s fascinated me as a kid. He and mom may not appreciate what I listen to with my headphones, however, that's okay because what bounces between my eardrums brings me pleasure. And from this joy has come my own fervor, my U2 fandom, which will stay with me to the bitter end.

Acknowledgements

Four years can seem like a lifetime, especially when it comes to working on one's life story and I couldn't have done it without the support, patience, and love given to me by my wife, Amy. She knew when we met how passionate I was about U2 and didn't fear that they would come between us. I married Amy for the love of music, laughter, life, travel, trying new culinary experiences, friendship and of course for date-night. She has stood by my side, through thick and thin, unwavering in her friendship and for that, I'm deeply grateful.

The book would not have been written if I weren't here. For that, I have to thank mom and dad. They each touched me in their own ways. Mom, the ever teacher, would wake me up at the crack of dawn to review my English papers in high school making sure the edits we discussed the night before were included. She was a champion of instituting education, a lover of travel, passionate about life and a mother soon to be missed. Dad had the same impact by making sure I was taken care of even when he wasn't there. His purchase of my first stereo is paramount to my eventual admiration for all things music, which began with his love for 50s music, the big band era, and classical work. Dad made sure the creative apple didn't fall too far from the tree as I took up his infatuation with all things creative. Both mom and dad knew that self-expression in art, whatever medium it may be, made one a more well rounded person. I can say, because of them, I came out all right.

Stepparents always seem to get a bad rap, but in my case, it couldn't be farther from the truth. Dad's wife, my Stepmom Linda, has been in my cheering section since the day she met me and has never given up the post. She has been the buffer when I needed it and a guiding light when lost in a sea of emotional confusion. A writer herself, she was a fan of this book even before I had a chapter worth reading. Berni, my stepfather, never read the stories gracing these pages, but did recognize my fandom when he sent me an article about U2 clipped from *The New Yorker* in the early 90s. It's hard to imagine what his response would be to all this U2 madness captured in this writing. Perhaps, he sits in a bar, on a street with no name, hanging out with his friend's Joyce, Yeats, O'Casey and Morrison all the while looking down and beaming with pride. His wonderful children, my stepsisters, Kevin and Erika were unselfish in sharing with me a father who loved them both. I also include my mom's current husband, Tom Goodmann, whose love and passion for music runs just as deep as mine. He is a saint among men taking care of my mother and has been a guide to life's challenges. I am very appreciative to have him in my life. The trio of Linda, Berni and Tom have provided me kindness and encouragement. They love me like I was one of their own as I circumnavigate life. To that, I am truly thankful.

I cannot walk away without thanking the Shivvers' side of the family. Aunts, uncles, cousins and grandparents who have made life's journey a little more special. Damon, Diana, Joseph, Kathy

Lynn and Alan have been a great group of cousins to hang with at the Iowa State Fair. My aunts and uncles – Doug, Carol, Kathy and Barb – have all impacted me. Especially my Aunt Barb, and her husband Ted, who took me in when I moved to Chicago and told me to chase a dream of painting jeans for U2. Without them, a piece of the story would have never happened. Martha and Woodrow Shivvers are grandparents who us cousins loved to have around. They each touched us by teaching us to fish, play cards, love music and enjoy reading. They were the founders of our education.

On mom's side of the family, the Gabrielson's, is my cousin Tony. We are the only grandchildren of Myrl and Dan Gabrielson and share the common bond of being only children. We are as close as brothers and share a passion for U2. Tony's mother, Roxie, made our relationship happen and for that I thank her. I appreciate her love as well. Tony's father, Steve, is the rock in the family who exemplifies hard work and character.

Speaking of family, I have an extended one who is as close to me as my own. My in-laws, Mary and Tom Bernstein, are the best you can get. Yes, Mary is still waiting for Bono's phone call since she knows we are so tight. And I enthusiastically welcome Tom's Nebraska Cornhuskers into my Big Ten conference. My brother-in-law, Andrew, graciously accepted me into the family and is a delight to converse with, especially when it comes to movies. As for Amy's aunts, uncles and cousins, I thank you all as well and appreciate the guidance and support.

There are a couple people who don't know me personally, but I want to thank them because they were instrumental in giving me direction and support to the project. To Bill Flanagan, I would like to thank you for picking up the phone and giving me six minutes of your time. The discussion we had about publishing helped push me to self-publish this work. I knew my story had to be told and your insight gave me the kick in the ass

I needed. To Bill German, I covet your book on The Rolling Stones and felt your work was the guide for me to tell my U2 story. I appreciate all of our e-mail communication and hope we continue.

I would like to thank those who helped me along the path of my U2 fandom. To Candida Bottaci and Jeremy Joseph, who took my calls and were gracious enough to put my custom-painted jeans in front of their client. I thank you ten fold. Meeting Bono years later and having him autograph my work made the life cycle of the project come full circle. To Sheri Salata, I will be forever grateful as you gave me a ticket to the show in which my custom-painted jeans granted me access to sit on Oprah's tan-colored couch minutes before Bono came out. For that opportunity, I am very appreciative. To Dave Silbar, what can I say, but thank you for believing in the project and helping me out along the way with great ideas and your public relations savvy. Rob Sullivan, I thank you for helping me craft my thesis statement and book proposal. Your guidance and friendship have been a wonderful addition to my life. Susan Krantz, thank you for guiding me to the Iowa Summer Writing Workshop. It was a great ten days at my Alma mater. Speaking of writing, I would like to thank my teacher and memoirist, Sarah Saffian, who taught my class in Iowa City. Sarah, your guidance and teaching have been very beneficial to my success. I thank you, and my classmates, for listening to my work. To Lila Stromer, thank you for helping me out on the journey of editing the first few chapters of the work and some last minute direction. You set a benchmark that I followed and for that, I am very appreciative of your help. To Mary Jones, I want to thank you for the friendship over the years and your eleventh hour guidance on this project. It is very appreciated. To Ed Paquette, thank you for getting us tickets to the lecture at UNL and being a great friend. Lastly, I want to thank Kimberley Johnson, a writer herself, who told me to go self-publish this book and share it with the world.

And finally, the list of friends I have made along the way of life. Kevin Berger, my first U2 date, thanks for going to the show with me in Iowa City. What a night to remember. To my childhood friends, Derek Peters and Greg Williams, thanks for helping me through the tough times. Monte Montgomery and Phil Bass, I appreciate the friendship ten fold. Keep the music coming. To my Evanston gang of Todd Stein, Suzette Chandonnet, Reed and Steve Anderson (and their respective wives Carolyn and Sarah) plus Terry Morton, thanks for making single life fun. Steve Pundzak, a ten fold thank you for the U2 introduction. Cathal McCarron, I hope my work can sit next to yours. Cliff Mahaney, thank you for the friendship over the years and giving me the push to get my work to the band the first time around. Steve Alford and Suzanne Ferriss, I appreciate the love. You are the best innkeepers in South Florida. I thank you Megan Ferenchak for drop-kicking my work back at me and "showing" me how to write a "telling" story. NASA Man, thanks for the great riffs. To John Cline and Vincent Giovinco for being the first true believers to the FB page. To the rest of my Half Acre cycling brethren, thank you for the friendships along the passion filled roads of cycling. To the greatest advertising mentors a kid could have, David Strandberg, Hank Hechtman and Phil Adams, I hope I did you proud. What's your favorite color Gregg Jaffe? Living Colour! Wes Morris, thanks for the friendship and joining me in the 360° Tour pit. To Phyllis Jones, what can I say girl? You come in and out of my life like the Mistral, but your friendship never leaves. Thanks for all you have done. Hit Man, thanks for posting the note on the school wall. Roo, you're the best damn dog a guy can have. Thanks for taking me to the park and getting me away from the computer. Matt McGee, you run one of the finest U2 fansites, atU2.com, and your support of this project is much appreciated. Keep on doing what you are doing. To Melanie Feerst, thanks for pushing me to create Bono's birthday hat. To Joe Bowen, thanks for the laughs and the introduction to your wife, Lila, who has been a great help with this project. To Deb Fell and Larry Boswell, thanks for the laughs. Pam Cibulski, Amy and I will never forget meeting you on the flight from Houston nor the long-time friendship. Jazzman, thanks for keeping the low end low. To my gang in Tulsa – Tim Staley, Sam Conner, and Barbie Jeffers – thanks for letting me watch your MTV! Alec Herring, you are the best Lego builder in the world. Thanks for the good times listening to KISS. To my I'm a U2 Fan Facebook followers, there are too many of you to mention by name, but thank you for the support. Bob Meinig, your coaching was the mental break I needed from the project. Dale Lewis, Ron Troester, Randy Carris and the rest of the Iowa crew, thanks for making those undergrad days a blast. Michelle Steenbergen, Laurie Lanham and Alison Lee thanks for letting me encroach on your pad and share in the post-college revelry. MacPhisto, God called and he would like his platform shoes back. Angela Hoops you get the "greatest achievement award" for slugging through the very nascent copy of this book. To my U2 hotel buds, Kimberly Coleman and Laurie Ayala, it's great to see you, and catch-up, at our favorite spot. To the rock gods above, whomever you are, I feel blessed to have your guiding spirit. Lastly, if I have forgotten to mention your name, I am truly sorry and I thank you.

In closing, I speak for all U2 fans who are touched by the lyrics, melodies, and stadium shows, thank you Larry Mullen, Jr., Adam Clayton, The Edge and Bono for staying true to your creative convictions, sticking it together all these years and making the world a better place.

Made in the USA
Charleston, SC
09 June 2011